Dr Bobbie Jacobson is a research fellow in health promotion at the London School of Hygiene and Tropical Medicine. She is the author of *The Ladykillers: Why Smoking is a Feminist Issue* (Pluto Press, 1981), the book which first drew attention to the issue of women and smoking. She is an active campaigner against the tobacco industry.

Bobbie Jacobson

Beating the Ladykillers

Women and Smoking

Pluto Press

First published in 1986 by Pluto Press Limited,
The Works, 105a Torriano Avenue, London NW5 2RX
and Pluto Press Australia Limited, PO Box 199, Leichhardt,
New South Wales 2040, Australia. Also Pluto Press,
27 South Main Street, Wolfeboro, New Hampshire 03894 – 2069

7 6 5 4 3 2 1

90 89 88 87 86

Set by Rapidset and Design Limited

Printed in Great Britain by Cox & Wyman, Reading, Berks

British Library Cataloguing in Publication Data
Jacobson, Bobbie
    Beating the ladykillers: women and smoking.
    1. Cigarette habit   2. Women—Tobacco use
    I. Title
    306'.4   HV5740

ISBN 0 7453 0209 2

Contents

To all the women who have nearly quit smoking, their daughters and all those who believe in promoting women's health

Acknowledgements

I could not have written this book without help from people all over the world, or financial assistance from the Health Education Council, UK. Eileen Crofton, Alison Hillhouse, Liz Batten and Mike Daube helped bring greater clarity and accuracy to it, and Patti White and Michele Vincent helped to open up the ASH information goldmine for me. I am indebted to Richard Peto, Steve Sutton, Jil Matheson and Alan Marsh for their advice and help in producing some of the information; to Cancer Research Campaign for funding my research on children and smoking, and to Channel 4 Television for permission to use excerpts from 'A Picture of Health'. I could not have presented the international perspective without help from Mira Aghi, Dee Burton, Virginia Ernster, Debbie Fisher, Margareta Giebels-Nilson, Judith Mackay, Ruth Shean, Simon Chapman and Steve Woodward. I have no idea what I would have done without Beryl Frost's ability to turn messy typescript into a finished manuscript.

To my friends and family I owe special thanks: to Jonathan whose support helped me to quit smoking in 1973; to my parents who believe in me without asking why; to Boris who watched over me in silent approbation; to Imelda who quit smoking after she read my book, and to Mike who tolerated so much and said so little.

Above all I owe a great deal to all the women – smokers, ex-smokers, non-smokers, activists and observers – who gave me the opportunity to discover what smoking really means to women, and how they are winning the battle against cigarettes.

PART I

The Sexual Politics of Smoking: Why Women Smoke

Introduction

Beating the Ladykillers started out in life as a second edition of *The Ladykillers – Why Smoking is a Feminist Issue* which I wrote in 1979. There are four main reasons why it rapidly turned into a new venture. First, the cigarette-induced death toll among women is still rising inexorably in the industrialised world. Second, smoking can no longer be regarded as a parochial problem – among either men or women – for a few rich countries; for the multinational tobacco companies have made sure that it has become an international epidemic. The cost of increasing tobacco use among women in poor countries has been neither acknowledged nor adequately documented. Third, recent research has uncovered new health risks which smoking imposes on women, and has shed further light on why girls are overtaking boys in starting to smoke and why women's smoking patterns are different from men's. Lastly, and most important, women are no longer silent on this issue and have taken both individual and collective action throughout the world to beat cigarettes.

1: Today's epidemic

The smoking and health campaign has come of age; it is now a generation since British doctors first alerted the public to the risks of smoking. And the results in Britain so far show that the tide has turned firmly against smoking. Cigarette sales have plummeted by an impressive 28 per cent[1] and seem destined to continue falling. Nine and a half million people have quit smoking,[2] and in 1982 women and men smokers from *all* backgrounds were in a minority for the first time in recent history.[3]

But the story of women's responses to the smoking and health message has been different from that of men. In the early years of the campaign, smoking declined much faster among men than women. And men responded more vigorously to the anti-smoking message, widely publicised following two major reports from London's Royal College of Physicians. In 1961 (the year before the first report) nearly 60 per cent of men smoked cigarettes. By the time the second report was published in 1971, this figure had dropped to 47 per cent.[4] Yet over the same period, there was no response from women at all, and smoking among them stuck fast at about 40 per cent.[5] This meant that the gap which used to exist between men and women has gradually closed. Today, nearly half of Britain's 14 million smokers are women.[6] In 1984 32 per cent of women smoked – only just outnumbered by the 36 per cent of men who smoked.[7] Not only did the *proportion* of women smoking catch up with men, but also the *amount* they smoked. In 1950 the average British woman got through half as many cigarettes as her male contemporary. Today they are neck and neck: she averages 14 to his 16 a day.[8]

During the second decade of the anti-smoking campaign, smoking started to fall among women too – albeit much more slowly at first (see Figure 1).[9] This trend is now accelerating and

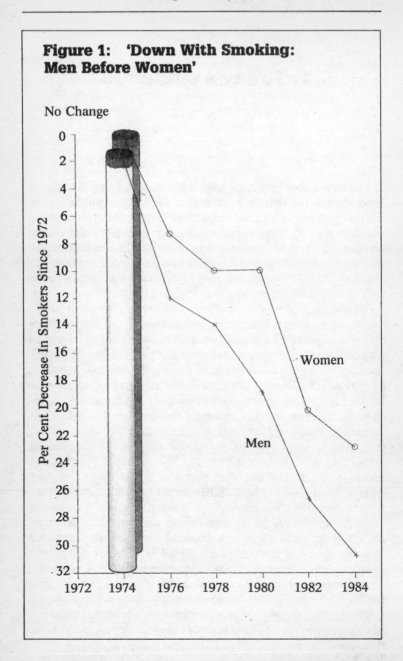

Figure 1: 'Down With Smoking: Men Before Women'

women are beginning to follow men on the road to freedom from cigarettes.

Britain is not the only country where men led and women followed. Compare the British trends with those of two other rich countries from different parts of the globe – the USA and Australia – but both with substantial anti-smoking campaigns themselves. And you get a similar picture. In the USA, initially, smoking also fell more quickly among men than women.

The proportion of US women smoking heavily has more than doubled since 1965, and they are now the world's heaviest women smokers.[10] The gap between men and women smokers is also closing, with 37 per cent of men and 29 per cent of women smoking in 1980.[11] The Australian woman smoker is potentially in the worst position of the three countries. Not only has her smoking remained at 30 per cent for the last 13 years, but it is actually *rising* among both young and middle-aged women, as well as in working-class women.[12] This is in direct contrast to Australian men, where there has been a small but steady decline in all these groups.

More impressive still is the consistency of these differences between women and men in most of Europe and the rest of the rich world. Table 1 shows that while the proportion of men who smoke is falling in 19 of the 22 countries shown, among women it is rising or stable in 11 of them.[13-33] And in the 10 countries showing a fall among women as well as men, the decline is *much bigger* for men in seven cases. Thus, with few exceptions, smoking has become a bigger problem for women and a smaller problem for men.

Girls make a lot of difference

Why the difference in smoking patterns between women and men? There are two processes which determine the total proportion of people who smoke: the number starting balanced against the number quitting. And fewer boys are starting to smoke, while girls have both caught up and are beginning to overtake boys. Second, proportionately more men than women quit smoking in the early stages of any given anti-smoking campaign. This dual process explains why some of the good news about women –

Table 1: Smoking Trends In The Rich World

Country	Year	Smoking Rates (%)		Direction of Smoking	
		Women	Men	Women	Men
Australia	1983	30	37	◀▶	▼
Austria	1981	22	33	▲	▼▼
Belgium	1980	21	53	◀▶	▼▼
Canada	1981	29	37	▼	▼
Denmark	1980	44	57	▼	▼
England & Wales	1984	32	36	▼	▼▼
Finland	1984	16	33	◀▶	▼▼
France	1983	29	52	▼	▼▼
W. Germany	1980	29	41	▲	▼▼
Greece*	1983	30	50	▲▲	▼
Ireland	1984	30	34	▼	▼▼
Italy	1980	17	54	▲	▲▲
Japan	1983	14	66	▲	▼▼
Netherlands	1982	33	41	▼	▼▼
New Zealand	1981	30	35	▼	▼▼
Norway	1983	32	42	◀▶	▼▼
Poland	1980	29	63	▲▲	▼
Scotland	1982	39	45	▼	▼▼
Spain (Catalunya)	1982	20	58	?	?
Sweden	1982	31	31	▼	▼▼
USA	1980	29	37	▼	▼
USSR (Moscow)	1980	10	44	▲	▲

Key:

▲   Proportion of smokers rising.

▼   Proportion of smokers falling.

◀▶   Proportion of smokers remains unchanged.

▲▲ or ▼▼   Big increase or decrease in smoking relative to opposite sex.

*   Estimate

there are three and a half million British women who have quit smoking,[34] for example – is partly obscured by increasing numbers of girls and young women starting to smoke, and a history of women being slower to catch up in quitting.

Looking again at Britain, the US and Australia, it is easy to see similar trends. British teenagers seem to have followed the path of their parents: while boys who smoke used to outnumber girls until the mid-1970s, the position has now been almost reversed. By 1984, nearly as many girls as boys smoked in all teenage groups. Like their mothers, 24 per cent of 14-to-15-year-old girls smoked compared with 17 per cent of boys.[35] And in Northern England and Scotland, girls have resolutely taken over from boys in their teens and are showing no signs of relinquishing their lead.[36-38] The reason for this reversal is not because girls are starting to smoke earlier, but because increasing numbers of girls compared with boys are starting in their late teens.

The rising tide of teenage girl smokers in the US mirrors what has happened in Britain. By 1979 more than a quarter of 17-year-old girls were smoking, compared with only 19 per cent of boys,[39] although the peak of the girls' smoking epidemic may be over. The Australian girl smoker did worse than her sisters. By 1983 she smoked more heavily, and had overtaken her male counterparts by the time she was 14. At seventeen, *twice* as many Australian girls as boys smoked.[40] Our three reference countries exhibit patterns of teenage smoking which also hold true for most of the world's rich countries. Table 2 shows that girls have become the new smokers in 10 of the 18 countries shown.[41-53]

Do women find it harder to quit smoking than men?

In Britain (as well as in the US and Australia) there are still proportionately more ex-smokers among men than women. And this relationship seems to hold for every occupational and age group.[54] Is this because women find it harder to quit smoking than men? Looking at those who have ever smoked in Britain, younger women seem to have had little trouble keeping up with the men who have quit. But once over the age of 25 the success

Table 2:   Challenging The Boys' Monopoly

Country	Year	Smokers % (Mid-teens)	
		Girls	Boys
——————— Girls Lead Boys ———————			
Australia (NSW)	1983	37	29
Belgium	1975	45	44
Denmark	1980	43	35
England & Wales	1984	24	17
Greece	mid-1970s	54	46
Italy	1972	55	51
Netherlands	1981	30	27
New Zealand	1981	30	27
Sweden	1984	22	15
USA	1979	26	19
——————— Girls/Boys Equal ———————			
Canada	1983	20	20
Ireland	1980	32	32
France	1980/81	43	43
W. Germany	1976	40	40
——————— Boys Lead Girls ———————			
Bulgaria	1975	30	79
Finland	1983	33	45
Norway	1980	21	22
Spain (Catalunya)	1982	68	78

gap widens, and in the over-50s nearly half of the men had successfully quit in 1982 as compared with only one-third of
women.[55] The latest government National Opinion Poll at the
end of 1984 suggests that women are getting better at quitting,
but the gap still seems to persist.[56]

Apart from being male, what else determines who will quit
successfully? This question was posed in 1982 by a government
research team at the Office of Population Censuses and Surveys
(OPCS). And in the largest piece of research of its kind, they
showed that the more positive your attitude to the health
benefits of quitting, the more likely you are to resolve to quit, to
actually try and – ultimately – to be successful.[57]

Is it possible that women are less likely to quit because they
have less positive attitudes to the health benefits of quitting and
are, therefore, less well-informed about the risks of smoking?
The OPCS study clearly showed that women were no less likely
than men to expect health benefits from quitting, and that
although most smokers tended to play down their own personal
risk of developing lung cancer and heart attacks, there were no
special differences between women and men. In fact, the only
women who seriously underestimated the risks more than others
were young, middle-class *non-smokers*. As middle-class women
are only a tiny minority of women who are also *non-smokers*, it
cannot explain the discrepancy between men and women which
persists in all other groups of *smokers*.[58] And it is also clear from
the OPCS research that women's relative lack of success is not
for want of trying. For women tried to quit as often as men.

In 1980 the US Surgeon General collected together the
world's information about women and smoking and came to this
conclusion:

Across all treatments, women have more difficulty giving up
smoking than men. No studies have been reported in which
women do significantly better than men. Several of the larger
studies show higher abstinence rates by men.

The conclusions are based on hundreds of trials of special
methods for helping smokers to quit. When comparing the
results for these equally motivated groups of women and men,
men are up to twice as successful as women – irrespective of the

method used.[59] Alongside these specialised projects lie hundreds of requests which Action on Smoking and Health (ASH) receives for help from ordinary smokers every day. Most – about three-quarters – come from women.[60] That women are more inclined to ask for help has been confirmed by researchers monitoring the effects of anti-smoking TV programmes. In 1978, nearly seven out of ten people responding to a TV *Reports Action* programme offering help to quit smoking, were women.[61] And in 1982, nearly two-thirds of those writing in for help in response to the BBC series *So you Want to Stop Smoking* were also women.[62] Even the clinics, set up by local health authorities to help smokers to stop, are peopled mainly by women.[63]

But the case is not yet proven because researchers have criticised the evidence, saying that smokers who attend special courses or clinics form a tiny group and do not represent the majority of ordinary smokers who go on to quit on their own. True, yet they have no explanation as to why women – within these special groups – are more likely to ask for help *and* have less success in quitting. The only acceptable source of evidence, they say, is from large national surveys which represent most smokers. If you look at such surveys in Britain, the US, Canada and Australia, all seem to confirm that men are better at quitting than women. Despite all this, one new piece of evidence from Martin Jarvis, a researcher at London's Addiction Research Unit (ARU), suggests that the differences are not so much because women find it harder to quit, but rather that men – about 5 per cent – are not as good as it as they seem, because they may have given up cigarettes but now smoke cigars.[64] If you take men's cigar smoking into account, says Martin Jarvis, the success gap between men and women under 50 closes. But whether the man who switches from cigarettes to cigars is the same as the regular cigarette smoker remains to be shown. What we can therefore say is that while some women – especially those looking for professional help – still lag behind men in their quitting rates, women are getting better at quitting all the time.

Not only a question of sex

Smoking patterns also reflect the politics of underprivilege – irrespective of whether you are a woman or a man. People with lower incomes, status and educational achievements are more likely to smoke. British men provide the clearest example of the gradient of underprivilege. Despite a small drop in all groups, middle-class professional men – doctors, lawyers and university teachers etc. – are nearly twice as likely to have quit smoking as compared with unskilled manual labourers.[65]

Underprivilege of a different kind

Black people in a white society are likely to have higher smoking rates than whites. In the US, racial and sexual underprivilege go hand in hand: white women are less likely to quit smoking than white men, but have higher quitting rates than black women.[66]

Roughly equal proportions of black and white American women smoke, but black women smoke more dangerously, with many still using non-filter cigarettes.[67] South Africa – the world's most brutal example of the deliberate segregation of rich and poor – boasts a society where black men smoke more than whites and coloured women have higher smoking rates than most white *and* black men.[68] In New Zealand, which claims to have 'less class consciousness than any Western country', Maori men *and* women are the country's leading smokers.[69] They are also among New Zealand's poorest people. Maori women have one of the world's highest smoking rates for women, nearly double that of their white female counterparts.[70] In Britain it seems that white women still smoke more than black women at present, and Asian women hardly smoke at all.[71] Although information is still scarce, soaring smoking rates among both men and women are the hallmark of the poorer Southern European countries. This applies to Greece, Italy and Spain, where smoking rises inexorably each year.[72] In Greece the increase has been attributed mainly to women and young people.[73] In Spain, as many as eight out of ten boys and seven out of ten girls under 15 now smoke.[74] This is nearly four times higher than the highest rate for all other European children *and* adults.

Women's work – a fuller story

Among women there exists underprivilege of a different kind: that of sex. For class alone cannot explain women's smoking patterns. Unlike men, women *at both ends of the social scale* are united by their rate of smoking. In the US, for example, in 1976 42 per cent of women with highly paid managerial jobs and 39 per cent of underpaid women service workers smoked, so the gradient of underprivilege seems to have disappeared.[75]

At first glance, British women do not follow the American pattern and reflect the same poverty gradient as men. This is because all information about the British woman smoker was based on her *husband's* and not on her *own* job. When the government translated the 1982 figures for women according to their own jobs, the picture that emerged was almost identical to that in the USA: 38 per cent of women with professional and managerial jobs, and a virtually *identical* (40 per cent) proportion of women in unskilled manual jobs smoked.[76]

German researchers have taken us a step further. By painstakingly recording the smoking habits and exact job of 500,000 people taken from their 1978 census, they found – as expected– that the men with the highest smoking rates were 'blue collar' or manual workers, whilst those with the lowest were professionals and academics.[77] They also uncovered a new smoking hierarchy among women. The women with the highest smoking rates were not necessarily manual workers; many had non-manual jobs. What becomes obvious from Table 3 is that the factor linking these women and their job rates is not just poor pay, but that they were all doing *women's work*.[78]

Women's unpaid work

If a woman's job tells us something about her smoking patterns, then perhaps her unpaid work can tell us more. The woman whose work it is to bring up a family and look after the home must be one of the most under-researched of human beings. Seen by society as 'economically inactive', she is dumped among all those people who are regarded as 'non-productive'. In 1982, 80 per cent of the 7.4 million British people in this group were women.[79] In the late 1970s, to be 'economically inactive' seemed to be a protection against smoking; so housewives in Europe and North America had lower smoking rates than women in paid, full- or part-time jobs. By 1982, this relationship remained the same everywhere except in Britain, where housewives' smoking rates seemed to have caught up with those of women in paid work.[80] Have the pressures on the British housewife grown out of all proportion to those of her counterparts abroad? Probably not. This apparent shift is more likely to reflect the more rapid rise of unemployment among British women – at least one-third of whom do not register as unemployed.[81] This means that more and more unemployed women, who have high smoking rates, are also being dumped into the amorphous 'economically inactive' category.

Table 3: Smoking and Women's Jobs

Smoking Rank	Job	Smokers %	% Women in this job
1	Waitresses/Restaurant Workers	50	72
2	Industrial solderers	48	87
3	Copytypists	48	93
4	Telephonists	47	80
5	Beauticians	46	96
6	Hairdressers	43	80
	All Women (1979)	**28**	—

But today's largest and growing group of women are not the 'economically inactive', but those who combine bringing up a family with paid work. So perhaps it is a unique combination of women's paid *and* unpaid work which can help explain why women's smoking patterns are different from those of men. Since men do not do much unpaid domestic work, the strain of having children to rear as well as a paid job is unlikely to have much impact on their smoking patterns. The research indicates that this seems to,be the case in both Germany and Britain.[82,83] German research among married women shows that those most vulnerable to cigarette smoking were city women who had children under 10 *and* who also went out to work. Table 4 shows that it is neither paid work alone nor having young children which produces the women with the highest smoking rates, but a *combination* of the two factors.[84]

Table 4: Smoking and Women's Work: A New League

Smoking Rank	Working Status (Married City Dwellers)	Smoking Rate %
1	In paid work with children under 10	48
2	In paid work with children 10-17	36
3	Housewife with children under 10	35
4	In paid work, no children	26
5	Housewife, no children	24
6	Housewife with children 10-17	24
All Women	—	33

In Britain the picture is not clear, and is probably confused by a higher unemployment rate which minimises differences between women in paid and unpaid work by swelling the ranks of the 'economically inactive'.[85]

2: The price women are paying

The 'Big Three' casualties

In 1983 cigarettes killed nearly 33,000 British women.[1-3] If it takes four hours to read this book, by the time it is finished, cigarettes will have claimed another 16 women from heart attacks, lung cancer and chronic bronchitis. These are the 'Big Three' cigarette diseases.

Although lung cancer is the best-known of the smoking-induced diseases, cigarettes are also a major cause of coronary heart disease (heart attacks) where the arteries which feed the heart muscle with oxygen and nutriments gradually become hardened and narrowed. The process starts in childhood and is also brought about by a diet high in saturated fat, high blood pressure and a lack of exercise. As it worsens, it leads to chest pains later on – angina – as the heart muscle 'screams' out for more oxygen. A heart attack is the end point of this process; it occurs when the narrowed arteries ultimately become blocked, causing part of the heart muscle to die. Heart attacks are not the preserve of the elderly and often occur in people under 50, when the risk of death is high. Although some survive their first heart attack, the writing is on the wall. But even then you can still act, because quitting smoking halves the risk of another attack.[4]

Women are still seen by many as relatively immune from coronary heart disease – assumed to be protected somehow by the blessing of female hormones. Yet coronary heart disease is the main killer of both women and men in all rich societies. In 1983 it claimed nearly 76,000 British women – *more than all forms of cancer combined*.[5-7] We are beginning to see a decrease in heart disease in both women and men, but there is still a long way to go. Although smoking is not the only cause of coronary heart disease, the woman who smokes 20 cigarettes a day is at least twice as likely to die of a heart attack as her non-smoking contemporaries – *irrespective* of any other risks.

Unlike heart disease, there is not much you can do about lung cancer once you have it. Fewer than one in ten people with lung cancer survive for five years. In 1983, it claimed over 10,000 British women.[8-10] Five years ago, I predicted in *The Ladykillers* that deaths from lung cancer could overtake those from breast cancer – then the No. 1 cancer killer in women – by the year 2010. That prediction is alarmingly out of date. By 1984 lung cancer had already overtaken breast cancer in Scottish women,[11] and the same was true of English women between 65 and 74.[12]

Although lung cancer rates are showing the first signs of decrease among younger women,[13] the overall direction is inexorably upward. Among men the story is quite different, however: the trend is downward in *all* ages.[14] It is true that lung cancer still kills three times as many men as women, but women have been catching up at a *much faster* rate. Between 1963 and 1983, lung cancer rates went up five times as fast in women as in men.[15] When lung cancer reached its peak in men in the mid-1950s, ten times more men than women died of it, but by 1983 this ratio had shrunk to three.[16]

The price women are paying worldwide

Scottish women – who smoke more than English women *and* men – are in the unenviable position of leading the women's world lung cancer league (see Table 5). American women come a close second, with 38,600 expected to die of lung cancer in 1985.[17] In 13 states, lung cancer rates have already overtaken those for breast cancer, and the American Cancer Society predicted that it would become the principal fatal cancer in women throughout the US by the end of 1985.[18] Because Australian women took up smoking much later, they come a little lower at twelfth in the league – at present. In 1983 lung cancer still claimed nearly 1,000 Australian women.[19]

Of the top 20 countries in the league, all but two have one thing in common: high cigarette consumption. What is more, all but two are industrialised countries which (with the exception of

Table 5:   The Women's World Lung Cancer League: The Top Twenty (Age: 45-54) (1980s)[20,21]

League Position	Country	Death Rate/100,000
1	Scotland	39.4
2	USA	33.8
3	Denmark	31.7
4	Hong Kong	26.9
5	Canada	24.2
6	England & Wales	23.5
7	Ireland	23.4
8	New Zealand	22.4
9	Singapore	21.8
10	Hungary	18.2
11	Netherlands	16.1
12	Australia	14.9
13	Norway	14.2
14	Sweden	13.6
15	Cuba	13.5
16	Yugoslavia	11.7
17	Brazil*	11.5
18	Austria	11.4
19	Belgium	10.6
20	Rumania	10.4

*An underestimate.

the communist countries) house powerful multinational tobacco companies. Why women in Hong Kong, Singapore and China (which would rank No.21 in the league)[22] have such apparently low smoking rates (less than five per cent)[23,24] and such high lung cancer rates is a mystery. But the women most at risk in each country tend to be Chinese/Cantonese in origin,[25] and the paradox does not extend to their male equivalents whose lung cancer risk is in keeping with the amount they smoke.[26] So whatever the factor is, it is not likely to be genetic or inherent, and whether Chinese women use other forms of tobacco or underestimate their own cigarette consumption for cultural reasons, remains to be tested. So far, researchers have tested and ruled out some of the other possibilities including exposure to kerosene gas while cooking,[27] and passive smoking (long-term exposure to their heavy-smoking husbands' cigarette smoke).[28] They are now looking at the possible role of dietary deficiency – especially vitamin A[29] which protects against several cancers. As yet they have not come up with any clear-cut answers.

In Hong Kong there is an uneasy alliance between two cultures. On the one hand there is the traditional oriental community in which women are expected to play a subordinate role, and on the other a highly technocratic society which operates according to the rules of the West. It is still regarded as 'not nice' for women to smoke, says Judith MacKay, a physician and leading smoking and health campaigner in Hong Kong. As yet, only four per cent of Hong Kong women smoke. But this may change soon. That Hong Kong women already rank number 4 in the world lung cancer league has not deterred attempts by the tobacco companies to expand what is obviously virgin territory with potential. In December 1984 the American company, Philip Morris, launched Virginia Slims Lights in Hong Kong with a huge, mass-media advertising campaign directed specifically at young women. The message is the same as in the US: smoking is the mark of an emancipated woman.

'You've come a long way baby,' say the commercials. 'Now there's a slim cigarette just for women: new Virginia Slims Lights. Tailored for the feminine hand, slimmer than the fat cigarettes men smoke, with a milder flavour you'll like. New all-American Virginia Slims Lights. Now in Hong Kong.' Both Chinese and Western women find these ads uniformly 'awful', reports Judith Mackay, but she sees the launch as a deliberate bid to create a market which did not previously exist. Her number 1 priority is to campaign for a ban on all forms of cigarette advertising in Hong Kong.

Chronic bronchitis and emphysema are the third of the 'Big Three' cigarette-induced diseases. These two names are interchangeable; essentially, if you've got chronic bronchitis you almost certainly have emphysema too. Whilst doctors search for the all-round scientific word to describe both processes, some simply call it 'cigarette lung'. Certainly people who suffer with 'cigarette lung' have no trouble describing what they experience: increasing and gradually debilitating breathlessness, along with coughing up phlegm, punctuated by increasingly severe chest infections and prolonged visits to the hospital. Cigarette lung used to be so common in Britain that it was called 'the English disease'. Although it causes fewer deaths than lung cancer, it is a *much bigger* cause of disability. It is now on the decline in women as well as men.[30] Less smoking, less air pollution and better treatment have all contributed to that steady decline. Like heart disease, if you already have cigarette lung, quitting smoking can slow down the deterioration in your lung function and improve your quality of life[31] – if you don't wait until you are too disabled for it to make any difference.

A lost cause?

Amid the sensational death toll from heart attacks and lung cancer, the disabling (if not killing) effects of smoking on the rest of the circulation are lost. Smoking has the same 'hardening' effect on the arteries feeding parts of the body other than the heart. When the leg arteries are affected it can cause a kind of angina of the legs – called intermittent claudication – and if you are also diabetic the effects are magnified. Claudication sufferers – over 90 per cent of whom smoke [32] – may eventually only be able to walk a few yards before the claudication pain stops them. If you have become incapacitated by the pain, quitting smoking can improve it. If not, you are faced with having a major operation to by-pass the blocked portion of artery, or (sometimes) losing part of a leg. Quitting smoking in time can help to avoid the operation in the first place. But failing that, quitting for the operation *still* maximises the chances of the operation's later success. Like the 'Big Three' cigarette diseases, claudication and its consequences are thought of as another archetypal male disease, which was true in the 1950s when nine out of every ten people with severe claudication were men.[33] But American research in the late 1970s showed quite a different picture: nearly *40 per cent* of people who needed operations for this disease were women.[34]

For women only – the new cigarette diseases

Cigarettes pose special problems for women, especially young women. The safety of the contraceptive Pill has been a matter for stormy debate for more than 15 years. The three million British women who use it,[35] their doctors and journalists have understandably been preoccupied with each new piece of research as it seemed to overturn opinion based on the last. Although this debate is by no means over, the effect of smoking on Pill users is now quite clear.

Of all the known risks of the Pill, the ones which cause the most death and disability are heart attacks and certain kinds of stroke. What emerges from the longest-standing study of 23,000 women on the Pill is that although the Pill *on its own* increases these risks in non-smokers, it is *smoking* which makes the Pill unacceptably dangerous for young women. So much so that all but two of the women in the study who died over a ten-year period were smokers.[36]

A woman who smokes and takes the Pill is ten times more likely to die of a heart attack or stroke than a non-smoker not taking the Pill.[37] More relevant is to compare the risks of smokers and non-smokers both of whom use the Pill at different ages (see Figure 2). If you are under 30 on the Pill – and even if you smoke– the risks are minimal. But the older you are and the more you smoke, the greater the risk becomes; it's a bit like stepping into the shoes of a woman ten years older than you are. Figure 2 shows that smoking does not simply add a little to the risk – it *multiplies* it.[38]

The total number of women who die of smoking and the Pill is a drop in the ocean of the 'Big Three' killers, but this is not a valid comparison. Lung cancer takes about 30 years to develop and its victims, therefore, are mostly over 50. The victims of the Pill and smoking – like the much-publicised heroin addicts – have not even lived half their lives. Not to mention the women under 40 who may survive a stroke only to live out the rest of their lives with permanent walking and speech difficulties. The tragedy of the young woman who smokes and takes the Pill is that it doesn't seem to matter much how long she takes the Pill and smokes, a heart attack can occur *at any time*.[39]

It now seems that smoking must also be added to the increasingly long list of risks which play a role in cancer of the cervix (entrance of the womb). Even though no one knows the exact cause of cervical cancer, researchers believe that it is transmitted by – and could be caused by – a virus. For many years they

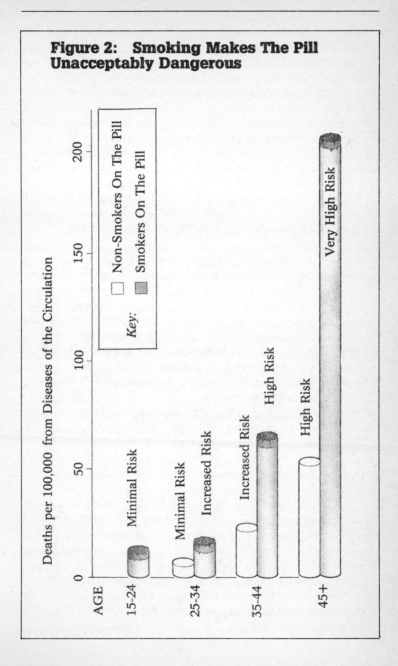

Figure 2: Smoking Makes The Pill Unacceptably Dangerous

thought it might be a special type of herpes virus – which causes genital herpes – but this has been difficult to prove.[40] The latest research suggests that certain new types of virus similar to those causing genital warts (also transmitted sexually) could be responsible,[41] as they are detectable in most women with cancer of the cervix.[42]

Because cervical cancer is likely to be caused by a virus that is transmitted sexually, anything which increases the chances of infection by the virus will also increase the risk of cancer. This is why the younger a woman is when she first has sex, and the more sexual partners both she and her partners have, are the two most important factors.[43] New worldwide evidence shows that the Pill itself – unlike the cap or sheath which probably provide a more effective barrier against the virus[44] – increases a woman's risk of cervical cancer.[45]

Even though the most inventive have difficulty in imagining how the smoke gets there, researchers have shown that nicotine is present in the cervical secretions.[46] They are convinced that the risk is real. Some argue that those who have large numbers of sexual partners may smoke more, so smoking cannot really be a separate factor. But even when researchers have accounted for sexual behaviour – if that is possible – smoking remains as an unshakable separate risk.[47] A partner's smoking may also be important, but not *as* important as the woman's.[48] It is hard to deny the evidence which faces us so far: the relationship between smoking and all stages of pre-cancer to fully developed cervical cancer,[49] increases the earlier you start smoking and the more you smoke.[50] So strong is the risk that an editorial in *The Journal of the American Medical Association* concluded: 'We can now add cervical cancer to the list of tobacco-caused diseases.'[51]

Despite the complexity of other factors involved in cervical cancer, there are several good reasons for focusing on smoking. It is probably easier to stop smoking than to remain celibate – for most. The number of young women under 35 in Britain dying of cervical cancer has *doubled* in the last ten years, and it is these same women who have above average smoking rates.[52] (See Table 6 opposite[53-57].) The Pill imposes its own set of risks on younger women and is also associated with cancer of the cervix *and* smoking.

Table 6:　Smoking and The Pill: A Double Burden for Young Women

Age	Women on the Pill % (1983)	Women Smokers % (1982)	Cervical Cancer[1] Death Rates (1963-1983)	Coronary Heart Disease Risk for Women on the Pill who smoke
Under 20	43	30	Not Applicable[2]	Minimal
20-30	48	37-40	Increasing	Small Increase
31-40	17	37-38	Increasing	Increased
40+	4	38	Decreasing	Very High
All Women	28	33	**Decreasing**	—

1. The figures for smoking and trends for cervical cancer and coronary heart disease are not published for exactly the same age categories as the per cent Pill-users quoted in each group above. The figures in the table are for *approximately* the same age groups.
2. The numbers of deaths in this age group are too small for comparison.

Table 6 points to the women currently at greatest risk from cancer of the cervix and they are *young women under 30* with above average smoking rates – nearly *half* of whom are on the Pill. These are the same women who will go on to risk heart attacks and strokes if they take the Pill and smoke as well.

Passive smoking – who are the victims?

Unlike the 'Big Three', passive smoking (inhaling other people's cigarette smoke) has always had female overtones. Evidence from countries such as Japan and Greece, where women still have low (but increasing) smoking rates, suggests that inhaling smoke from their heavy-smoking husbands can increase their chances of developing lung cancer.[58,59] Second, smoking during pregnancy and afterwards can harm the unborn baby and young child, who is more likely to develop chest infections as a result of its parents' smoking.[60]

As research on the effects of passive smoking rapidly accumulates, it is obvious that women who don't smoke are not the only victims. In rich countries, where women smoke nearly as much as men, both men and women are at risk. Moreover it is *smokers* and *not* non-smokers who are at greatest risk, for they are the ones who inhale most of the drifting (or sidestream) smoke from both their own and other people's cigarettes.

The effects of smoking on the unborn baby, although mishandled in past health education campaigns (see Chapter 9), are undoubtedly real. Poverty and poor diet have a bigger impact,[61] but women who smoke during pregnancy are more likely to give birth to an underweight baby than women who do not. And an underweight baby is often a sicker baby.

A risk underemphasised

Researchers have recently discovered that women who smoke have their menopause, on average, two to three years earlier than non-smokers.[62] You may say that some women would consider this a blessing – but the earlier your menopause, the more likely you are to develop thin bones – or osteoporosis.[63] This means more broken bones – especially your wrist, hip or back. It is true that women who have had their menopause are more likely than men to break bones anyway, but an early menopause for *any* reason *accelerates* the bone-thinning process.[64] It affects older women, most of whom outlive their spouses and may have no one to depend on for help if they break a bone, which often means staying in hospital for a long time.

Tomorrow's casualties

Today, cigarettes are already the biggest single cause of premature death and ill-health in women as well as men in the rich world. Although it is difficult to predict exactly how many cigarette casualties there will be next century, and who they will be, for some it is already clear. At the moment women from Britain, the US and Australia live for about seven or eight years longer than their male compatriots.[65] Most researchers reckon that much of this difference – perhaps 50 per cent – can be attributed to the lower smoking rates of women in the past.[66] So if men and boys continue to turn away from cigarettes, and if girls and women do not, that gap in life expectancy could close during the next century.

Which women?

If smoking patterns continue as they are, the cigarette will claim most of its future victims from two main groups of women: the underpaid and underprivileged working mothers in rich countries (see Chapter 1). Among this group are the doubly underprivileged women from minority ethnic groups who are often poor and almost always poorer than white women. It can be no coincidence that lung cancer rates among Black American women have increased faster than among their white neighbours.[67] Cigarettes are already claiming both women and men who can least afford to smoke, but who are nevertheless amongst today's heaviest smokers. They will continue to be the prime casualties in the next century.

Although still a small group, today's so-called independent career women will also succumb to the cigarette in increasing numbers. Hailed by advertisers as their most lucrative target since the last war (see Chapter 4), these women are just as vulnerable to the cigarette as their working-class sisters.

3: Third World women – a market waiting to be tapped?

Both women and men from the world's poor countries will undoubtedly swell the cigarette casualties most in the next century. Tobacco problems in the Third World used to be called 'Tomorrow's Epidemic' but they are fast gaining ground on the major diseases of poverty: malnutrition and infectious diseases. The World Health Organisation (WHO) estimates that smoking causes one million premature deaths throughout the world,[1] and one-third of the people who die from lung cancer *today* come from Third World countries.[2] Unlike the industrialised world, deaths from lung and other cancers account for more of tobacco's death toll than coronary heart disease. This is because one of the main causes of heart disease – aside from smoking – is a diet rich in saturated fat which is part of a lifestyle peculiar to the affluent world. The majority of Third World people would neither want nor be able to afford such a diet. Many do not live long enough to have a heart attack anyway.

The world's poor countries already consume more than half of all the tobacco produced,[3] and this proportion is growing. Global cigarette consumption is increasing by 2.1 per cent a year, and most of this is in Third World countries. As much as half the global increase in smoking in the last decade was in China, whereas consumption in most affluent countries is now falling.[4] Falling cigarette sales in the rich world have been one of the biggest incentives to tobacco companies to export the smoking epidemic to the Third World. In 1978 the American tobacco trade magazine *Tobacco Reporter* described Third World countries as 'potentially lucrative' and 'receptive new markets'.[5] Patrick Sheehy, Chairman of British American Tobacco (BAT) – the world's largest tobacco company – has made the industry's intentions towards the Third World quite plain. In BAT's Annual Report in 1983 he said, 'The whole world is our market-place and if we seize the opportunities which the market-place offers then I am confident of our ability to flourish and prosper.' In that year BAT made £542m profit from tobacco alone.[6] A combination of an ever-expanding population, no controls on tobacco advertising, and in addition governments which put too much emphasis on the short-term economic benefits of tobacco rather than its health hazards, makes the Third World a tobacco industry dream come true. As *Tobacco Reporter* put it: 'It seems inevitable that expansion [of cigarette smoking] will continue.'[7] Because the tobacco companies have bases throughout the world and can afford to spend more than $2 billion globally selling smoking each year,[8] it has been easy to gain a foothold in many Third World countries, where cigarettes usually rank among the top three most advertised products.[9]

Selling opulence and ill-health to the poor

The Third World today is the theatre for the tragic re-enactment of the adoption of cigarette smoking which started in the rich world more than 50 years ago. Only this time the tobacco companies have full knowledge of the effects of cigarettes, and the scale is unprecedented. What is happening is this: if the poor cannot have opulence, then the tobacco companies sell them an image of it through cigarettes. It is a tribute to the power of cigarette advertising that growing numbers of Third World people learn to associate cigarettes with wealth, status and male sexual prowess. Boosted by a bevy of brand names such as 'Hero', 'Rich', 'Master' and 'Champion', men who can afford it take the bait first. Sure enough, the Filipino brands Champion and Boss Super Kings were the No.1 and No.3 bestselling brands in 1983.[10]

Then – cultural and economic norms permitting, and with a bit more help from advertising – the cigarette culture is next passed from men to city women. By using advertising as widely as possible, the ultimate aim is to ensure that rural men, followed by women, will discard their traditional types of tobacco and become hooked on cigarettes too. Cigarettes caught on in rich countries in exactly the same way. Widespread advertising helped to sell the new cigarette culture to cigar-smoking, tobacco-chewing men, and later to non-smoking women in the 1920s (see Chapter 4). Rich first and poor later! The irony is that both rich *and* poor smokers are destroyed which could not be further from the image of the State Express 555 ads in Ghana which sell 'the very special taste of success' or Kenya's International Embassy: 'The smooth way to go places.'

The tobacco companies have a doubly powerful hold over Third World countries, which produce 63 per cent of the world's tobacco.[11] They have helped to persuade poor farming families – and governments – that growing tobacco is good for them. Yet in the long run it makes poor people poorer. In many tobacco-producing countries, food is the commodity in short supply, not short-term cash from tobacco – most of which disappears straight back into the tobacco companies' pockets. In the Third World, growing tobacco destroys the environment as well as the people. Vast areas of tropical and other forest are being cut down to provide wood to cure tobacco. One in eight of Tanzania's trees are being chopped down in the interests of manufacturing a product[12] which kills one in four of the people who use it.

Tobacco and Third World women: a unique tragedy

The WHO estimates that as yet few Third World women smoke cigarettes (about 5 per cent overall), whereas more than half of the men smoke some form of tobacco.[13] But this hides the true picture. In many poor countries women smoke as much as – if not more than – men. Cigarettes are only *part* of the tobacco problem for women from poor countries who use a variety of other – often more dangerous – forms of tobacco. Alongside the increasingly evident signs of lung cancer, smoking imposes unique problems for Third World women. The stark comparison between what kills rich and poor women is obvious from Table 7,[14,15] which looks at the importance of three key tobacco-related diseases in women in different parts of the world: lung cancer, cervical cancer and perinatal deaths – babies dying at or around birth. Here the difference between rich and poor is striking: the richer the country, the more likely a woman is to die of lung cancer (or breast cancer, which is not caused by smoking). Cervical cancer does not rank high on the list in rich countries and perinatal mortality is also low. As you move down

Table 7: Poor Women, Rich Women and the Smoking Epidemic (early 1980s)

World Region	The No.1 Cancer Killer (Relative to 12 cancers)	Lung Cancer Rank (Relative to 12 cancers)	Perinatal Mortality (Deaths at or around birth)
———————— Holocaust ————————			
Northern Europe	Breast	3	Low
North America	Breast	3	Low
Australia/NZ	Breast	3	Low
———————— Epidemic ————————			
Southern Europe	Breast	4	Moderate
USSR	Stomach	5	Not Known
Eastern Europe	Breast	5	Moderate
Temperate South America (e.g. Chile)	Breast	5	Moderate
———————— Growing Epidemic ————————			
Tropical South America (e.g. Brazil)	Cervix	7	High
China	Cervix	7	Not Known
———————— Future Epidemic? ————————			
Southern Asia (e.g. India)	Cervix	9	Very High*
West Africa	Cervix	11	Very High*
East Africa	Cervix	11	Very High*
North Africa	Breast	11	High*

Key: Lung Cancer Ranking System (of 12 major cancers)

Holocaust	1-3
Epidemic	4-6
Growing Epidemic	7-8
Future Epidemic	9-12

Perinatal Mortality

Low	Under 15/1000
Moderate	15-30/1000
High	30-50/1000
Very High	Over 50/1000

* = Infant Mortality (Perinatal mortality not known.)

the table, the countries become poorer and lung cancer becomes less important, only to be overtaken by cervical cancer which tops the list in all but one of the poorest countries. Yet the tobacco companies are directing more of their ever-rising promotional budget at Third World women; so we can expect not only a rising death toll from lung cancer but also an untold extra burden of perinatal deaths and cervical cancer, both of which are already outrageously high.

Three recipes for ill-health

The battle to win over Third World women to cigarettes is being fought between the tobacco giants and the forces of religious, cultural and economic control. The tobacco companies' access to women depends on a combination of geography and existing cultural norms which determine a woman's status in any given community. Ironically, in most communities the lower a woman's status, the greater her protection from their commercial assaults – although she may not be protected from the hazards of traditional forms of tobacco.

Religion – the great protector?

In traditional, male-dominated Moslem communities, it used to be rare to see women smoking cigarettes. A Moslem woman who smokes is not only breaking the law set out in the Koran, the holy book of Islam which forbids addictions, but also risks being labelled a 'fallen woman'. Yet times are changing, and today not even a yashmak is enough armour against the cigarette. One shocked doctor visiting Kuwait reported that 'for the first time recently, I saw Arab women, often in traditional dress, smoking cigarettes in front of their menfolk without any apparent inhibition'.[16] The latest WHO estimate suggests that up to 10 per cent of Kuwaiti women smoke cigarettes.[17] Another observer in equally Moslem Morocco described how she had noticed increasing numbers of women students wearing Western clothes and smoking cigarettes.[18]

Too poor to smoke?

Thanks to modern India's steadfast refusal to be dominated by any other culture, her people remain largely beyond the reach of the tobacco multinationals – for the moment. Some of the more affluent city men smoke cigarettes, but only a handful of women students and women who work for international companies or the media do so. These women, says Mira Aghi, one of India's leading health education specialists, 'identify themselves with their counterparts in the western world'.

India's real tobacco problem is in the villages where 80 per cent of the country's 750 million people live. There are as many ways of using tobacco as there are to tie a sari. Northern Indian women smoke bidis – small, locally made cigars whose smoke has a higher tar and nicotine yield than commercial cigarettes.[19] A packet of 20 bidis – which look much like small, conical fireworks – costs only a few paise, so everyone can afford to buy them. In Western States women rub powdered tobacco under their lips or inside their cheeks. In the Southern tip of India they chew pan – tobacco mixed with red betel nut and lime, which is neatly wrapped up in a betel leaf. Here, as in most other parts of rural India, the village streets and walls are stained – like the users' teeth – with the garish red spittle of pan chewers. Women from the Southern State of Andra Pradesh boast the most spectacular method of smoking. A bit like flame-swallowing, it is known as reverse chutta smoking. They put the lit end of a long, locally made cigar into their mouths and puff incessantly.[20] In Andra, nearly 60 per cent of the women smoke reverse chutta;[21] they say it is 'more feminine' than the non-reversed chutta which the men smoke.[22] If the women who smoke reverse chutta met those who smoke the equally 'feminine' Virginia Slims Lights, they would undoubtedly be mutually bemused.

The rural Indian woman's attitude to tobacco is one of 'benign tolerance,' says Mira Aghi, mixed with a belief in its magical and medicinal properties: 'They are blissfully unaware of any ill-effects of tobacco.' Even if there were health warnings on bidis – which there are not – few could read them, she says. The price Indian women are paying is not in the high lung cancer rates which characterise cigarette smoking, but in cancers of the mouth, throat and gullet (in the case of reverse chutta smokers).

Between 50 and 70 per cent of all cancers in India are in the mouth and throat.[23] Reverse chutta smoking – not surprisingly – carries the highest risk of death of all forms of tobacco in India, followed by bidi smoking which is about as risky as commercial cigarettes.[24] Even chewing pan – with and without tobacco – carries an increased risk of death which is only partly explained by the mouth cancer it causes.[25] The effects of betel are little understood, but it is a mild stimulant and can cause cancerous changes in animals on its own or with tobacco.[26] Indian researchers have counted seventeen different ways of tobacco chewing and smoking; the most risky combination for women is pan chewing with smoking, which increases the risk of mouth cancer 36 times above that of someone who does not use tobacco at all.[27]

Amid this tale of rural, tobacco-induced suffering there is good news. Unlike some of their counterparts in the rich world, rural Indian women are much better at quitting tobacco than men! In a rural health education programme in Southern and Western India, nearly twice as many women as men gave up tobacco over a five-year period.[28] The programme itself was an ingenious mixture of mass media approaches backed up with one-to-one support from a travelling health team. It relied heavily on using local art forms and the ubiquitous Indian cinema. Villages without electricity were no deterrent to the health education team intent on getting its message across: they simply plugged their films into the team's jeep batteries! Mira Aghi, the programme's media specialist, has a theory on why Indian women seem better at quitting tobacco than their Western sisters – despite the obvious poverty and malnutrition, she believes that the rural Indian woman is more emotionally secure. There is no threat to her wifehood; she has the comfort and peace of mind that her husband will always be with her and that her children will support her. India is still a country of arranged marriages, dowries, widow-burning and high illiteracy, yet it places enormous value on the family and the woman's role within it. Women's work is not devalued as it is in other societies. As Mira Aghi puts it, 'Rural Indian women do all the important work. Not only do they raise and feed their large families – they also produce all the food as well. The men, after all, are only the breadwinners.'

In Nepal poverty is extreme. Outside Kathmandu, where most people live in hill villages, there is no electricity and no clean water. Life is a constant struggle to grow enough rice and a few vegetables against extremes of temperature. Nearly all Nepalis smoke, including about 60 per cent of the women.[29] Young boys, hoping to put up an authentic Western front to tourists, buy American cigarettes in ones and twos. Everyone else smokes local tobacco. Village women smoke bidis. Cupping their hands around the whole cigar as they inhale, they direct the smoke straight into their lungs so that none escapes into the air. Their incessant 'smoker's cough' is undoubtedly worsened by inhaling the smoke from the fires which fill every tiny Nepali house. By the age of 40 the cough has turned into cigarette lung. Unlike rich countries, where cigarette lung is much more common in men, a house-to-house survey discovered that more than half of Nepali *women and men* were afflicted with it.[30] Lung cancer is not a problem in Nepal, for Nepalis don't live long enough to get it.

In Bangladesh, the combined forces of poverty and the Moslem patriarchy partially protect women from smoking. Men appear to exempt themselves from the Islamic laws, for official estimates suggest that 70 per cent of them smoke, compared with the official estimate that only one per cent of women do so.[31] The true picture according to Nazia Khanum, a Bangladeshi journalist, is that middle-class women tend to be 'deeply religious' and do not smoke, but bidi smoking among poor rural women is much commoner than the official estimates suggest. They have 'neither the time nor the education to be as religious as their more affluent sisters', says Nazia Khanum.[32] This may explain why nearly 80 per cent of women as well as men report regular cough and phlegm – the beginning of cigarette lung.[33]

The most obvious effect of smoking in Bangladesh is that it makes poor families poorer. Bangladesh's rural poor are farmers and earn their money from small landholdings. The landless – up to 15 per cent – are the poorest of all and are often women widowed early with large families to feed. Up to 5 per cent of a Bangladeshi's income may go into smoking.[34] This may not sound much, but in a country where at least one in four children are malnourished, an average family which gets through five cigarettes a day is equivalent to allowing nearly *25 per cent* of the precious calories needed to feed a young child to go up in smoke.[35] The average Bangladeshi woman can expect to live to the ripe old age of 47 – a full *thirty years* less than her sisters from the rich world.[36] Dying in childbirth is common, and her baby is *ten times* more likely to die at or around birth than a baby born in Britain or the US.[37] Poverty, leading to malnutrition and anaemia worsened by repeated pregnancies and lack of ante-natal care cause this tragically high death toll. Smoking during pregnancy merely adds to this large and untimely death rate. It has a much greater effect on Bangladeshi babies – doubling the already huge risk of a baby dying around the time of birth[38] – than on richer, better-fed women from the industrialised world.

Under the urban influence

In Nigeria there is a constant exodus from country to city. People in search of a better life often exchange rural for urban poverty, but urbanisation makes life easier for the cigarette salespeople. As the history of the cigarette repeats itself, smoking is now a common sight in Nigeria's cities; nearly half the men in Lagos now smoke cigarettes.[39] The strength of Nigerian culture has held back this generation of women from leaping into the Western mould, and less than 3 per cent of Nigerian city women smoke,[40] but the tobacco companies are rapidly investing in their daughters. Cigarette ads now feature smart young women as well as men. In 1973 less than 3 per cent of Nigerian women students smoked,[41] but by 1982 the figure had reached 21 per cent and a stunning 52 per cent among teacher-training students.[42] The tobacco industry sees these figures as 'particu-larly important . . . since they are the marketing base for the future'.[43]

Today's Nigerian woman is still too poor to die of lung cancer. She is the victim of infectious diseases – the diseases of poverty. Her children are *ten* times more likely to die before their first birthday than their British or American counterparts.[44] If stand-ards of living improve, lung cancer will be a disease of her daugh-ters, while she succumbs to cervical cancer.

Brazil, like Nigeria, has a growing urban poor. Together with its teeming populace and 200 per cent inflation, the last thing it needs is a cigarette epidemic. In 1979, *Tobacco International* offered some insights into why Brazil is one of the most lucrative, growing cigarette markets in the world:

1. Consumers' purchasing has increased, as a result of the country's economic boom. [They were wrong on that: the boom has since turned into recession.]
2. Women make up a good part of the market now, where formally [sic] the social acceptability of their smoking was questionable.
3. With the shift to the cities, such rural habits as rolling-your-own have declined, since city-dwellers tend to prefer tailor-mades.
4. Distribution of cigarettes has improved greatly.
5. The health issue is not strong in Brazil. There are no warnings on cigarette packs, nor are there advertising restrictions.[45]

Added to this are the unlimited opportunities for the tobacco companies to draw Brazil's burgeoning youth into the cigarette net. Forty per cent of Brazil's 120 million people are under 15,[46] and will become vulnerable to the idea of buying Western culture with cigarettes – even if they can only afford to buy one at a time. By the turn of the century, the population is expected to have grown to 200 million[47] an alluring prospect for tobacco sales-people. British American Tobacco (BAT), through its subsidiary Souza Cruz, controls 80 per cent of the Brazilian cigarette market.[48] In Brazil more money is spent on advertising cigarettes than on *any other single product*.[49] Brazil stands out among other Third World cultures because it is the most industrialised. Seven out of ten of its people now live in urban areas, and TV reaches nearly 80 per cent of households.[50] This makes Brazilians an ideal, receptive audience for the tobacco companies. Brazil is also a step further ahead in the transmission of smoking from men to women. In the urban Rio Grande area nearly 60 per cent of men and as many as 26 per cent of women smoked cigarettes in 1978.[51] As US women work their way down from the 29 per cent who now smoke, Brazilian women will shortly overtake them on their way up. As far as the size of the smoking epidemic and its consequences is concerned, Brazil is beginning to look like a rich country. Brazilian women already rank fourteenth in the world lung cancer league (see p.19), although this is an underestimate as death statistics for a quarter of this vast country were not then available. Doctors in Brazil have since been able to gain access to more comprehensive figures which show that lung cancer in women ranked second only to cervical cancer as the biggest cancer killer of Brazilian women in 1979.[52] So Brazil is misplaced in Table 7 (see p.31) as a 'growing epidemic' – it is already a 'holocaust'. What is more, heart disease – the archetypal disease of affluent societies – has taken over from infectious diseases as the principal cause of death in Brazil.[53]

The irony is that for all its industrialisation, life in Brazil still bears the hallmarks of the Third World too: the average Brazilian woman still dies 15 years before her US sisters, while large numbers of Brazilian children do not survive their first birthday.[54] Cigarettes, doctors believe, make a substantial contribution to this death toll; they estimate that smoking is responsible for 20 per cent of the underweight babies born in Pelotas,[55] deep in tobacco-growing Southern Brazil. So Brazil is a poor country which suffers not only the health burdens of the poor, but also a cigarette epidemic that is as big as any in the affluent world.

The potential for selling smoking to Brazilian girls and young women is not lost on BAT, whose brand 'Hollywood' leads the market and is now as aggressively directed at women as at men. Peter Taylor, author of *The Smoke Ring* – a comprehensive and meticulously researched account of the politics of tobacco – had this to report from Brazil:

> I turned on the television in my hotel room. A suntanned beauty leapt onto a surfboard and plunged into the waves. Another surfer swept into the shore to the beat of the music. Another beautiful girl [*sic*] drew a packet of cigarettes from the side of the briefest of bikinis. Another slides a cigarette from her boyfriend's lips: '*Ao successo com Hollywood*,' – 'To success with Hollywood', was the message. It was as if the Surgeon General (the author of the first US report on the health hazards of smoking) had never put pen to paper. The same slogan 'To success with Hollywood', appeared in huge letters on the baseline of the Davis Cup team tennis match between Brazil and Argentina which was being sponsored by

Hollywood and carried on the nation's television screens. Having seen it on the screen I went along to the event. Again, there were cigarettes everywhere. More beautiful girls, now wearing mini-skirts and blouses emblazoned with 'Hollywood', moved among the audience giving away free cigarettes and lighting them between the lips. Children gazed open-eyed at the performance.[56]

Peter Taylor asked Alan Long, President of BAT's Souza Cruz, why the Hollywood commercials equated smoking with glamour, affluence and success. Long's answer was that glamour could not be subjectively measured and that success referred to the success of the brand only. But he did admit, says Peter Taylor, that 'the commercials were effective and that is what they were trying to achieve'.[57]

Another Souza Cruz brand, Charm, is aimed exclusively at women, and was Brazil's twelfth bestselling brand in 1983,[58] which means about a quarter of a million women smoke it. Depicting a mixture of bubble-gum-chewing young US and dusky Brazilian beauties with cigarette in hand, the message reads: *'O importante e ter Charm'* – 'What really matters is to have Charm'. When it comes to selling smoking to women, no hoarding is left unpasted. Peter Taylor even found a village store in the mountains above Rio Grande Do Sul boasting an ad for Sudan 85 depicting a bronzed city woman basking in a carelessly untied bikini. Its message to local women was: *'O prazer mais perto de voce'* – 'Pleasure comes close to you'.[59]

4: The ladykillers – a history

What are the forces which are driving women to follow men to an early grave? Faced with what we know about cigarettes today, how can history repeat itself? Looking back to the origins of cigarette smoking, there can be no doubt that of the many factors affecting its growth, cigarette advertising has played a central role in creating and modifying each successive generation of smokers – both women and men. If cigarettes were a new product today, their advertising would undoubtedly be prohibited. But they have been manufactured and advertised since before the beginning of this century – a time when people were ignorant of their ill-effects. It is this history which will help us to understand today's modern tragedy.

The tobacco advertiser's methods are the same the world over: associate your product with something desirable (no matter how irrelevant); suggest that it fulfils a genuine need, or is an essential accoutrement of the modern trendsetter, and if possible make it sound like an agent of progress. In the case of women, cigarettes have always been – and still are – promoted as a route to sexual success, sophistication and slimness as well as emancipation or subordination (whichever virtue is more in vogue at the time). The history of cigarette advertising in Britain, Australia and the US is remarkably similar.

The development of machine-made cigarettes in the 1880s enabled the tobacco companies to turn cigarettes into big business. Men were won over first. Any proper lady of the time who dared prostitute herself to such a habit risked the ostracism of Victorian society – even though the new slender white cylinders were regarded as an effete version of the cigar. While the time was not yet ripe to persuade women themselves to smoke, they proved to be an excellent vehicle for selling cigarettes to men through a

series of now-celebrated cigarette cards. So effective were the
women and the words in British brands such as Wild Woodbine
and Cinderella, that there was no need even to display the product itself.

By the 1920s, the time was right to exploit the new generation
of women, liberated from the rigid grip of Victorian morality.
Women had organised politically and won the vote, as well as
new sexual freedoms heralded by the flapper. The scene was thus
set for the tobacco companies, which had begun to experiment
with mass media advertising so as to reach women in a big way.
The early route was paved with misguidedly coy attempts. Mis-
reading the new feeling of confidence among women, the US
company Lorillard tried to redirect its old Turkish brand Murad
at women by featuring the new smoking flapper alongside the
old non-smoking Eastern beauty whose job it had been to entice
men to smoke. The new slogan was: 'Why be embarrassed! Be
nonchalant – Light a Murad.' In 1926 Lorillard had another try
with Chesterfield, whose new ads showed a fashionable woman
not smoking herself, but ecstatically inhaling the smoke from her
male companion's cigarette. 'Blow some my way' was the new
message. In 1927 the then London-based company Philip Morris
(later to become the world's most renowned recruiter of women
smokers) tried a different tack with a new brand called Marlboro
which had red cork tips. 'Red tips for ruby lips', it suggested
hopefully. Although this approach failed, Marlboro was later to
be reborn with a new macho image which would help to make it
the world's bestselling cigarette.

None of these methods proved successful until American
Tobacco, led by its ambitious president George Washington Hill,
pulled off one of the biggest advertising coups in history. Hill hit
the female jackpot by re-launching America's No. 2 brand Lucky
Strike with a completely new approach directed at women. Hill's
strategy depended on a well-orchestrated use of the mass media.
First, his specially hired psychologists and advertising team devised a new green pack. Then they paid a series of models and
high society women to smoke Lucky Strike in key places. This
was followed by a series of massive advertising campaigns, using
testimonials from film stars and famous women. But it was the
new Lucky Strike slogan which won the day. There are several

versions of how Hill dreamt up the memorable theme; according to his own account, he was sitting in his car in New York when the idea came to him:

> There was a big stout negro lady chewing on gum. And there was a taxi-cab coming the other way. I looked and there was a young lady sitting in the taxi-cab with a long cigarette holder in her mouth, and her skirts were pretty high, and she had a pretty good figure . . . But right there and then it hit me; there was this coloured lady that was stout and chewing, and there was this young girl that was slim and smoking a cigarette.[1]

And it was thus that the unforgettable slogan was born: 'Reach for a Lucky instead of a sweet.' Within two years of its re-launch, women helped Lucky Strike surpass its opponent Camel and become America's bestselling cigarette.[2]

Lucky Strike's success was a turning point, after which there was no stopping the attempts of Hill and his competitors to reach down every possible female avenue. There were ads for the health-conscious woman: 'Luckies are always kind to the throat.' For older, middle-class women, 'Lucky Strike is a light smoke.' Even brides clutched Luckies saying, 'I do.' America's arch rival R.J. Reynolds followed suit and exhorted women to 'Smoke Camel for your throat's sake.' And Chesterfield even featured a knitting granny saying, 'Land sakes – I do believe I'll try one.' By the 1930s, mass media advertising had encapsulated its view of the female persona – described in *Campaign*, the leading magazine of the UK advertising industry as a synthesis between 'female freedom and free enterprise'.

> It might reasonably be assumed that it was advertising pure (and then reasonably simple) that had led an entire generation of women to the conviction that the most important task they could expect to perform each day was the creation of an alluring self-image: so products – the magical, the mythical and the *right* products – became a way to express yourself. You *were* what you *wore*.[3]

And it was the same with cigarettes: you were what you smoked.

The powerful impact of Hollywood's heroines was not lost on

the tobacco companies either and many, like Jean Harlow, appeared in their ads testifying to the virtues of cigarettes. At the same time the new mass medium of cinema immortalised the bodies, faces and cigarettes they smoked. Marlene Dietrich, Greta Garbo, Lana Turner and Betty Grable smoked their way through roles representing women from all walks of life. Sadly, the women who learned to worship the nascent cigarette culture from Hollywood could not have known that two of its leading disciples – Betty Grable and Humphrey Bogart – would later die of cigarette-induced cancers. The hitherto male images of the cigarette had been successfully converted into female ones. In 1924 hardly any women bought cigarettes, but by 1935 18 per cent of American women smoked cigarettes.[4]

The British manufacturer's similar venture into the world of the potential woman smoker also bore fruit. The Carreras tobacco company took the plunge in the early 1920s by re-adapting its Craven A brand to feature a smoking flapper saying: 'My word, they're good! No wonder you men are so enthusiastic about them.' 'Players Please – the Ladies too' beckoned the more coy-looking Imperial Tobacco ads, which showed the head and tastefully disappearing shoulders of a woman who *almost* dared to hold a cigarette. She was soon replaced by the short-skirted, independent-minded young woman boasting a Players Bachelor in her hand. By the 1930s Carreras made no bones about the reasons why cigarettes were an asset for women. Their seductive woman in red looked you straight in the eye and raised her Craven A (from a matching red pack) almost to her mouth. In 1920 women did not figure at all in British cigarette sales figures, but by 1939 they smoked 500 cigarettes per head per year.[5]

Thanks to what was probably a unique combination of Antipodean machismo and a manly emphasis on roll-your-own tobacco, the Australian tobacco industry's plunge into the women's market came later. Its early attempts to introduce women to the joys of the cigarette were like Chesterfield's, but open to other more modern interpretations: the ads for Ardath cigarettes featured a non-smoking flapper hungrily inhaling the smoke from her man's cigarette which was 'A Satisfying Blow'. Later approaches closely followed tactics elsewhere offering 'feminine' tipped cigarettes which were 'kind to the palate'. Although smoking became what was described as 'perceptible'

among Australian women in the 1920s, young women did not
seriously follow their male counterparts until the 1930s.[6] Many
tobacconists refused to sell cigarettes to women, and even as late
as 1971 the 'feminine' etiquette of the past lingered. Women who
smoked were advised not to:

Blow smoke in anyone's eyes.
Talk with a cigarette hanging from your mouth.
Exhale like an out-of-work dragon.
Walk along the street smoking.
Light your own cigarette if there's a man around.
Roll your own.[7]

By the end of the 1930s women had been led up what started to
look like an irrevocable cigarette path. The colossal stresses of
the Second World War – along with Roosevelt's declaration
(with an equivalent in the UK) that cigarettes were as essential as
food and should be issued with rations – undoubtedly boosted
cigarette sales to both men and women. But it had a much more
profound effect on women. Ironically, the War was a great liber-
ator of women. Many joined the forces or took on paid work
and, for the first time, large numbers of women had their own
money to spend. So the tobacco companies rapidly ditched the
old, peace-time message of the slim, sexy, woman smoker and
replaced it with the new emancipated female patriot. Lucky
Strike offered women in uniform a new white pack with the message: 'Lucky Strike has gone to War.'

In her analysis of the history of cigarette advertising directed at
women, Virginia Ernster, Associate Professor of Epidemiology,
University of California, offers further examples of the new approach.

Chesterfield offered women in the Forces 'help to make your
job more pleasant' as well as delivering 'more pleasure' . . . to the
men on the Front. Even the brashly 'masculine' Players Navy Cut
on the other side of the Atlantic took the final 'feminine' plunge
and featured women members of the mythical ship HMS *Excellent* smoking with new-found patriotic fervour. During the War,
cigarette consumption per head increased fourfold among
women in the UK, but only 1½ times among men.[8] The prize for
using the most emancipated image of the time must surely go to

Chesterfield for featuring 'Rosie the Riveter' – that memorable symbol of female liberation – in her working overalls with a cigarette hanging out of her mouth: 'When you're doing a bang-up job you need a bang-up smoke.' After the end of the War (1950) 25 per cent of American women,[9] 40 per cent of British women[10] and about 30 per cent of Australian women[11] had become cigarette smokers.

The end of the War took women back to the kitchen sink – but with it began a period of unprecedented affluence. Cigarettes were still cheap and women could afford to buy them. Sales continued to climb. Sensing these changes, cigarette advertising also restored women to their former glory as wives and lovers enjoying life's little pleasures – and smoking cigarettes. Chesterfield's post-war advice to women was: 'Everything's going to be just the way he'll want it. His easy chair . . . His slippers and his Chesterfields.' The post-war implication was that people's wives also smoked Chesterfield – and affluent brides slipped boxes of Chesterfields into their honeymoon cases. In the UK women also climbed out of their uniform and straight back into State Express 555 ads in full evening gowns. Women's magazines began to portray pairs of young lovers frolicking in the countryside, both smoking their Players Navy Cut: 'Whatever the pleasure, Players completes it.' Gallaher was alone in its attempt to appeal directly to women by reminding them of their short-lived, highly-paid war work. Its Du Maurier ads showed women offering cigarettes to men. This campaign was not regarded as a success. By the 1950s cigarette smoking had stopped increasing among men, but was still climbing among women. It peaked in Britain at 44 per cent in 1957[12] and at 33 per cent among American women.[13] About 30 per cent of Australian women smoked in 1950, and this figure remains the same today.[14]

Having helped to establish smoking as a widespread phenomenon in women as well as men, the tobacco industry had to find new ways of reinforcing as well as increasing its sales. This led to a new era in which the consumer was submerged in a constant tide of new brands each promising unique new qualities. Even more important was the growing emphasis on filter-tipped cigarettes. At the time the industry denied that this was in anticipation of the health warnings, but said that filter-tips would appeal more to women; they were apparently reminiscent of the

slender 1920s cigarettes in holders, and they avoided the unlady-
like practice of spitting out bits of tobacco which escaped from
non-filtered cigarettes. There is some truth in this because the
prototype filter-tipped cigarette, 'Silver Spray', with the 'cotton-
wool tip', was launched as early as 1909 with exactly this message: 'It absorbs nicotine and leaves no bits in the mouth.' The
manufacturers quite clearly had women and not health in mind
as early as the 1920s and 1930s, when Australian Cork tips for
'ivory lips' and British Players Navy Cut Cork tips were introduced with the new advertising message for women: 'Thanks for
the tip, I prefer them too,' said the Players 'lady.'

By the 1950s, reports on the health effects of cigarettes began
to trickle through in a small way. The industry's emphasis on
filter-tips changed radically – especially in the US. Cigarette
companies now competed to provide the consumer with a filter
cigarette which offered 'greater protection against nicotine and
tars than any other brand'. 'It [the filter] is the greatest health
protection in cigarette history,' proclaimed the ads.[15] Women, it
seems, fell for both messages and in 1961 twice as many British
women smoked filter cigarettes as men.[16] But as health concerns
grew inexorably, so did the number smoking filter cigarettes and
now more than 95 per cent of smokers in many Western cultures
– both women and men – smoke filter cigarettes. Likewise, the
ads for non-filter cigarettes are few and far between.

In 1962, when London's Royal College of Physicians published its first report on the effects of smoking on health, the
period of ignorance for both the tobacco companies and the
public was over. Both took the warnings seriously. In Britain
cigarette sales dropped by 10 per cent that year but the tobacco
industry has never officially acknowledged the evidence and
continues to advertise cigarettes as if it did not exist. But the huge
publicity and political concern generated would not go away. In
Britain it resulted in legislation to ban cigarette advertising on
TV and radio in 1964 – followed by similar bans in the US and
Australia in 1971 and 1976. But tobacco interests are not so
easily beaten and blocking one means of advertising, although
valuable, has simply redirected it through other, equally effective
channels. In 1983 the US tobacco industry was still the country's
main advertiser, spending at *least* $2,000m promoting cigarettes
– more than 100 times the money available to health agencies to

combat smoking.[17] (The British and Australian industries spend at least £100m[18] and A$65m respectively doing likewise.)[19,20]

Despite its huge resources and powerful paid allies among politicians and big business, today's tobacco industry has never been more threatened and not only by health activists but by the biggest lobby of all: the public. Witness the American Tobacco Institute's (TI) increasingly panicky responses to the growing concern about the rising cigarette-induced death toll in women. Following the US Surgeon General's 1980 report on smoking, which was devoted to women, the TI immediately circulated a synopsis containing its own version of the truth. 'The current increase in lung cancer in women,' it stated, 'may not be due to smoking but to some as yet unrecognised cause.'[21] This desperate attempt to refute the irrefutable would be laughable but for the fact that smoking kills about 350,000 Americans a year. An ever-increasing majority of people – especially women – now want to see a ban on tobacco advertising[22] as well as other action to reduce smoking. It is no longer a question of whether but of *when* our governments will act. But in the meantime – which may still be long enough to produce another generation of cigarette casualties – the industry will fight tooth and nail to preserve its most powerful weapon: cigarette advertising. It will continue to lobby politicians, buying support where it can, and silence governments more interested in raising tax revenue than preventing ill-health. It will buy allegiance and credibility through sport and cultural sponsorship as well as silence from the so-called free press which earns money from cigarette ads. It has even bought British scientists and doctors by providing money for 'health promotion' research which can cover any topic as long as tobacco is played down.

Women – a key asset

Today the tobacco companies are banking on women more than ever before. The male market has plummeted and looks more and more like a lost cause, so the women's market is an obvious target. And as in the 1920s, there has been an unprecedented liberalisation of attitudes to women in Western cultures. The time is again ripe to harness feminism to sell ill-health to women.

The aims are still the same: getting us started (see Chapter 6), and delaying us quitting. The industry's new focus on women is no secret, and the tobacco press is littered with learned articles and advice to retailers 'with women in mind'.[23] 'Women top Cigarette Ad target', read the headline in America's *Advertising Age*.[24] According to Gerald Long, R.J. Reynold's chief executive officer in 1981, 'The women's market is probably the largest opportunity for Reynolds.'[25] Women, especially the 'go-getters', are seen by the American advertising industry as the 'newest mass market'.[26] And their advice to European 'marketing men': 'Women are a prime target' for cigarettes.[27]

Although a little slower to catch on, the British Tobacco press could not agree more: 'Is there not a manufacturer set to win or consolidate a share of the woman smoker's habit?' asked *Tobacco* magazine in 1983.[28] The industry's justification for focusing on women leaves no doubt that profit and a cynical disregard for humanity are its guiding principles. The argument goes like this: thanks to the women's movement, women are worth more than they ever were before, because more have jobs with better pay, which means more money to spend on cigarettes. Think too, says *Tobacco* magazine, of the increasing numbers of women now in part-time work; they are worth some attention too – they earn nearly as much as women in full-time work.[29] 'Everyone,' concludes *Tobacco*, 'seems set on gaining a share of what purses and handbags are contributing to the tills of the nation . . .'[30] After all, there's more to be earned from women than men in the long term – because they live longer, says *Tobacco*.[31] And the case does not rest here. There are a few additional factors which make women an even more attractive proposition. US market researcher John Maxwell observes: 'Women are now experiencing the same job pressures that men experience. As a result they are smoking more.'[32] And finally, women are more important to the retail trade than men because, 'Our type of trade centres around women who are often more dedicated smokers than the average. For as we read the statistics,' says Ray Donovan, Marketing Manager of Bishops, a British wholesale and retail chain, 'once hooked, women are far less likely to abandon the habit than their husbands or boyfriends.'[33]

Cut-price heart disease

Marketing to women depends on an understanding of the balance between the emancipation which has led to financial independence despite continuing inequalities in pay and other aspects of life. It is still women who buy the food, and are most conscious of having to make ends meet for the family long before beginning to consider what's left over for themselves. This is why cut-price (discount) cigarettes are an effective way of attracting women and anyone else who can ill-afford to buy them. The importance of the small tobacconist is slowly being reduced by burgeoning supermarket chains where bulk-buying of cut-price cigarettes by the carton – especially in the affluent US and in Australia – has become the norm. And there is much more scope in supermarkets to promote cigarettes to women. First, it is still a predominantly female arena – an ideal place to tempt women under 30 too.[34] The supermarket shopper spends much more time looking at products rather than talking to an assistant, and is likely to buy her purchases on impulse.[35] Teenagers and young women spend at least three times as much on cigarettes as they do on confectionery and one and a half times as much as on cosmetics.[36]

The tobacco companies recognise the importance of the supermarket as a retail outlet. Tobacco sales in the British Co-op chain of stores are worth £50m a year, and they represent 40 per cent of the takings in the Bishops chain.[37] British American Tobacco owns the International chain of supermarkets in Britain. The Tesco chain now sell their own brand of cut-price cigarettes. In Australia too, shopping malls have become a focus for reaching women directly – often jointly with in-store promotions. So the shopper is beset with free cigarettes and 'special offers' outside the supermarket and further cut-price deals within. As successive budgets have made British cigarettes more expensive each year, sales of cheap 'own-name' cigarettes by supermarkets – especially in the US – are booming. The British Spar chain sells £60m worth of its 'own label' cigarettes from its cash and carry stores at 20 per cent off the retail price.[38] 'Customers,' says Ray Donovan, 'are much more likely to buy on price. Discounts of six pence on list price can be a real customer draw.'[39]

Lung cancer – and other special offers

If you were to ask a group of women shoppers what kind of product incentives they prefer, they would probably say price cuts, free samples and coupons, in that order. The tobacco manufacturers offer them all. The coupon business has always been dominated by women looking for bargains. Until the mid-1970s, when tax changes made it unprofitable, collecting cigarette coupons was one of the hallmarks of British smoking tradition. The ban on TV cigarette advertising led to heavy investment in gift coupon schemes with expenditure increasing from £8m in 1965 to £50m in 1975.[40] Collecting coupons was a good way of keeping people smoking and provided an ideal incentive to postpone a decision to quit. Gallaher's Kensitas gift catalogue offered 'Something for every member of the family'. If the average woman smoker got through 20 cigarettes a day for 30 years – the average time it takes to develop lung cancer – she could collect an electric sewing machine along with a cot and mattress for her baby. 'You get more out of life with a Kensitas,' said the ads. When ASH pointed out that you get lung cancer, heart attacks and chronic bronchitis, Kensitas withdrew the ad series.

Cigarette coupons have given way to an unending series of new incentives like special offers and competitions. Even the package holiday business has been annexed by cigarettes, as a way of advertising them without using the supposedly compulsory health warning. Bargain holiday hunters – 40 per cent of whom are now women[41] – can go on a package tour courtesy of Peter Stuyvesant, John Player Special and Silk Cut. And for those who could not afford the accoutrements of a summer holiday in 1983, cigarettes were there to save the day with their 'Summer Savers Vouchers' scheme. In exchange for 50 packs of Embassy King Size, you could be the proud owner of a pair of sunglasses, a hairdrier, a beach towel or inflatable dinghy. If you were one of the four million unemployed and couldn't afford a holiday at all, at least you could lie on your beach towel in the back-yard and enjoy a cigarette. If holidays did not appeal, there was the Mini Metro car for the 'go-ahead girl' who smoked More cigarettes or the Embassy Super Bingo or Superkings (Low Tar) Blackjack Competition – all especially designed to keep you interested in cigarettes.

5: The evolution of the female cigarette

Having identified some of women's strengths and vulnerabilities, the industry has evolved a series of strategies – not all successful – for incorporating 'feminine appeal' into what are uniform, cancer-causing products.

The macho cigarette

Despite the undeniably successful campaigns directed at women so far, the overriding image of successful post-war cigarette advertising was of the virile he-man smoking his Marlboro, Chesterfield or Camel. Having failed dismally as a woman's cigarette in the 1920s, Philip Morris re-launched Marlboro in 1955 with the now immortal (in fact, dead) Marlboro cowboy who enticed you to 'Come to Marlboro Country'. So successful was this re-launch that it now sells more cigarettes than any other brand in the US[1] *and* in the world.[2] Although its macho image has undoubtedly won it more male smokers, large numbers of women also smoke it. In Australia it is the eighth best-selling brand among women[3] – commanding a comfortable 3 per cent of the market.[4] Why do women smoke a product clearly intended for men? Do the Marlboro women really want to be men? Not at all. There is no threat to their femininity because the ad symbolises more than crude masculinity, but everything that goes with it: power, status, success and confidence, which is why Marlboro is so successful in poor countries.

The death and subsequent reincarnation of the Marlboro cowboy in Britain is a good example of how tobacco companies have adapted their tactics to get round restrictions on advertising. Compared with Australia and the US, they seem almost benign, but they are no less hard-hitting. In the early 1970s the

Marlboro cowboy rode roughshod over Britain, followed closely
by the more refined high-class pilot whose job it was to persuade
you to smoke Rothmans 'When you know what you're doing'.
But ASH had begun to make life difficult for the tobacco companies and government, and showered both with a constant flow
of complaints about these and other ads. This led in 1975 to the
Advertising Standards Authority (ASA) – a supposedly independent watchdog of the advertising industry – adopting a Code of
Advertising Practice for cigarettes. In it was a clause which specified that cigarette ads should not suggest that smoking or to
smoke a particular brand is 'a sign or proof of manliness, courage
or daring'. This meant instant burial for the Marlboro cowboy
and the Rothmans pilot. But such is the ingenuity of the ad
agencies that they were both rapidly resurrected as more effete
versions of their former selves. The cowboy was transformed
into a blond young man of ambiguous sexuality, and the pilot
lost his former hallmark of masculine achievement – the four
gold stripes on his cuff – and reappeared with a plain one.
Today's Marlboro and Rothmans ads show only the pack and its
symbols, but so strong are their 'after-images' bolstered by Marl-
boro-sponsored sportsmen, that teenagers who have never seen
the cowboy in the ads, still see Marlboro smokers as 'Marlboro
men'.[5]

Although Marlboro itself does well in Australia, Rothmans
came up with a more popular, uniquely Australian brand:
Winfield. Launched in 1972, its mass appeal was based on comic
hero Paul Hogan whose brash Australian humour was discovered on a TV talent show. 'Anyhow', he beckoned to all Australians who shared his working-class origins: 'Have a Winfield'.
And they did. Winfield has been Australia's biggest selling brand
since 1978.[6] Hogan's appeal was different from the macho fantasy offered by the Marlboro cowboy; he was just the kind of man
every Australian could identify with. So powerful was his influence on children that a public interest group MOPUP (Movement Opposed to the Promotion of Unhealthy Products) com-
plained as a matter of urgency to the Advertising Standards
Council, which is supposed to monitor cigarette ads through a
code based on the British model. However, it took 18 months of
stalling before Hogan was finally removed from the billboards.[7]
And like Marlboro, his 'after-image' remains.

The androgynous cigarette

The next obvious step in appealing to the yin as well as the yang among potential cigarette consumers was to match the hitherto male symbols with female ones. The beauty of this strategy is that it had been well-tested in the 1920s, and it was a safe way of enticing both women and men. The virile cowboys in the US began to make way for this new androgynous cigarette. Women as well as men began to tell us to 'Taste Winston Lights' or that 'Now is a satisfying decision'. Hand in hand with the new androgyny went a novel and apparently egalitarian form of advertising. Women were no longer helpless, pretty things waiting for strong men to light their cigarettes; the women in the new ads were their own mistresses. Benson and Hedges went so far as to depict a woman who was so emancipated that she smoked *and* put a protective arm around him. The Vantage woman equals her male counterpart in advocating, 'The taste of success'.

What the cigarette advertisers have done is to take women seriously and depict them as people with clear, independent interests. But here is where the egalitarianism stops. The themes of equality are merely used to *subordinate* women to cigarettes. Australian androgynous ads play safe in two ways. They incorporate the idea that it is desirable for women to smoke alongside men, but at the same time avoid any challenge to existing sexist prejudices. So the men are more likely to do the smoking and the women to do the watching – in the ads at least. In his analysis of Australian cigarette advertising, Simon Chapman – from Australia's National Health and Medical Research Council – finds that this back-door approach to women is a recurring theme: 'The advertisers feel it permissible to show men smoking' but the women can 'only be inferred to be smokers' by the men and the cigarette paraphernalia that surrounds them. This, he suggests, may be due to the lingering 'sexist ideology' that actively smoking women look 'bad' or 'cheap'.[8]

Take Philip Morris's Peter Jackson, whose ads brim with ecstatic young people, all teeth and smiles, proclaiming: 'I'm for Peter Jackson.' The name is male, but women go for it as much as men and it is the fourth most popular brand among both women and men.[9] For women are accustomed to supporting a male cause. Simon Chapman's 1982 analysis showed that the Peter

Jackson men were the smokers, and their women hoped some would blow their way.[10] More recently, Philip Morris have thrown sexist caution to the winds and the women now smoke as well as the men: 'With Peter Jackson You're Laughing,' they say. Benson and Hedges offers its special yin appeal through its Sterling and Extra Mild brands. Sterling, which is far more popular among teenage girls than among boys, puts its androgyny across in a series of ads where male and female hands symbolically exchange cigarettes. 'What a Sterling idea,' they say. And like the early Peter Jackson ads, they play safe: she never offers, but only accepts.

Black and White is one of Australia's cheapest brands and is directed at the women and men who can least afford to smoke. The theme running through the ads, says Simon Chapman, is 'powerlessness', matched with the fantasy of revenge against the powerful.[11] With the money they 'save' smoking Black and White, he can get rid of 'the wife' *and* mother-in-law by sending them on a holiday, and she can send her husband on a 'washing-up course', say the ads.

Until the late 1970s, the androgynous approach offered British manufacturers an extra bonus. It was a way of getting round the masculinity clause in the ASA's Code of Cigarette Advertising Practice. Characteristic of this period was the Player's No.6 series which was then Britain's bestselling cigarette. Women were already attracted to No.6 because it was cheap, but the new series of advertisements gave them female images with which to identify. The successful slogan, 'People like you are changing to No.6', remained the same; only the cast of characters was expanded. First, attractive young women began to appear alongside the laughing young men. They were soon followed by women of varying ages from all walks of life.

In 1976 changes in the way cigarettes were taxed meant that king-size became only marginally more expensive than the hitherto popular smaller varieties. This led to a flurry of new king-size brands to compete with Benson and Hedges, which became the new brand leader. Today, all the leading brands are king-size. Imperial Tobacco brought out John Player King Size and its lower-tar version portraying the successful career woman (or man) extolling the virtues of the new 'egalitarian' cigarette. By the time Imperial launched its king-size John Player Special

(JPS) in 1980, the smiling people of the 1970s had disappeared. The JPS series is based on the clever misuse of the word 'black', derived from the new black and gold pack: 'Black Chat', was the general introductory message, followed by 'Black Hander', featuring the well-manicured female hand which accepted the new JPS. Today, JPS is smoked equally by women and men[12] and is second only to Benson and Hedges.[13]

The female cigarette

To label a cigarette as 'female' means death to the potential male market. While it is possible to thrive on selling a male image to women, it simply doesn't work the other way round. After all, what man would be seen smoking a mere woman's cigarette? Hoping to ride the crest of the 1960s wave of liberation, both British and US manufacturers felt the time was right to go all out for a woman's cigarette. Their early fumblings led to several non-starters. Liggett and Myers tested the water in the US first with Eve, which bade 'Farewell to the ugly cigarette . . . Smoke pretty Eve – a cigarette as feminine as the ring you wear.' The cigarettes came complete with flowery pack and filter. But Eve was a failure, and commanded less than the minimum one per cent of sales needed to make it.[14] The same was true of Silva Thins and Max sold as fashion accessories: 'Wear a Max today.' In Britain both Silva Thins and Reyno Menthol – promoted as an aid to slimming – failed to make the grade too.

But out of these crude experiments grew a strategy that was to take women by storm. If modern women could no longer be persuaded to buy cigarettes in the interests of beauty and slimness alone, then perhaps they could be enticed by marketing a cigarette exclusively for women which was promoted as the hallmark of equality in a man's world. So Philip Morris took the ad industry's advice for targeting women: 'Aim where women are going, not where they have been.'[15] Never mind the continuing inequalities in women's lives – it was *equality* that women were dreaming of – so why not offer it to them through a cigarette 'they can call their own'? In 1968 Philip Morris launched Virginia Slims, the first ever 'all-female' cigarette with the 'immortal' slogan: 'You've come a long way, baby.' The early Virginia Slims

ads depicted slightly coy and giggly young women, but their confidence soared with sales. Today's ads are hard-hitting and usually compare the poor oppressed wives of the past with today's
jet-setter or executive whose cigarettes form an integral part of
her liberation from all forms of drudgery – even marriage.

The 'beauty' of the Virginia Slims woman is that she may have
'come a long way', but she is still someone's 'baby'. So she's only
playing at being the independent woman, and her Virginia Slims
are still a passport to slimness because they are 'Slimmer than
the fat cigarettes men smoke'. By appealing to women in two
conflicting ways, the campaign exploits both their strength and
their vulnerabilities. The magazine and billboard ads are only
part of the whole new Virginia Slims jamboree created by Philip
Morris. There's the world of Virginia Slims tennis, art exhi-
bitions and the 'Ginny jump-jackets'. There's even a Virginia
Slims football outfit so that women can 'Call the shots, play the
game and suit up just like one of the boys'. In 1970 Virginia Slims
introduced an annual Women's Opinion Poll as a reflection of
Philip Morris's sense of 'responsibility' and 'continuing commitment to the American woman'.[16] In 1983, 15 years after its
launch, Virginia Slims was still America's eleventh bestselling
brand[17] with nearly 1½ million women smoking it. Its initial success surpassed all of Philip Morris's 'fantasies', and its recent
growth is described in advertising circles as 'spectacular'.[18]

Keen to cash in on the 'women only' market, other companies
entered the fray. R.J. Reynolds first took the plunge in the US
with More cigarettes, launched in the 1970s for the 'confident,
sophisticated woman' who would be attracted to long, slim,
brown cigarettes. 'I'm more satisfied,' was the introductory inn-
uendo in the message. By 1983 there were four varieties of More
which together were the thirteenth bestselling brand family in
the US,[19] and are now leading R.J. Reynolds's sales.[20] By 1982
American manufacturers were lining up to develop 'dozens of
new brands with women in mind'.[21] The current shift is away
from the mock-independent Virginia Slims and back towards
the old, well-tested images of 'confident, sophisticated, feminine
luxury'.[22] The apotheosis of this strategy has been Lorillard's
1983 launch of Satin with the biggest (but undisclosed) advertising budget in the history of the company.[23] 'Spoil yourself', read
the unintentionally accurate headline which accompanied the

ads depicting glamorous women clad in satin on a white satin background savouring their 'Satin moments'. Lorillard sent all members of the press a large satin-lined box containing a cigarette lighter in a satin pouch, a bottle of champagne plus tulip glass to drink it from and a box of Godiva chocolates – all to be enjoyed while listening to Lorillard's promotional tape to the accompaniment of 'Satin Doll' by Duke Ellington. And what was Satin's unique appeal to women? It was, according to the advertisers, 'the smooth, satin-like filter tip' which added a 'special touch of femininity and luxury'.[24] The message women's magazines bring home to their readers is of the Satin woman who has 'great taste'. These advertisements are inadvertently accurate, since the woman is now portrayed as the smoker accompanied by her *non-smoking man*. Like Virginia Slims, it is not enough to use every available section of the media, Satin has managed to reach the front page of *Cover Girl* magazine by offering a range of 'Spun satin [eye] shadows' and lipsticks for the teenager who is advised to 'stroke it on and look radiant'. Insulting to women, you may say, even trivialising – but it works. In its first 12-week test launch sales reached nearly 1½ per cent of the market[25] and were holding strong by the end of the year.[26]

To the advertisers there is no limit to the expansion of their 'feminine' armoury. In March 1985 R.J. Reynolds launched Ritz cigarettes, deliberately aimed 'at the fashion-conscious female'.[27] They carry the Yves St Laurent logo – a new presentation of an old idea used by Imperial Tobacco in Britain to sell cigarettes to women in the 1970s. Virginia Ernster, speaking at the American Cancer Society's press conference to alert the public to the burgeoning female lung cancer epidemic, had this to say about the launch of Ritz: 'Does this mean that our society, in which designer products thrive, will soon tolerate – even pay for – "designer death"?'[28]

The female cigarette that had to go

In 1976, Philip Morris, still dizzy from its successful launch of Virginia Slims in the US, decided to try to lure British women into the Virginia Slims habit. In the interests of British female sensitivities, they used a different blend of tobacco, and even modified the sexist 'baby' slogan which had so offended *Ms* mag-

azine. October 1976 saw the aggressive £1½ million launch[29] of
the anglicised version of Virginia Slims with the slogan, 'We've
come a long, long way.' The theme of the woman who discovers
her emancipation through her cigarettes was otherwise the same
as the American version.

ASH was incensed. It was the first overt attempt in Britain to
use women's liberation to sell cigarettes and Mike Daube, then
director of ASH, protested immediately to the ASA. 'The ads deliberately attempt to exploit the women's movement and are thus
trying to recruit new smokers,' he said. 'The Virginia Slims
advertisements are directed at a specific sector of the market
where there is still room for expansion.[30] Despite appearing to
break nearly every rule in the ASA code, there was no 'femininity' clause to go with the 'masculinity' clause. The ASA said it
could not see 'how the campaign could be said to seek to persuade women to start smoking'. It did, however, express 'considerable reservations' about the ads, which it saw as being 'in
doubtful taste because they exploited the campaign for women's
rights'.[31] However, finding the ads objectionable on these
grounds was not sufficient reason to reject them.

Not satisfied with plastering hoardings, magazines and newspapers, Philip Morris approached the editor of *Ms London*, a
magazine aimed mainly at working women aged between 16 and
24, who agreed to let them use the magazine to run a competition. All readers had to do was answer some questions about
such 'female revolutionaries' as Princess Anne, and complete the
slogan: 'Virginia Slims are perfect for the modern woman because. . . .' The six best entrants won prizes which included an
elegant pen and propelling pencil set.[32] The incident provoked
immediate parliamentary questions from two MPs, Laurie Pavitt
and Lynda Chalker, and a sharp condemnation from the then
Health Minister, Roland Moyle, who was concerned that the
ASA did not consider the *Ms London* ploy in breach of the cigarette code: 'This strengthens our view . . . that the present [ASA]
Code does not go far enough.'[33] It is ironic that this first official
parliamentary recognition of the growing smoking problem in
women was prompted by a tobacco company's own efforts to sell
cigarettes. When the ASA code was revised in 1977, ASH made
sure that, alongside the virility clause, there was an equivalent
femininity clause which, theoretically at least, protected women

against any similar future ads. Today, ads are not allowed to suggest that 'female smokers are more glamorous or independent than non-smokers' or that 'smoking enhances feminine charm'.[34]

But a mere 'femininity clause' was not to get in the tobacco industry's way. In 1982 British American Tobacco (BAT), encouraged by the sales of its Kim brand in Italy and W. Germany, unleashed Kim on British women with a £3.5 million initial advertising campaign.[35] Its distinctive colour scheme of orange, yellow, red and gold was emblazoned on the pack, the filter and the seductive young woman whose complementary orange lips peeked out at you from under the brim of her Kim hat. Like Virginia Slims, Kim was also 'Long, Slender, Light and Mellow'. The ASA, which by then had begun to examine all cigarette ads in advance, let the ad slip through its Code. But didn't it break the new 'femininity clause'? Yes, agreed the ASA following a complaint from the public. BAT was asked to withdraw the ad – which it did *six months* after the campaign had already had its major effect. By this time it had been superceded by a similar series of obviously female images and silhouettes, as well as special offers in women's magazines which the ASA no longer saw as breaking the femininity clause. Although smoking and health activists were able to congratulate themselves when BAT finally withdrew Kim from the British market in 1984, we will never know how many teenage girls and young women were introduced to smoking during the two years that Kim was most heavily promoted (see Chapter 6).

The Alpine woman

Philip Morris, 'committed' as it is to the American woman, has shown a similar dedication to the Australian woman in the shape of Alpine Menthol cigarettes. Reminiscent of Britain's long-banned ads for Consulate which were 'as cool as a mountain stream', Alpine offers the Australian woman a unique opportunity to unite herself with Mother Nature. 'Fresh is Alpine' proclaim the ads which feature her with her inevitable man in the great Australian outdoors – swimming, walking, cycling or just plain frolicking. The early Alpine ads did not dare pollute such pristine beauty by showing her smoking. But they have

learned to overcome the contradiction – and get away with it.
Now her cigarette – and occasionally his – are part of the snowy
landscape. Alpine has been astoundingly successful and is
Australia's fifth bestselling brand[36] – second choice only to
Winfield among women[37] *and* teenage girls.[38,39] With the current
upward trend among girls and young women smokers, Alpine's
future looks as healthy as the landscapes in its ads. Alpine
Luxury Length, which combines Satin's seduction with Virginia
Slims's pseudo-liberation, was launched in 1983. It is Philip
Morris's urban answer to the ordinary Alpine woman who en-
joys the simple pleasures of nature. It depicts a woman whose
eyes, satin dress, jewellery and cigarette pack reverberate
together in shimmering turquoise. She no longer needs her Alpine lover – her extra-long cigarette is enough.

The low tar trap

Women proved to be an ideal target first for the filter, then for
lower tar cigarettes; in Britain three times as many women – especially older women – smoke them.[40] According to a government report, it is middle-class older women who are also most
likely to believe in the 'health advantage' of low-tar cigarettes.[41]
In the US more women than men have always smoked them, but
because the industry's low-tar strategy is more highly developed,
men are beginning to catch up. By 1983 26 per cent of men and
29 per cent of women smoked low-tar cigarettes.[42] Australia is
ten years behind the US and UK: only about one in ten smokers
smokes low-tar cigarettes, but still this involves twice as many
women as men.[43]

The development of the lower-tar cigarette – like the accept-
ance of the health warning on each pack – is the tobacco industry's tacit, if not overt acknowledgement of the cancer-
producing capacity of tobacco. It has staked its future profits and
our future health on what it has described as the 'low-tar
boom'.[44] What are lower-tar cigarettes, and what are their effects? Lower-tar cigarettes produce smaller amounts of the tars
which are known to be cancer-causing agents. If you smoke a
lower-tar cigarette, your chances of developing lung cancer are
reduced, but nowhere near as much as for a non-smoker.[45] The

recent growth of lower-tar cigarettes explains, in part, why male lung cancer rates have begun to fall.[46] But this is an over-simplification of a complex issue, for cigarettes contain thous-ands of other constituents most of whose effects are still a com-plete mystery. What we do know now is that lower-tar cigarettes *do not reduce the risk of a heart attack or of chronic bronch-itis*[47,48] (cigarette lung). Heart attacks, *not* lung cancer, are the principal killer of both women and men. Consider the effects of rearing a generation of young people on low-tar cigarettes. Brit-ish trends suggest that lung cancer rates in younger men brought up on lower-tar cigarettes have been reduced by about 40 per cent since the 1960s.[49] Although a lower-tar generation would lead to fewer people dying of lung cancer, *at least* 90,000 people would continue to die of cigarette-induced heart attacks and cigarette lung. In 1981, the US Surgeon General commissioned a report on the effects of lower-tar cigarettes. His conclusion was:

> In the case of lung cancer some cigarettes appear to be less hazardous than others, although the reduction in risk is min-imal and limited. No such conclusion can be reached for card-iovascular disease [heart attacks], emphysema, bronchitis [cigarette lung] or pregnancy effects.[50]

In other words, the only safe cigarette is an unsmoked one. The low-tar route benefits no one except the tobacco companies.

Low-tar disinformation

The tobacco industry says it is committed to reducing the level of tar in cigarettes, and it insists that the only way to encourage people to smoke lower-tar cigarettes is by 'informing' them through advertising. In practice the story is somewhat different. Among the bewildering array of 'mild', 'mellow', 'extra mild' and 'ultra light' cigarettes advertised in Australia, Simon Chapman could not find a single specific piece of information about tar content in more than 1,000 ads he analysed.[51] The picture is the same in Britain. When an ad agency attempted to calculate advertising expenditure on cigarettes in the low-tar category, it included all the brands which were described 'mild' or 'low tar', but only half of them actually fell within the government's des-

cription of low tar.[52] More important still, why are British
tobacco companies spending more money promoting cigarettes
in every category other than low tar, if they are committed to
persuading people to smoke lower-tar cigarettes? It can come as
no surprise then that the proportion of people smoking low-tar
brands has remained static at 15 per cent since 1977.[53] Average
tar levels have dropped impressively over the last two decades,
not because of advertising but because of extra taxes on high-tar
cigarettes, together with pressure brought by governments on
the industry to modify the levels of tar in all brands. But they will
not do so unless forced. According to *Tobacco* magazine, the
'manufacturers would have little difficulty in reducing tar de-
liveries by several milligrams. That they do not do so shows a
realistic approach to the commercial dangers of sudden changes
to the formulation of an accepted product.'[54]

The US tobacco manufacturers boast that 60 per cent of their
advertising is devoted to 'low-tar' cigarettes and claim that 58
per cent of smokers smoke low-tar brands.[55] But the reality is
that the true low-tar brands (cigarettes yielding less than 10mg of
tar) are smoked by only 19 per cent of smokers.[56] Many of the
so-called 'lights' sold in the US would not even fall into the low-
tar category in the UK. One of the few countries in which the
market for low-tar cigarettes is genuinely expanding is Finland,
where nearly one-third of all smokers smoke low-tar brands.[57]
This has been achieved by exactly the methods the industry fears
most: a ban on all cigarette advertising, together with effective
legislation and long-term strategy which forces the manufacturers to reduce the tar yields (as well as nicotine and carbon
monoxide yields) in all brands every two years.[58]

How are low-tar cigarettes aimed at women? The tobacco
companies are understandably reluctant to reveal marketing information. When I contacted the five major companies operating
in Britain, only Gallaher – makers of low-tar Silk Cut – were
prepared to talk to me. Silk Cut, Britain's No.3 brand,[59] two-
thirds of whose smokers are women,[60] is 'definitely not seen as a
female brand', said Martin Mulholland, Gallaher's public affairs
manager. The aim for Silk Cut, he assured me, was to reach
everybody. But Silk Cut has to protect its *existing* market as well,
he said. Reaching women without appearing to do so seems as
attractive an option as that of the androgynous strategy which

was used to advertise Silk Cut and other low-tar brands in the 1970s. As today's ads are devoid of human figures, women must be attracted by devious means. Low-tar Superkings does it by offering a longer 'feminine' cigarette, concentrating its ads in women's magazines and using competitions. While it is true that Gallaher advertise Silk Cut in all media, they have a history of carefully placed advertising designed to appeal to women. In 1983 they sponsored a series of fashion design competitions through women's magazines 'to help keep the Silk Cut name in front of women smokers', as well as an Autumn fashion collection.[61] Their 1984 leisurewear collection was dominated by female models too. Within their sports sponsorship programme, which covers cricket and tennis, there is also some strategically placed show-jumping sponsorship at Hickstead – a sport that is popular with women. 'Promoting to women without upsetting men,' concluded an article on Silk Cut and other low-tar brands, 'can be varied and subtle.'[62]

In the US, where it is considered normal to spend $50m–$150m launching a new brand, the battle in the lower-tar arena is well-advanced. In an article on marketing to women, six of seven new brands aimed at them were either 'light', 'ultra light' or 'low'.[63] Even Lucky Strike, the prototype women's brand of the 1920s, has re-launched a new, low-tar version of itself: 'Lucky Strikes Back'. Each major brand now owes some of its success to a more recently launched 'light' or 'ultra-light' version. This growth of brand 'families' enables companies to direct their lower-tar versions – especially 'ultra lights', such as Vantage Ultra Lights, Pall Mall Lights, Benson and Hedges Lights, Merit Ultra Lights and Kent Golden Lights – to women without risking unnecessary losses among dwindling male smokers who might smoke the major brand in the family.

In Australia the seeds of the low-tar strategy were sown many years ago. An analysis of ad expenditure in the press for the first half of 1984 showed that the top ten spenders in women's magazines were on brands which were all described as 'mild', 'extra mild' or 'light'.[64] Of the 21 'mild' brands listed, 13 were heavily advertised in women's magazines. More than twice as much was spent promoting 'mild' brands in women's magazines than anywhere else in the press.[65,66] The latest addition to the Alpine family, Alpine Lights, depicts the Alpine woman – cigarette in

hand – helpfully undressing her non-smoking man on the beach.
While the regular Peter Jackson ads boast both men and women,
the ads for the 'extra mild' version depict only women and
appear in women's magazines.

The three L's – a 'feminine' synthesis

According to *Tobacco* magazine, what women want in a cigarette is 'the three L's: Low Tar, Longer [length] and Low price'.[67]
If packaged in a mentholated flavour, you have the 'ideal'
modern woman's cigarette. Just as women first led the way with
king-size cigarettes, so they now lead with the extra-long cigarette – seven out of ten of whose users are women.[68] 'This is what
ladies prefer,' according to research done by R.J. Reynolds.[69] The
longer cigarette is 'in some way linked to the lost elegance of the
even longer cigarette holder', say tobacco pundits.[70] But are
today's young women really harking back to the long-forgotten
image that many have never even seen, or is it merely an image
offered to deflect any serious concern for health? Does the new
More Lights 100s, whose ads show a woman in gold lamé pros-
trate next to the matching beige and gold pack, really 'allow the
consumer to make a statement about her personality and her
lifestyle', as *Tobacco Reporter* suggests?[71] Are the long, slim,
100mm low-tar Satin and Virginia Slims Lights really what
women are demanding? Why should women *deliberately* expose themselves to more tobacco per cigarette than men unless
they have been coaxed into doing so?

The post-human era

Restrictions on British tobacco manufacturers have forced them
to think again. Human images have all but disappeared from
Britain's billboards, to be replaced by no less eye-catching racing
cars and surreal images, guaranteed to get past the ASA Code.
They appeal to women, men and children. Intellectuals (and
advertising executives) elevate the most surreal to an art form.
Benson and Hedges leaves a trace of recognisable gold in a Sun-
dew, a candelabrum and a shed snakeskin. People – especially
children – marvel at them and wonder what will come next in the

series. Silk Cut now uses a series of slashed expanses of silk with the health warning transformed into advertiser's copy. 'Do you think they meant it to be a vulva?' the young man asked me nervously at a conference. 'It doesn't matter what they intended. As long as we keep talking about it, then they are getting the message across,' I replied.

6: Growing up in smoke

What makes a girl start smoking? Research has so far confirmed what you might expect to be true: smoking parents, friends and teachers tend to produce smoking children.[1] Girls tend to copy their mothers and older sisters, and boys their fathers and brothers.[2] If you are a parent, the weaker your stance against smoking, the more likely your children are to start.[3] For children smoking is one of the forbidden fruits of adulthood; it seems to be associated with things only grown-ups do.

Tanya is 30 and smokes 20 cigarettes a day. She remembers her first cigarette very well: 'I started when I was 12. My father had remarried, and although my stepsister was only a year older than me, she seemed so much more mature in her dress and her ways. My stepmother let her smoke, and she took the mickey out of me because I couldn't smoke properly. I got my own back by stealing her cigarettes and going into the bedroom to practise smoking until I could do it without looking stupid.'

Catherine's reasons for starting were similar. She first started when she was 18 – just before her 'A' level exams – partly because she associated smoking with 'calming the nerves and relieving anxiety' and partly because 'it made me feel that I had, in some way, graduated to adulthood; I felt quite proud of myself.'

Smoking also appeals to a child's sense of curiosity. The girl who tries on her mother's lipstick and clothes when she is out may find her cigarettes lying around and try them too. Nancy had her first cigarette just before appearing on stage when she was 18: 'There was no pressure from anyone to do so . . . I had an almost disinterested curiosity in cigarettes. I wanted to know if what they said about cigarettes was true. I was trying to discover if smoking really did help one overcome anxiety at such times.'

Although Tanya's early experiences with cigarettes were anything but pleasant, she was determined to tread the path to adulthood: 'I even remember the brand of the first packet of cigarettes I bought, because they had such a bloody horrible taste. I didn't enjoy them; they made me feel sick. But I felt incredibly grown-up buying them. They made me feel that I was a big girl.'

Claudia, a 37-year-old secretary, started smoking when she was 11: 'I remember being bored one night and finding my mother's cigarettes lying around. I tried one because I wanted to mimic what I had always seen her do. Smoking was always very important for her, and I felt somehow closer to mum by copying her. It was always curiously reassuring to see her light a cigarette.'

Smoking is also a friendly thing to do; it is a way of saying 'Hello, I like you' – especially to boys. Most girls who smoke also have friends who do so, and the cigarette is a way of making those friendships special, a means of identifying with a special group and feeling part of it. Susie is in her last year at school and started smoking two years ago. For her it was a conscious decision – a way of joining the local elite: 'My image at school was that I was too good. I found that frustrating because I felt it didn't show me up for the little rebel I thought I really was. When I started smoking, people began to be nicer to me – especially those who had laughed at me before. I used to skulk off with them every break and lunch hour for that fag we all so desperately needed.'

Helen, who is 21, began smoking at 13. She viewed smoking as a means of narrowing the gap between herself and her fellow students, whom she saw as intellectually less able: 'I started primarily because it was forbidden, and therefore quite exciting for a couple of us to smoke behind the back of authority. I began to inhale and smoke more heavily at the age of 15. I think it was an attempt to prove to contemporaries lower down the "intelligence ranks" at school that the snobs (such as myself) could smoke just as well as everyone else. Meeting in the school lavatories for a surreptitious smoke helped to break down the unpleasant intellectual barriers between us at the time. It helped to provide some common ground between us.'

Kathy started smoking a year ago: 'The first time I smoked a whole cigarette was when I was with a boyfriend who was older than me. There were two other boys there, one of whom offered me a cigarette. Everybody took one – including me. I felt that it somehow brought me closer to them and also defined me as a person rather than a silly girl. The initial offering and sharing of cigarettes, to me, forms an immediate social bond.'

These are some of the main reasons why girls start experimenting with cigarettes. They are the same for boys, and therefore cannot *alone* explain why girls are now overtaking boys in beginning to smoke (see Chapter 1). How else can the difference in trends between girls and boys be explained? Certainly, proportionately more men have quit smoking than women so perhaps it is simply that today there are more women around than ever before to act as models for their daughters and younger sisters. But smoking is declining among women in the UK and US too, and there are still more men than women who smoke in the community as a whole. So why *is* smoking dropping among boys and increasing among girls? Of the other forces which could explain this discrepancy, cigarette advertising is one of the most powerful. So pervasive is its influence that it often escapes research altogether. Unlike the tobacco companies who take this subject seriously, many health researchers avoid it because it is too difficult a topic for 'orthodox' study.

Adults only?

Real knowledge about the effects of cigarette ads on children is obscured by a vast wall of denial. In Britain the voluntary agreement between the tobacco industry and government (as in Australia) requires young people to be protected from inducements to smoke. It is hardly surprising then that the industry argues forcefully that its ads are directed only at adults.[4] The American Tobacco Institute (TI) has gone as far as '*proving*' its honourable intentions by sponsoring a booklet – which is mysteriously unavailable when you ask for it – called *Helping Youth Decide*. In it, Vice President Walker Merriman proclaims:

> The industry does not want youngsters smoking cigarettes . . . That has been our policy for many years which has guided and will continue to guide our industry's marketing, promotion and advertising practice. This effort should actively discourage youth smoking.[5]

Successive British governments which earn more than £5,000m from tobacco tax each year are also understandably reluctant to admit to the influence of advertising on children, because to do so would mean conceding the need to take action against their friends. They are also in the uncomfortable position of having banned advertising on TV and radio because of its acknowledged effects on children, yet continuing to permit promotion through sponsorship and in other media.

You don't have to be an advertising executive to recognise that the tobacco industry's future lies with young people – getting them to start smoking to replace each generation of older smokers as they quit or die (prematurely in many cases). As we have already seen, women – especially girls – are the logically expandable parts of the market. Never has it been more important to reach girls than today. In the innocent days of the 1930s, women of all ages responded to the new advertising messages directed at them and started to smoke.[6] Today, public knowledge about the dangers of smoking is such that, if you escape inducements to smoke by your early twenties, you are unlikely ever to start.[7,8] So the tobacco companies – as well as health educators – need to reach us while we are as young as possible.

The tobacco industry's own market research paints a picture which is quite different from its public statements. In 1976 the American Federal Trade Commission – a government regulatory body – used its powers to subpoena all advertising documents kept by American tobacco companies and their agencies. From the mountain of material submitted, there emerged some revealing advice given to Brown and Williamson (the third largest tobacco company in the US) and first of the BAT empire to attract 'young starters':

> For the young smoker, the cigarette is not yet an integral part of life ... in spite of the fact that they try to project the image of a regular run-of-the-mill smoker ... In the young smoker's mind a cigarette falls into the same category with wine, beer, shaving, wearing a bra (or purposely not wearing one), declaration of independence and striving for self-identity. For the young starter, a cigarette is associated with introduction to sex life, with courtship, with smoking pot and keeping late studying hours.[9]

This was how Brown and Williamson was advised to attract 'young starters' to its brand Viceroy:

— Present the cigarette as one of the few initiations to the adult world.

— Present the cigarette as part of the illicit pleasure category of products and activities.

— In your ads create a situation from the day-to-day life of the young smoker, but in an elegant manner have this situation touch on the basic symbols of the growing up, maturity process.

— To the best of your ability (consider some legal constraints) relate the cigarette to 'pot', wine, beer, sex, etc.

— Don't communicate health or health-related points.[10]

We do not like to admit that we are influenced by any kind of advertising – least of all for a product which we know can kill us. We prefer to feel that we are free to make our own decisions about whether or not to smoke. Yet stop for a moment and think back to the first pack of cigarettes you ever bought. Was it simply because you needed them much as you might a bar of soap, or did they say to others that you were grown up and sophisticated? Did you choose the long, 'glamorous' ones or the minty ones because they looked good when you smoked them? Or the 'mild' 'feminine' ones to go with your image? Where did you get the idea that some cigarettes are 'feminine' and 'sexy', while others are 'tough' and 'macho' when they all contain the same lethal products? Was it your friends? Your parents? And where did *they* get the idea? Such is the impact the tobacco companies have on our decision-making.

Getting the message loud and clear

Although the research is still scant, there is ample evidence that not only are children aware of cigarette advertising, but they are more vulnerable to it than adults. Scottish research among 6 to 16-year-olds show that cigarette ads enter a child's consciousness as early as the age of six[11] – long before most would even contemplate smoking. Visual images are crucial in the young, and the words become more important as they get older. By the age of 12, nearly nine out of ten recognised the surreal Benson and Hedges ads and could name the brand.[12] This is at an age when both girls and boys are most likely to believe that smoking 'looks tough' and is 'grown-up'.[13] By the age of 14, children are not only immediately able to recognise cigarette ads, but are very good at discerning which brands are for girls and which for boys.[14]

An important part of getting an advertising message across is to win the consumer's approval and admiration for the advertising. Research the world over shows that children like cigarette ads. Three-quarters of Australian teenagers thought such ads made smoking look better than not smoking,[15] and in another study children who approved of cigarette ads were twice as likely to start smoking as those who disapproved.[16] The results of the American Cancer Society's research on teenage girls were similar: over two-thirds thought the kind of people shown in ads 'enjoyed themselves' and were 'attractive' and 'well-dressed'. About half thought they were 'healthy', 'young' and 'sexy'.[17] Children are not only best able to identify the most heavily advertised brands; they also smoke them. In Australia, Winfield is the most heavily advertised brand and is also the bestseller among adults.[18]

It is not surprising that research in both New South Wales and Western Australia shows that Winfield, with its Paul Hogan appeal to children, was also their favourite brand.[19,20] In the UK the pattern is the same. Gallaher's Benson and Hedges was the brand leader in 1983[21] and was the most advertised of all brands with more than £6m in its press advertising budget alone.[22] It is also the No.1 brand chosen by children.[23,24] This, according to Martin Mulholland from Gallaher, was simply stating the obvious: children smoke the brand 'because they see it advertised and smoked'.

My own research into 15-year-olds showed that their favourite brand was Benson and Hedges – also heavily advertised through sponsorship and elsewhere at the time of the research. These teenagers were unanimous in their view of what Benson and Hedges smokers were like: 'Young people', 'everybody', 'normal people', they said. Why was this? 'Because it is popular,' said Helen, a non-smoker. 'You see Benson and Hedges around all the time.' Maria started smoking two months ago and smokes six Benson and Hedges a week. Despite trying to quit with her

boyfriend, Benson and Hedges is her favourite ad: 'It's such a
good ad; it really impresses me. I'd like to hang a picture of it in
my bedroom.' Dave, who smokes 15 a week, says: 'I buy B & H
and Silk Cut because they're the ones I know.' Steve smokes 60
Benson and Hedges a week and he thinks they're 'popular with
kids' because 'they are the most well-advertised – so people start
smoking them'.[25] If cigarette advertising were banned, would
children still see Benson and Hedges as the 'normal' thing to
smoke? Indeed, would they smoke at all?

Consider, too, the Alpine campaign in Australia. Is it really
meant for adult women only? With its carefully positioned promotions and special offers in young women's magazines, it has
become one of the most successful 'women's brands' in the
world. Not only do twice as many adult women smoke Alpine as
compared with men,[26] but *four times* as many teenage girls as
boys smoke it too.[27] None of the British brands aimed exclusively at women has been as successful as Alpine or Virginia
Slims, but BAT was happy with Kim's success in Britain at the
end of its first year of heavy advertising. Mike Reynolds, then
Marketing Manager of BAT, told me that Kim was aimed at
'Women who were independent, self-confident and who were
looking for a cigarette that reflects their lifestyle.' And sure enough, the teenagers in the Scottish study reiterated this description of the Kim smoker as if they were reading straight from
BAT's advertising brief. They saw Kim was 'young, female and
lively'; the Kim smoker was someone who wore 'fashionable and
trendy clothes and liked pop or disco music'.[28] A recipe for attracting young girls, you might think. But according to BAT, Kim
was deliberately *not* aimed at the under 18s. Kim smokers, said
Mike Reynolds, were intended to be between 20 and 40: 'There is
no evidence that it [Kim] appeals to young smokers.' Yet a
Channel 4 documentary on women and smoking showed a
group of 15- and 16-year-old girls smoking Kim in the summer of
1983, when it was advertised everywhere from billboards and
women's magazines to Wimbledon tennis. Harriet, one of the
girls in the film, said:

> Kim came out last summer when I started smoking, and it was
> a new cigarette. It was quite mild as well – it wasn't strong like
> B & H or any other brand really . . . It was the new fashionable

cigarette for girls 'cos they were all on the adverts with girls on the front. So I just started smoking those [Kim] 'cos it was the new thing – the latest thing.[29]

Donna, one of Harriet's friends, also smoked Kim:

When I came home from holiday, we were driving through London and I saw these great bill-posters with this Kim; and I thought what is this Kim thing? When I came home Harriet was the first person I saw and she said: 'There's these new cigarettes called Kim.' I said, 'Oh, I'll try them.' They looked an attractive packet – it seemed feminine. Because it's Kim, you think of it as a girl's name . . . and we just tried them from then on 'cos they were quite mild to start off with.[30]

Renee Short, Member of Parliament for Wolverhampton West, raised this issue in parliament with John Patten – then junior health minister – who promised to look into it. In a letter to him she said, 'The remarks made by the young girls show how strongly affected they were by the advertising campaign.' And Mr Patten agreed: 'I accept that some of the women interviewed on the programme appeared to have been influenced by advertising to smoke Kim, though in none of the cases cited is it clear that they were persuaded to actually start smoking rather than simply switch from another brand.'[31] Such advertising, said Mr Patten, was 'perfectly legitimate'. It is this 'legitimacy' which is the tobacco industry's central defence of cigarette advertising. The claim is that somehow cigarette advertising – unlike advertising for any other product – does not persuade people to *start* smoking, but merely persuades those who *already smoke* to *switch* their brands.

However, when it comes to children this whole argument is a fallacy. Brand-switching is acceptable, says the industry (and the government), because it only affects *established* smokers and not, of course, the vulnerable teenagers whom they are pledged to protect from starting to smoke. Yet my own research with 15-year-olds who had recently begun smoking shows that switching brands is *a central part of the process of becoming a smoker*. Although they all had a favourite brand, nearly three-quarters smoked other brands as well. And more importantly, a majority had changed their brand up to *five times* over the preceding year,[32] much like the girl who experiments by presenting new images of herself to the world with each new hairstyle or fashion clothes. Mary smokes only at night and has gone through several brands. She smokes Benson and Hedges at present: 'I like to try all of them when they first come out. You'd get bored just smoking one brand . . . You experiment at first, until you find what you like, then you stick to it.'

Laura has been smoking for six months and changes her brand each time a new one is advertised: 'I started on B & H. Then I tried Raffles when it came out, but didn't like it. Then I tried Marlboro because all my friends smoked it, but I didn't like that either. So now I'm back to B & H.'

Unlike the long-established adult smokers – 80 per cent of whom are loyal to one particular brand[33] – the teenage girl (or boy) experiments with each new brand as it is launched. This is an integral part of learning to smoke.

The transition from young non-smoker to established smoker does not happen overnight. Think back to that first puff again – you were about ten, maybe younger. This was probably followed by a long period experimenting with the odd cigarette, accepting them from other people at discos and parties and getting used to the image. During this stage many girls do not even consider themselves to be smokers. Take Debbie, who is 15: 'I don't really smoke. It doesn't look nice. It tastes 'orrible, looks 'orrible and stains your fingers.' Yet she smokes at weekends when she goes to discos. It is this experimental group of smokers – what the industry calls 'young starters' – who absorb the ad messages religiously and experiment with each new brand. The more heavily it is promoted, the more likely it is to reach a teenager's consciousness. Even though most new brands fail to make the grade in terms of overall sales, it is worth the expenditure if it keeps teenagers experimenting – especially as a high proportion (up to 80 per cent) of children who try cigarettes will eventually become regular smokers.[34]

Starting low and working up

The role of low-tar cigarettes and their advertising in persuading girls to start smoking is not immediately obvious. Certainly the bulk of people who smoke them tend to be women over 25.[35] Yet if you look a little more closely at the figures, more girls than boys smoke them as well. British researchers have found that nearly twice as many young women under 24 are likely to have changed their brand – up from a low-tar to a higher-tar brand.[36] Do girls use low-tar cigarettes as an hors d'oeuvre to higher-tar smoking – and if so, why? First, higher-tar cigarettes tend to taste more acrid and seem more likely to make inexperienced smokers cough and feel sick. But why should this affect girls more than boys? Some American researchers believe the explanation is biological and that girls are more sensitive to higher-tar cigarettes (which also contain more nicotine), and therefore choose a lower-tar brand.[37] But high-tar cigarettes did not stop women starting 50 years ago. This again ignores the obvious: lower-tar cigarette advertising, as we have already seen, is directed more at women than men. But why do girls go for low tar? The clue lies in the way in which their advertising, especially in the US and Australia, cleverly suggests that 'mild' and 'light' cigarettes are more 'feminine' than the strong cigarettes which men smoke. My own research with teenagers clearly shows that not only did they have no idea of the real meaning of tar, but that many had acquired an image of the 'weak', 'weedy', 'mild' cigarettes which were for girls, and the 'strong' 'macho' cigarettes suitable for boys.[38] More importantly, there were suggestions that girls (and some boys) used low-tar cigarettes as a way of acclimatising themselves to stronger brands. And because this stage is transitory, it never shows up in the figures. This is how Mary started smoking: 'I thought when I first started, I'd better pick a low-tar brand because they're better. But I wasn't getting enough out of it so I switched to Benson and Hedges.' Jane is also 15 and has been smoking for about a year; she smokes about 15 cigarettes a week – not low-tar because she thinks those are for 'kids of 11 and 12'. I asked her why: 'They want to keep their grown-up image, but if they have a middle [tar] one they'd probably cough themselves to death. So they go for low [tar] ones. That way they can still keep up the image.'

Lower-tar cigarettes first gained currency with women in the mid 1970s. Research into London children's smoking habits over this period showed that they took longer to penetrate teenage consciousness. In 1975, less than 1 per cent of girls (and boys) under 18 smoked them, and by 1979 this figure had only increased to 6 per cent.[39] But the discrepancy between girls and boys emerged clearly amongst the 'experimental' smokers – those smoking fewer than one cigarette a week. In 1975, less than 4 per cent of all the experimenters smoked low-tar brands. But by 1979 – a time when investment in lower-tar advertising was growing and girls were beginning to overtake boys in starting to smoke, as many as 22 per cent of the girls were experimenting with low-tar cigarettes compared with 16 per cent of boys.[40] If it is the *advertising* which explains why girls are more likely to go for low-tar cigarettes, then you would expect the sex differences to disappear if advertising were banned – which is exactly what has happened in Finland, where slightly more teenage boys and girls now smoke low-tar cigarettes.[41] So the advertising for low-tar cigarettes seems to kill more than a few birds with one stone: it keeps consumers' minds off the dangers of cigarettes, helps girls to get started and may also delay a decision to quit.

Smoke gets in her eyes – but how?

The tobacco companies are clearly getting their message across to girls, but how do they do it? It is obvious that any child – unless she is blind or illiterate – will absorb the advertising messages which surround her on the billboards, newspapers and magazines, as well as through sponsorship. But what better *direct* route to a girl's or woman's heart and lungs than through her favourite magazine? At least half of teenage girls and women read magazines regularly,[42] and many rely heavily on them for information and advice about health, jobs, lovers and fashion – which explains why expenditure on cigarette advertising rose by nearly 50 per cent in women's magazines between 1977 and 1982.[43] British tobacco companies spent nearly £7m advertising cigarettes in women's magazines in 1984.[44] In a survey I conducted with health education specialist Amanda Amos on advertising policy in 53 women's magazines, all but two of them told us they were very fussy about taking ads and vetoed any which were 'hazardous', 'offensive', 'misleading' or 'anti-female'. Yet nearly two-thirds said 'Yes' to cigarette advertisements (almost) without question.[45]

The 'essence' of the ASA Code on cigarette advertising is to protect young people from inducements to smoke. Its rules state quite clearly that advertisements 'should not seek to persuade people to start smoking' and should not appear 'in any publication directed wholly or mainly to young people'.[46] If these heart-warming declarations – along with repeated assurances from the tobacco industry that their ads are directed only at adults – are true, yet our survey showed that cigarette ads appeared in *nearly 60 per cent* of the magazines whose readers were mainly teenagers and young women?[47] We analysed 14 of these magazines (half of whom took cigarette ads) and found that over one million teenage girls *under 19* were being exposed to cigarette ads in this sample alone.[48]

Our conclusions have since been tacitly accepted by both the Department of Health and the tobacco industry. For their latest voluntary agreement on tobacco forbids cigarette advertising in women's magazines where a third or more of the readers are 15-24 (where circulation is over 200,000).

A quick flip through Australia's bestselling woman's magazines will help you – and their proprietors – to forget that cigarettes kill 16,000 Australians each year. Their advertising pages are stuffed – to the tune of A$9m a year[49] – with ecstatic women (and the occasional man) extolling the virtues of the cigarette which has liberated them from their drab, oppressed lives to a world of beautiful people who drive fast cars and live and love to the full. Philip Morris spent nearly 60 per cent of Alpine's press advertising budget on women's magazines in the first half of 1984.[50] *Australian Women's Weekly*, Australia's bestselling women's magazine, has more than four million readers.[51] Its March 1985 issue included an innocent-looking four-page 'advertorial' called 'Do you Mind if I smoke?' written jointly by *The Weekly*'s advertising staff and the Australian Tobacco Institute. In 'the interests of fair and open discussion', it asked: 'Are Australians now being misled by people determined to stop us smoking at any cost?' These 'self-appointed guardians' were not giving us 'the truth', it asserted. Yet nowhere did it even acknowledge that the product it was defending is responsible for more premature death and ill-health than any other known to human society. Ruth Shean, director of the Australian Council on Smoking and Health, wrote to *The Weekly*'s editor, Dawn Swann, saying that the ad was misleading, and in the light of the growing smoking epidemic among women hoped that *The Weekly* would 'redress the balance' by inserting a feature of similar length on the effects of smoking on women's health. In a one-sentence reply, *The Weekly* said that the same issue contained an ad on 'How to Stop Smoking'. The ad in question, which was near the back of the magazine, was for a peppermint-flavoured spray of unproven value which contained the following detailed information on smoking and health: 'You know what cigarettes are doing to your health.' When Ruth Shean complained to the Advertising Standards Council (ASC), even they ruled that *The Weekly* and the Tobacco Institute were 'equally culpable in committing the breach' and her complaint was upheld.[52]

New Idea is read by three million women, nearly half of whom are under 25.[53] It has carried Alpine 'Win the holiday of a lifetime' competitions on its back page, and *Cleo* – also a magazine for young women with 1½m readers under 25[54] – has offered readers the Alpine 'Fresh Ideas Diary'. Thirty per cent of the advertising pages in *Cleo's* April 1985 issue – most of whose regular features were on sex – were devoted to cigarettes. This proportion is twice as high as any single other magazine on record in the UK, US or Australia. Among the ads was a 16-page promotional supplement on Alpine cigarettes. Cleverly dressed up as a 'Special Report' reminiscent of Philip Morris's Virginia Slims Women's Opinion Poll, it claimed to provide 'insight' into the character of the Australian woman. It even got a plug on the magazine's front cover. Looking for all the world like an editorial endorsement of the Alpine Woman, it identified five types of woman: the Modern, the Traditionalist, the Background Woman, the Suburban Superwoman and the Activist. All were neatly juxtaposed between Alpine cigarette ads. My letter to *Cleo* about the 16-page Alpine insert went unanswered.

Buying editorial silence

Do magazines which take cigarette ads keep quiet about smoking and health? The omission or de-emphasis of smoking risks occurs too often to be accidental. In the late 1970s American *Harper's Bazaar* – which earned $1m from cigarettes in 1981[55] –

commissioned Elizabeth Whelan, Director of the American
Council on Science and Health, to write an article on cancer. As
smoking is responsible for one-third of all American cancer
deaths, she logically opened the piece with a section on cigarettes, but when it was published this section had been relegated
to the end. According to the health editor at the time, the editor
had asked her to move it 'so that it wouldn't jump in the face of
every cigarette advertiser'.[56] There is a continuing 'unspoken
pressure' to 'consider the advertisers', she said in an article in the
Wall Street Journal.[57] Undeterred, Elizabeth Whelan again approached 11 women's magazines in 1981 – including *Ms* and
Harper's Bazaar – asking them if they would support her Council's anti-smoking campaign by writing an article in their July
issues. *Seventeen* – which doesn't take cigarette ads – was the
only magazine to reply.[58] In 1981 Carol Wheeler, a regular freelance journalist for *Savvy* magazine, reviewed *The Ladykillers*
when it came out in the US. According to the *Wall St Journal*,
Wendy Cripps (*Savvy*'s editor) admitted that the review had
only got through because she had not read it beforehand: 'We've
got a very young magazine. I don't want to get hurt by one lousy
book review,' she said.[59] So Wheeler's name was removed from
the magazine's masthead for fear of offending cigarette advertisers. This pattern of non-accidental reshaping of health information about smoking has occurred in the general press as well in
the US, UK and Australia.

Hollywood's legacy

Gone are the days when Hollywood's cigarette heroines appeared interchangeably in films (and later TV) and cigarette ads.
Cigarettes are rapidly becoming 'non-U' for the heroines of the
1980s who either don't smoke at all, or are busy trying to quit.
Apart from the teenage heroine of *Flashdance*, cigarettes have
become strictly unglamorous. Leading British TV serials such as
Crossroads and *Coronation Street* specifically avoid showing
their characters smoking, while new serials such as *Brookside*
on Channel 4 and *EastEnders*, take a firm anti-smoking stance.
But there are always those whose commitment to the nation's
health is open to negotiation. It is well known that there are
agents whose job it is to get products – including cigarettes – into

films. Take *Superman II*, whose hero is widely known in Britain
for his services to smoking and health. Whose idea was it to
make a 'Marlboro Woman' out of Lois Lane, his human heroine? And who engineered the heroic scenes where Superman
fought the Evil Three against a backdrop of Marlboro vans? Was
this yet another advertising ploy designed to reach millions of
teenage Superman fans the world over? Absolutely not, said
Philip Morris (the makers of Marlboro) when questioned by
Paul Magnus, Associate Medical Director of Australia's National Heart Foundation. They simply provided the 'authentic
background props' when approached by the Superman production team.[60] But informants connected with the film told Paul
Magnus a different story: the Marlboro star appearances were
'no accident', they said.

A bit of a racquet

Any advertiser who can afford it knows that there is no substitute for a captive TV audience of millions of young people. In
1969, shortly before direct TV advertising was banned in the US,
Joseph Cullman – then chairman of the Tobacco Institute – stated that the manufacturers 'recognised that the broadcast media
had grown to a position of unique appeal for young people'. In
evidence to the Senate Commerce Sub-Committee, he said:

> Young people are exposed to broadcast advertising differently
> than [*sic*] they are to print advertising. It is well known that
> young people spend a great deal of time viewing television
> and listening to radio; it takes an affirmative act on the part of
> the viewer or listener to avoid broadcast advertising.'[61]

This explains why the tobacco companies are now investing increasing sums of money – estimated at £15m in the UK[62] and
$13–20m in Australia[63] – in the sponsorship of heavily televised
sport, which thus enables them to get round the ban on cigarette
advertising on commercial TV and *all* advertising on non-
commercial TV for relatively small sums of well-placed money.
In 1984 tobacco-sponsored sports received more than 300 hours
of UK television coverage.[64] It also buys access to the healthy
image of sport and its personalities, as well as silence and even

respect from its advocates. More important still, it sells cigarettes! In Britain there is another voluntary code governing tobacco sponsorship in sport but, like its sister codes, this acts more as a charter to protect televised tobacco advertising than to curb the industry's activities.

Today's most heavily sponsored sports – cricket, rugby, snooker, golf and motor racing – are still largely a male preserve for both participants and viewers. But there are also ways into women's coronary arteries; athletics, enjoyed equally by girls and boys, would be a good option. But the Olympic Games and British athletics bodies have refused to associate themselves with cigarettes. Some companies like Gallaher have gone for the more female dominated show-jumping; and Philip Morris have personally sponsored Helena Dickinson – a potential Olympic hopeful – in a new £100,000 series of show-jumping events to be called the Raffles Classics.

Tennis is an even better bet; it gets good TV coverage, has an elegant, affluent image, is enjoyed by girls as much as if not more than boys – and its young women champions offer an excellent opportunity to associate cigarettes with glamour.

Philip Morris, as always, was the first to recognise this potential, and created the first Virginia Slims Tennis Circuit in the US which has now escalated to an all-year-round World Series with prize money of $10m. Its young women participants wear sweatshirts adorned with the Virginia Slims logo: a flapper with a cigarette (in a long holder) in one hand and a tennis racquet in the other, as if to say: 'Cigarettes got me where I am – how about you?' Of course most tennis champions are the last people who would ever dream of smoking, but top players like Rosie Casals have paid tribute to cigarettes: 'We respect Virginia Slims and what they have done for women's tennis,' she told the *Miami Herald* in 1970. And physician and tennis player Renée Richards assures us through the columns of the *New York State Journal of Medicine* that top players like herself, Martina Navratilova and Billie-Jean King are 'totally opposed to smoking'.[65] However Billie-Jean, when questioned more closely by Rita Addison of GASP (Group Against Smoking Pollution) in Boston, said she believed in 'free enterprise' and letting women choose to smoke or not.[66] Women have only their lives to lose, but a professional tennis player's livelihood is at stake: 'As professionals we had little choice but to play the Slims circuit . . . To not play would be tantamount to stop earning a living from professional tennis,' said Renée Richards.[67] Philip Morris have achieved what *Tennis* magazine described as 'the public relations man's dream': Virginia Slims, known simply as 'Slims', became 'synonymous in the public mind with women's tennis'.[68] And they continued that tradition – until recently, when Ford took over – with A$1.25m worth of sponsorship for the Marlboro Open Tournament in Australia where Marlboro women and men tennis champions helped to get the cigarette message across.

What better female ambassadors for the cigarette could you hope for? Most of the top players who meet one another at the Virginia Slims, Marlboro and other tournaments are under 30, and many have acquired a media stamp of approval for bringing back fashion-conscious 'femininity' to tennis. Hana Mandlikova reminds us, said the *Sunday Times* in its preamble to Wimbledon in 1984: 'Tennis girls can still, alluringly, be girls. The charms of this baby-faced 22-year-old from Prague were captivating.' Mandlikova won the Marlboro Open in 1980 – when she was 18 – and five Virginia Slims titles in the first quarter of 1984. Zina Garrison (20) – 'a beautifully natural athlete'[69] – reached the semi-finals of the Marlboro Open. Will emerging champions like Catherine Tanvier (19), described by the *Sunday Times* as 'pleasant on the eye', Manuela Maleeva, 'the pretty 17-year-old' and Carina Carlson (17) 'the attractive blonde'[70] be the paid cigarette advocates of the future? In February 1985, Philip Morris achieved what no other tobacco company has been able to do since knowledge of the effects of smoking became public. It was able to buy its way into health care by sponsoring the San Francisco Virginia Slims circuit 'in association with and benefiting the Children's Hospital Medical Center of Oakland'.

The Kim racquet

Martina Navratilova, herself a non-smoker and seven times Wimbledon champion, recently became notorious as a human ad for Kim cigarettes. Kim was launched in Britain just before Wimbledon in 1982 with an aggressive campaign aimed at young women. At Wimbledon that year, Navratilova and three other leading women players wore outfits bearing the distinctive Kim colours and logo. The ink was barely dry on the paper enshrining the new sports sponsorship code which was supposed to prevent players from displaying brand names on their clothes at televised events.[71] There was an outcry and even *Campaign* magazine, mouthpiece of the advertising industry, was shocked: 'The real tragedy of the affair,' it said in an editorial, 'is that young people may be encouraged to believe that success in tennis is achievable even if they smoke.'[72] British American Tobacco (Kim's makers) insisted that it was nothing to do with them. Navratilova and Co. were *not* sponsored by BAT, but by an Italian fashion company called 'Kim Moda' which had licensed another company 'Topline' to use the Kim name in its range of sportswear. That 'Kim Moda' had originally been licensed by BAT's German subsidiary was also purely coincidental. Even the then Sports Minister Neil Macfarlane, who was not known for his outspoken statements on smoking and health, agreed that a breach of the new sponsorship code had occurred. BAT apologised to the Minister and promised that it would not happen again.

In 1983, amid heavy advertising, Navratilova again appeared at Wimbledon in her Kim outfit. She still wore the distinctive Kim colours and only the tiny logo had changed from Kim to 'Topline'. This time Macfarlane was 'quite satisfied' there was no breach of the sponsorship code.[73] Navratilova, however, was intensely embarrassed by the bad publicity she was getting and discarded her Kim uniform, appearing at the semi-final in a plain white dress. By that time the damage had been done: she had already been seen as a walking endorsement for Kim by an estimated TV audience of 350m people in 90 countries.[74]

Drumming up smokers

As we have seen, banning tobacco advertising in one medium merely drives it to others. The medium of the future will be rock and pop music; seen as 'the key to the youth market', its potential to reach girls as well as boys is obvious: if you want to turn your product into a youth cult, buy a rock star and they'll do the rest. Rock stars, say marketing people:

. . . are already there, in the middle of hot dreams of pub-

escents up and down the country. Discussed in schools, glued
to walls, making their noise on one thousand and one stereos,
these faces are a ready-made medium. They are blank billboards waiting for brand names to be attached.[75]

Which is why Pepsi Cola sank $60m into a Michael Jackson tour
in the hope of raising a new 'Pepsi generation'.[76] Understandably, the tobacco industry is keen on a piece of the action; in the
US, R.J. Reynolds has already sponsored Eric Clapton concerts
and the 'Kool Jazz Festival' – popular amongst young people. It
is accompanied by ads for Kool cigarettes in *Ebony*, the leading
magazine for black people. Their message is: 'Where the music's
hot, the taste is Kool.'
   But megadollars won't buy everybody and when Peter, Paul
and Mary refused to perform at 'Camel Concerts on the
Common' because they were sponsored by tobacco, R.J.
Reynolds had no choice but to pull out.[77] Elsewhere, rock sponsorship is still in its infancy. In Britain, agencies specialising in
matching the products to the stars are springing up like mushr-
ooms overnight. Some record companies like Arista Records
want nothing to do with tobacco, but it is only a matter of time
before a tobacco megastar will help rear a new cigarette generation.

Doing the job properly

The ultimate responsibility for controlling cigarette advertising
lies with governments. In Britain and elsewhere there is ample
evidence that voluntary agreements between tobacco companies
and government are a sick joke. Both Norway and Finland
brought in laws to ban all forms of cigarette advertising in the
mid-1970s – a time when smoking had increased so much
amongst girls that they had overtaken boys. Since the ban, smoking has declined among all teenagers, but more sharply among
girls whose smoking rates are now below those of boys again.[78,79]
The reason for this striking effect, according to Matti Rimpela –
associate professor of medical sociology at Helsinki University,
and one of the architects of the Finnish legislation – is that
women took up smoking much more recently than men. This
meant that the growing women's market was much less 'stable',

and thus more susceptible to the effects of advertising – especially when the industry was aiming brands such as Mary Slim directly at women. The corollary to this was that women – especially girls just starting – were equally responsive to the ban on cigarette advertising for the same reasons. What is required of governments is now clear, but how much longer must we wait for them to act?

7: What really keeps women smoking?

How does the teenage girl who occasionally experiments with cigarettes become a confirmed, regular smoker? And more important, how does she differ from the boy who grows up to become a regular smoker too? While women undoubtedly see themselves as more dependent on fewer cigarettes than men, this cannot be explained by a simple physical craving for nicotine. For if this were so, you would expect all heavy smokers to feel addicted; a majority would find it hard to quit and most would need considerable support to do so. In practice, the opposite is true: many heavy smokers do not see themselves as addicts – about 90 per cent of the 9½m ex-smokers in the UK quit without any help, and a majority find it *easy* to quit. Perhaps the strongest challenge to the idea of straightforward nicotine addiction is the simple observation that social status is a more important determinant of who smokes and who quits (see Chapter 1) than either psychological or physiological make-up. To invoke nicotine dependence to explain why doctors have found it easier to quit than labourers, and why women feel more dependent on cigarettes than men, you would have to support the unlikely proposition that there is something about being a doctor (or a man) that confers physiological resistance to the 'addictive pull' of tobacco.

Not so much an addiction, more a way of life

Following a fruitless search for the 'smoker's personality', researchers found the first important clue which distinguished women from men who smoked: women were much more likely to smoke when under emotional pressure, whereas men preferred to do so in more relaxed or neutral circumstances.[1] The picture which began to emerge was one in which women depend on cigarettes to cope with their anger and frustrations much more than men.[2] Further pieces of the puzzle have fallen into place more recently; research in the UK shows that quitting smoking is a process which depends on the interaction of at least three crucial factors: perceptions of stress, self-confidence and dependence on cigarettes.[3]

Not only do women feel less confident and more dependent on cigarettes than men, they see themselves as being under greater stress than men as well – which in turn boosts their sense of dependence on cigarettes. From this spiral of lack of confidence, greater stress and dependence on cigarettes, there emerges a new explanation as to why women smoke for different reasons from men, and why they have different fears about quitting. A closer look at how women *themselves* understand their need to smoke takes us beyond the research to what is really happening.

Suppressing the unacceptable

Annie is 28 and smokes 20 cigarettes a day. When she feels bored or 'under stress' she smokes an extra ten. 'I couldn't contemplate stopping,' says Annie, 'because my biggest fear would be having nothing to rely on in a stressful or frightening situation.' Like Annie, Pauline also smokes at emotional high-points in the day: 'Cigarettes are a comfort and a cover-up for the many fears and embarrassments I encounter in my life. The moment I feel under any kind of stress, my first thought is to resort to smoking.'

Pauline and Annie, like so many women and some men, use their smoking as a safety valve, an alternative to letting off steam. They smoke not to accompany expressions of frustration or anxiety, but *instead of expressing these feelings*. As some researchers have said, women smoke to 'reduce negative affect'. Why? Claudia soon began to recognise the motives behind her smoking. She smoked heavily in all highly-charged emotional circumstances:

My cigarettes were a barometer of how I felt. If I was tense, I smoked more cigarettes. If I wasn't sleeping, I smoked more cigarettes. There was a predictable consistency in my self-destructive behaviour. If I was feeling relaxed and good in relation to myself, I would probably cut down on the number of cigarettes I smoked. It all seemed to hinge on how I viewed myself. I increased the amount I smoked to 60 a day after a very unhappy relationship with a man. After that point in my life, whenever I hit any kind of distress I would deal with it with a cigarette.

As a secretary, Claudia often felt powerless and frustrated at work:

If you watched me with a cigarette, you could see that I usually smoked when I was feeling anxious or distressed. I always found it difficult to express my anger and anxieties. Cigarettes were important to me because they helped to suppress a lot of these feelings. They were the only outside evidence of my feelings I was able to tolerate.

Aileen is a 57-year-old cook who smoked up to 40 cigarettes a day before her heart operation, but how smokes between 15 and 20 a day. She and her husband are separated. When her six children were young, Aileen had neither the time nor money to smoke much; the number she smoked shot up about five years ago as things deteriorated between her and her husband:

What upset me most was knowing that he'd made a right fool of me all these years. When I was sitting at home looking after the children, he was out enjoying himself or working overseas. And I'd sit at home thinking and thinking about how I'd been left to bring up the family on my own. And, of course, I'd smoke cigarette after cigarette to help calm me down a bit. I think my smoking went sky-high then because it was such a difficult period in my life. We couldn't afford a baby-sitter until six years ago. So I had no choice but to stay in. I had to wait until the eldest was 18 and a capable baby-sitter before I could allow myself to go out to the pictures.

Even when the children were old enough for us to be able to start going out together again, he still went off with his cronies. And he liked his drink too much; he came home drunk no end of times. When he started ranting, I used to be scared he might kill the kids. I remember one time when he hadn't been home all weekend, I'd been doing some washing – using the spin-drier. Suddenly everything in it seemed to go red; he'd hit me in the mouth, and I'd bled into the machine. I had to have three teeth out, and I've still got a loose one. I should have left him years ago, but I couldn't because of the kids. We've now been separated for three years, but I only get £1 through the separation order. I'm glad he's left, because he's still unemployed and claiming sickness benefit, but it's been hard to make the money stretch far enough.

Aileen would love to stop smoking and has every health incentive to do so. But, like many other women, she needs her cigarettes to maintain her calm.

Women have a bigger emotional investment in smoking than men. Cigarettes represent one of the few ways of uncorking those feelings that society teaches them to suppress. Mrs X, who is 64 and smokes 20 cigarettes a day, puts it another way: 'Cigarette smoking not so much calms the nerves as dulls the sensibilities so that I, at least, do not care so much that I am frustrated.'

Men do not, of course, escape similar frustrations, but there are more channels through which they can express these pent-up emotions. Society may not like a drunken man, but it approves even less of a drunken woman. Aggressive behaviour – whether desirable or not – is always an easier avenue for release of tension for men. This does not necessarily mean that women are innately less aggressive than men, but rather that women are *expected* to be so. Despite living in an age of 'sexual liberation', sexual freedom does not apply equally for men and women. Even exercise – a seemingly innocuous outlet – is still a more acceptable activity for men than for women.

Women not only smoke to keep their emotions in check; many dare not stop for fear of what may happen if they can't prevent their emotions from leaking out. Will her boss sack her if she answers him back next time instead of having a cigarette? Will her husband leave her if she gets fed-up and irritable about holding down a job as well as running a home? Will her children stop loving her if she turns from the loving mother into a momentarily angry woman?

Mrs S. is 46 and smokes 20 cigarettes a day. She admits to

using her cigarettes as a safety valve and has smoked a lot more since having a hysterectomy which left her feeling 'forlorn and run down'. Her cigarettes were a comfort to her, a way of dealing with being depressed. But her main problem is that she cannot stop smoking because her family finds her impossible to live with when she is not smoking. 'My family find me so irritable that, despite hating smoking themselves, they beg me to go out and buy cigarettes.'

There has been little research into what many women like Mrs S. are afraid will happen if they stop smoking. One small study of 16 middle-class housewives attending a stop-smoking programme in Connecticut concluded that one of the main barriers to stopping smoking was indeed a fear of losing control and expressing hostility. One woman on the regime said: 'Getting angry hurts others. When I smoke, I feel a release in my whole body from anger and tension. The cigarette won't hurt anybody but me.' 'Our husbands,' said another participant, 'can explode when they come home, but we can't. We are supposed to absorb the frustrations of everyone else in the family and still maintain the image of the superwife and supermother. I don't want to scream and yell at the family, so I smoke.'[4]

But housewives do not have a monopoly on the fear of losing control. Madeleine is a writer who has recently quit smoking and is slowly winning the battle to stay that way. She remembers why she smoked all too well and described her feelings on a Channel 4 documentary on women and smoking:

> Looking back . . . there was the fantasy of being in control, being cool, being sophisticated and being liked. I now see that the main driving force for my wanting to smoke was that the cigarette allowed my fantasy to take over. And the fantasy is that I'm in control of my life. I'm in control of other people. I'm in control of what happens to me. I'm in control of how I feel. So it's a fantasy of omnipotence. And without cigarettes (I mean trying not to smoke) I'm coming very painfully and very late to the awareness that I'm imperfect, that I'm not in control of my life, that things happen to upset me, that I'm alone.[5]

A question of stress

I'm not a women's libber, but I do feel that women have to give more of themselves in this life than men. The majority of women work at a full-time job, and then accomplish miracles in the house – cleaning, shopping, cooking and laundry etc. in the few short hours left in the day. Their husbands often help, but the ultimate responsibility for decisions made in connection with organising a home rests with the woman of the house. I don't honestly think a woman has time to concentrate on trying to give up smoking.

This is how Alison understands the difficulty she and other women smokers experience. She is 48 and works as a full-time secretary to the director of a small engineering firm. 'I am also a "girl Friday" at the office, and have to worry about everything in the running of a smooth operation from the most detailed of confidential correspondence to ensuring there is enough toilet paper.'

Smoking became a serious problem for Alison four years before her husband died. At 25 cigarettes a day, she was 'beginning to feel the stress and strain of the rat-race, especially holding down a full-time job and running a home'. She reached a stage where she 'couldn't seem to relax even when there was an opportunity'. Since her husband's death, it has become increasingly difficult to make ends meet. 'There is always the nagging fear at the back of my mind of being out of work, and wondering how I would manage. I get mentally tired at work and don't feel like tackling any domestic work when I go home.'

Alison used to enjoy running her home when her husband was alive, but postpones housework for as long as possible now so that she can keep up with the demands of work outside the home. She desperately wants to stop smoking. 'I hate myself for doing it, and feel constantly guilty about not being able to stop.' The difficulty for her is not so much the stopping itself, but staying off cigarettes. 'I always revert back to cigarettes because the alternative is to get fired from my job or to crash my car.' Known as 'Auntie Alison' by her workmates, she feels she has to live up to her gentle calm image. Her cigarettes are the only outward sign of the inner harassment she often feels.

Alison's need to smoke is a gauge of the conflict of loyalties in her life; if she devotes time and effort to stopping and staying off cigarettes, she must ignore other demands. Her predicament is familiar to most women smokers. She is torn by conflicting social pressures that maintain her need to smoke, and they are not the same as the pressures on most men.

Philippa is 37 and runs a holiday home for underprivileged children; she smokes 20 cigarettes a day. She has a non-smoking husband and three children who regularly put pressure on her to stop smoking. Family pressures seemed to work – for a while at least. But a disaster at home brought her rushing back to cigarettes. 'We were flooded out at home for three weeks and I couldn't cope, fighting the craving for cigarettes *and* running the home.' Philippa has clear ideas about why women need cigarettes:

> The biggest factor in women's lives is stress. Smoking is highest in poor areas, so is stress. More women are taking on the responsibilities that men traditionally carried alone. And more women are smoking: stress again. Many women in creative careers smoke. Creating is stressful if you've got a family to think about too.

Philippa's answer is certainly an oversimplification. But there is good reason to believe that smoking patterns do reflect – at least in part – the amount of stress in people's lives. For a woman, marriage and family responsibilities usually reshape any hopes she may have for herself. Society still expects her to devote herself primarily to her children and her husband, thus maximising the conflict between pursuing a career and caring for her family. The cigarettes many women keep lighting are one of the outward signs of their attempts to cope with that stress as best they can.

The multiple stresses on women are highlighted by Shirley's life. She is a single parent with two children aged three and five, and finds it difficult to make ends meet as a filing clerk. There is little time to relax and each day is a series of unending tasks. Before going to work herself, she dresses, washes and feeds the children, takes one to school and one to the nursery. After work she collects the children, gives them dinner, puts them to bed and does the ironing, washing and cooking for the next day. Shirley smokes to escape the unyielding demands of her daily routine:

I haven't got anyone to help me. It's just me that has to do it – I'm the only one that's there to do it. I mean, their dad comes and sees them when he's here, but he just sits there and gives orders. So it's not a matter of him washing, cooking, cleaning and looking after the kids, is it? It's a matter of reprimanding when he feels it's necessary. You know it's *me* that's got the 24 hours a day tension and pressure on my head that forces me to smoke – to get away from it all.[6]

The happy housewife?

While women like Alison, Philippa and Shirley use cigarettes to cope with the pressures of their multiple jobs, women who devote most of their energy to bringing up a family and looking after a home do not lead stress-free lives either. Viv has finally managed to quit smoking now that her children are grown up:

When the children were younger and I was at home all day, cigarettes became very important. They were the only treat I ever had. We didn't go out very much for a drink or to the pictures, so my cigarettes were my treat in life. They also meant an occasional bit of peace from three children under three living in an old house where we were all confined to living in one room.[7]

The old black fireplace in Viv's kitchen has a special place in her memory. It provided both the warmth and the focus for those much-longed-for cigarettes:

I can remember when the children were very young, I learned that if ever I sat down, they immediately came and crawled all over me. So to try and have some peace, I used to prop my library book on top of the black fireplace, and have my cup of tea and cigarette standing up. That was the only time I felt I'd got some space on my own – doing my thing . . . *That* was the real highlight of the day.

Although Ali is an actress, she regards looking after the house and her two children as her work: 'It's not my professional work, but it's the work I do a lot of!' She sees her reasons for smoking as a reflection of the changing pressure in her life. She started as 'a gesture of defiance' against a boyfriend who made her angry and unhappy. Having children gave her new reasons to smoke:

> When they were little I often had a cigarette because of the children. I wanted to wallop them, and I knew I mustn't; I knew it was completely unfair of me to feel like that. So I would rush out into the garden and have a cigarette to remind myself that I was an adult and I could do grown-up things, and wasn't forever having to cope with nappies and crying, and that kind of thing.[8]

Sarah is 26 and spends most of her time at home looking after her baby. She smokes between 20 and 30 cigarettes a day, she badly wants to stop and has made 'countless' attempts to do so. She describes herself as 'completely dependent' on tobacco:

> The guy I live with – the one with the income – is careless about money, and we always run short about the middle of the month. One month there was only just enough left for food – I just had to stop smoking. I was full of helpless rage and bitterness at being brought so low by his improvidence. In the end I adapted and managed by scrounging six cigarettes a day.

But Sarah soon returned to her former 20 a day. She sees her smoking as 'stupid and needless', yet she feels that women in her position need to smoke.

> A cigarette is the only pleasure you can indulge in without the kids pestering you for their share – especially if you've had no break from them for hours or days and couldn't afford to go out even if you did have a babysitter. You're tired, they're whiny, bored and awful. Ten fags may be the only pleasure you can (just) afford. They are your substitute for leisure, pleasure and ordinary adult activities.

Women from the Birmingham Women and Health Group saw smoking in a similar light. They smoked most when minding their children. Smoking, they felt, 'enables a woman to separate herself off from her children. The children have to wait until their mother finishes her cigarette. It makes her feel different and "grown-up", because smoking is an adult activity. It is a treat to relieve the monotony of being at home with small children all day.'

To Ali, Sarah, Viv and the women from Birmingham, cigarettes offered a way of identifying with the adult world from which they were largely isolated – a way of reminding themselves that they each had an identity separate from their children's. Many women choose to devote their energies to bringing up children, and willingly give up their jobs to do so; but this does not lessen the impact of the lack of adult support and the unchanging yet demanding routine of the world of children and babies. Smoking thus creates a space within this routine and while cigarettes may damage the women *themselves,* they are also a way of *momentarily* escaping from the pressures of home without appearing to damage their idea of what constitutes being a good mother.

Career and children: a difficult marriage

Myra is 46. She has four children and a non-smoking husband. She works for her local Family Planning Association as a 'general dog's-body', and is taking a full-time course in social work. Myra is convinced of the risks to her health, and her husband and children have all put pressure on her to stop. Yet she continues to smoke 40 cigarettes a day. Why? She is convinced that she is addicted to tobacco and is unable to muster the willpower to stop. Yet she sees her addiction not in chemical but in social terms, and has noticed that she is not alone with her cigarette problem.

> My friends and colleagues at work are mainly women under the double pressure of work and home commitments. They are all smokers. They devote a lot of time to half-hearted methods of cutting down. On the other hand, I have known several men who seem to have been able to give up with the greatest of ease.

Myra has to fight a battle to balance priorities between her own work and her children's and her husband's needs:

I desperately don't want to bring up latch-key children. I have to try to combine being a good mother with keeping up with the work expected of me at college. My husband doesn't like me working and would much prefer me to be the little woman at home. He is often disgruntled and feels hard-done-by if meals aren't ready on time and the house is untidy. Although he is happy to benefit from the extra pay packet I bring home, he still wants to play the conventional male role where he dominates and I take charge of domestic chores.

Myra's thoughts reflect the experience of every mother who faces the problem of finding child-care during her working day. Will they suffer from so-called 'maternal deprivation? Should she be leaving them at all? Deadlines at work seldom make allowances for motherhood, and the anxiety generated by these pressures can often be measured by the amount a women smokes. It is no accident that smoking rates among women who are most uneasy with this two-role conflict are as high, and sometimes higher than among men.

Ms Independent

What of the so-called independent career woman so beloved of the advertising men? For many such women, smoking becomes an indispensable means of hiding the underlying stress imposed by a society that disapproves of the choices they have made. Barbara fits the bill as 'Ms Independent'. At 28, she is ambitious and competent in her work as an architect. There is every chance that she will be promoted alongside the best of her male colleagues. Yet beneath the tough exterior, she feels insecure and has a constant nagging sense of being unfulfilled. She is not married and sees her smoking as a sign of failure – a feeling aggravated by her being the only woman working with four male architects who neither smoke nor approve of her smoking:

I look around in my office and see that my male colleagues are married with children. They seem to experience a kind of contentment I have never known, which makes me feel even more abnormal. Most of my female friends have left their jobs to have children. I think I find it hard to come to terms with the idea that if I pursue my career with the kind of single-mindedness that this male-orientated profession demands, I may never have time for children. Nobody has ever said that I've got the wrong priorities; they just think it. It makes me feel even more ill-at-ease with the choices facing me. Either I settle down and have children, which means sacrificing my career, or I follow my ambitions much like my male colleagues. The difference between them and me is that they are doing what is considered to be the norm in our society, and I am going against the grain. I suppose there must be something in me which chooses to oppose accepted female norms. I enjoy my work, but I feel restless at the same time because I feel I ought to be settling down. I feel tense at work, so I smoke. I feel lonely at home, so I smoke. In fact, I think I smoke wherever I feel abnormal because I am not somebody's wife or mother.

Maisie had her first cigarette at 14 when she started in a factory; she has now worked her way up to being a shop steward. She quit once for 7 weeks, but has not tried again since:

When we're called in to management, the first thing that comes out are your cigarettes – and on go their fans. By the look on their faces you know you're not going to get what you want, so another cigarette comes out. But the funny part is that none of the men smoke in there. They can't be smokers can they? . . . I think men have got it easy. I mean, a man retires at the age of 65. A woman doesn't retire at all – not until she's in a box.

Learning to be dependent

'I am an addict who cannot get off the hook . . . I am chemically addicted to it [tobacco]. I know I am weak-willed. I could have taken up the bottle when my husband died, but I took up nicotine instead.'

This is how Ronda – and nearly every other woman who talked to me about her smoking – sees her need to smoke. Yet at

the age of 60, Ronda has just as many convincing social and emotional explanations for why she smokes. She started 25 years ago
when her husband died, leaving her to cope with bringing up
three young children. Her second husband was 'an alcoholic
who made life intolerable for us all', leaving Ronda lonely and
depressed. Like all the women I interviewed, she opted to see
herself as 'a helpless addict' rather than a woman with good
reasons to smoke.

How can Ronda and so many other women be certain of their
'addiction' when research itself shows that there is much more to
smoking than chemical dependence on nicotine? British gov-
ernment-sponsored research tells us that the more dependent
you feel you are on cigarettes, the less likely you are to quit successfully.[9] But more importantly, it also shows that women feel
more dependent on cigarettes than men, and that this feeling of
dependence is 'more an abiding state of mind' than a chemical
dependence on nicotine.[10] This is supported by Liz Batten's research into smoker types, which shows that for women (and not
for men) there is an underlying core of 'addictive' smoking
within *each category* of smoker. 'Women's dependence,' concludes Liz Batten, director of 'Operation Smokestop', 'seems to
be tied up with *all* their reasons for smoking. Women associate
their craving for cigarettes with mood control and men do not.'[11]
Which is why quitting presents different prospects for women
and men. Alan Marsh, one of the authors of the government report, concluded that 'smoking is a *learned* dependence' and that
it can also be 'unlearned'. So if cigarette dependence is more a
reflection of our attitudes than simply the screeching of nerve-
endings, why are women more strongly influenced by such
attitudes than men?

Tanya quit smoking for three weeks, but now she is back to 20
a day. Like many other women, she recognises that she has
learned to use smoking to fulfil different functions at different
times in her life. As a teenager, she smoked out of sheer bravado.
Now, one husband and two children later, she has a different
story to tell: 'I used to smoke because I wanted to, now I smoke
because I need to.' Mrs D., who also smokes 20 a day, sees the
origins of her dependence as social. As a young woman she only
smoked occasionally and never felt deprived or particularly in
need of cigarettes – even at work, where smoking was not

allowed. 'My true addiction began when my husband broke out in a rash [*sic*] of schizophrenia. No help was available to us then [20 years ago] and the tensions became unbearable.' From then on, Mrs D.'s life was punctuated by her husband's deterioration and periodic stays in hospital. She managed to stop smoking quite easily following a stroke which put her into hospital for some time, thus separating her from her difficulties at home. 'I did not think of smoking again until my husband's aggro one day sent me rushing to buy cigarettes.' Mrs D. has continued smoking ever since. Although her difficulties are extreme in some ways, her account shows clearly how her dependence on cigarettes can be seen in the context of her life, rather than within the narrow confines of a chemistry which is beyond human control.

Thin is beautiful

With my smoking now ceasing
My food was increasing
And the bills which came in were immense;
My vital statistics
Were unrealistic
Things just didn't seem to make sense.

The problem of dieting
Was very disquieting,
I existed for weeks without dinner.
My physique I exerted
And snacks I deserted,
But nothing would make me get thinner.

This 17-year-old girl's musings won her a poetry prize in a magazine for young women.[12] In her own way, she reflects the plight of many, especially teenagers and young women.

These concerns are twofold. First, girls are much more likely than boys to see smoking as a means of losing weight,[13] and later on, women are more likely than men to be worried about gaining weight after quitting.[14] In the face of perpetual bombardment with cigarette ads portraying smoking as the ultimate aid to slimness and glamour for women, it is easy to see why girls are more likely than boys to take this view. The double irony is that smoking does not keep you slim, it makes you sick. Although most of the research is inadequate and was done only on men, there is no evidence whatsoever that smoking reduces weight in young people.[15,16] What it does is make older people ill (usually with chronic chest disease) and they lose weight as they become too breathless and unwell to eat properly.[17] What is more, US research into 57,000 women on weight reduction courses shows smoking to be an ineffective appetite suppressant as those most overweight were also the heaviest smokers.[18] More recently, Dutch researchers looking at a group of young women and men who were more representative of the general population, came to the same conclusion. They actually found that some of the heaviest smokers weighed more than either non-smokers and ex-smokers.[19]

Susie is 17 and is working for her A levels. To her, smoking is a lesser evil than eating:

> I would have a cigarette instead of nibbling and picking at food between meals when I'm not supposed to be hungry anyway . . . to stop smoking would mean not only that I would have to break away from my smoking friends, but that I would go back to picking food from the larder. What is needed is another form of oral satisfaction which has no bad social or health effects.

Helen is a 21-year-old student who smokes up to 25 cigarettes a day. Although she started at 13 out of bravado, she feels she now smokes for quite different reasons. 'One very significant reason is the fear of gaining weight. After a six-week period of giving up, I found my appetite for chocolate and biscuits increased phenomenally. I began smoking again to subdue my appetite. I equate smoking with weight loss.'

Olga is 41 and smokes 20 low-tar cigarettes a day. She responded to the publicity on smoking and health five years ago and stopped. Delighted that she had managed to 'break the habit', she was so afraid of gaining weight that she did not dare eat anything either. 'Imagine the hell. I stuck it for as long as I could – not smoking and hardly eating anything either – but finally succumbed with great remorse and started smoking again, having lose 28 lbs.' Olga managed an extraordinarily punitive regime for three months, displaying strong if misdirected willpower. It had all been channelled into keeping thin.

Many women find they smoke to reduce their weight, and eat compulsively at the same time. Cigarettes help Pauline to get through the day without eating anything, but by the evening she 'can't avoid those horrifying binges where [she] will eat a Mars Bar, a Kit-Kat and 14 biscuits with milk'. Pauline recognises that smoking is a serious health risk, but cannot stop because of wanting to control her weight. Yet smoking does not control her compulsion to eat and she finds that, despite smoking, she still gains weight. To leave the vicious circle, she must face the prospect of further possible weight gain.

Jane is a 30-year-old architect and smokes up to a pack of cigarettes a day. The fatter she feels, the more she smokes, sometimes she hardly smokes at all:

> When I feel thin, I can cope with the world and men in particular. It is only then that I have enough confidence to deal with my male colleagues at work. My cigarettes help me to make up for this ridiculous sense of inadequacy I have. Rationally, I know that I am as intellectually able as my colleagues, but I don't seem able to convince myself of my abilities.

Jane badly wants to be part of their male world and she competes in the only way she knows how:

> At work I get men to listen to me because I feel thin and attractive. I don't want to be treated as a sex object, yet I can't believe that men will take me seriously. So I force them to pay attention to me through my body. I want to stop smoking but I can't afford to lose the self-respect my thinness gives me. My cigarettes have become my food, my source of strength. My need for food is more threatening to my life than my need for cigarettes.

A confidence trick

Research in Britain clearly shows that if you want to quit successfully, then confidence in your ability to do so is of the essence.[20] This may seem a truism, but what is not so obvious is why survey after survey shows that despite an equal desire among women and men to quit, women are much less likely to feel confident of their success.

B. is a former government minister with a special interest in health. She smokes 20 cigarettes a day. She managed to stop smoking for a year before taking on her ministerial duties, at a time when she was actively campaigning on smoking and other health issues. Once appointed a minister, she began smoking again intermittently:

> As opportunities and, therefore, pressures in my job grew, I gradually increased my consumption to 20 a day. As a woman in parliament you are in constant competition with men – with men who are confident and assured of their roles as legislators and opinion-leaders. As women parliamentarians, we haven't yet had the time to develop the same confidence. When women speak in the House, they are always well-briefed and have done their homework. They rarely jump up and say anything off the cuff. That is a prerogative that stems from being a confident male.

Smoking is a confidence-barometer for B. just as for Jane. The more her competence came under scrutiny, the more she smoked, feeling that any political error would be taken as evidence of her female inferiority: 'I was always beset with the inner worry of never wanting to slip up. If a male colleague slipped up, you could always say it was "bad luck" or an "off-day". But if a woman made a mistake, they would say "What else, after all, can you expect from a woman?" '

Since leaving government, B. has returned to her former career as a writer; she still smokes, albeit the lowest-tar cigarettes available. She wants to stop now more than ever, but doesn't yet have the confidence. 'I sit at my desk each morning trying to write. But I don't believe I shall be able to write well, so I smoke instead.' So, like Jane who denied her talents by focusing on her body, B. denies her abilities by smoking instead of writing.

Heather is a 29-year-old clinical psychologist who used to smoke 60 cigarettes a day. She had wanted to stop for years and began to get increasingly frequent bouts of bronchitis. On a student grant, she had to sacrifice holidays and clothes to spend £10 a week on cigarettes. She had no respect for smokers and, as a smoker, was in a minority at work. She made several serious but unsuccessful attempts to stop and even attended a smokers' clinic, using every trick and diversion she could think of – including rewarding herself, scaring herself and even disgusting herself by collecting all her cigarette ends in a messy heap in her bedroom. Yet none seemed to have any impact. After she finally succeeded in the summer of 1978, the reasons for Heather's past failures became clearer:

> I simply didn't feel that I was *ready* to stop at the time or on subsequent occasions . . . I knew I was always fighting something in myself during these attempts: that's why I always capitulated to the little voice that said 'Go on, be nice to yourself, make yourself feel better, you need that fag.'

At the time, Heather was depressed. She had her training and qualifying exams to face and felt socially inadequate because she didn't have a boyfriend. Once she had passed her exams and got a good job, life changed radically. 'I suddenly had several reasons to feel good about myself.' She found a new, non-smoking flatmate and formed a relationship with a man who not only encouraged her to stop, but was prepared to support her efforts to do so.

> I suddenly realised that I really didn't need another cigarette. My friend helped me to tip the scales towards listening to the 'third force' in me which said 'you are strong, and you don't need to crave that cigarette'. . . This time I knew that *all* of me wanted to quit. I felt convinced that I would succeed . . . Smoking for me was tied up with some very basic feelings of not being able to support myself or 'feed' myself adequately. It was my dummy and my badge of defeat. The anti-smoking part of me was the critical voice, the mocking, unhelpful part. I couldn't stop until I felt stronger.

Unlike Heather, Tanya made her first serious attempt to stop smoking when her confidence was at its lowest ebb. As far as her health was concerned, Tanya had even better reasons than Heather to quit: her doctor had told her after her second child was born that if she carried on smoking, she would be dead in ten years. Tanya had a chronic cough with a persistent pain in the chest. She went to a local smokers' clinic, but managed to stay off cigarettes for only two-and-a-half weeks. The key factors preventing success in her case were a lack of confidence in her ability to maintain her resolve, and 13 years of unhappy marriage. 'Even when I stopped, I never dared think I'd be able to stay off permanently. I kept thinking in terms of weeks, and then going back to cigarettes.' Tanya felt her husband's attitude also undermined her self-confidence:

> I didn't feel as if I was getting any encouragement from him. He thought going to the clinic was stupid. He didn't see why I couldn't manage on my own. He thought I should be able to click my fingers and stop – just like him. He always seems to me to be the kind of person who is always able to do what he wants to do. He gave up smoking for three months because he wanted to, and he started again because he wanted to.

In the first two weeks after quitting, Tanya gained some weight, which reduced her confidence even further – her husband had told her how 'horrible and fat' she had become after having her second baby. She then discovered that he had secretly been going out with another woman, who had become pregnant. She threw him out of the house and took up cigarettes again.

Hospitals – a microcosm of male dominance

Hospitals provide one of the clearest illustrations of how social forces shape the smoking habits of those who work within them. Although there is no research on smoking among non-professional hospital workers, smoking patterns among doctors and nurses clearly reflect the consequences of working within a society where we are divided not only by race and class, but by sex as well. Both doctors and nurses have a double incentive to quit smoking. Not only do they repeatedly see the effects of cigarette-induced diseases, but they are expected to set an example to the rest of the community. Doctors, both male and female, have responded to this pressure and probably have lower smoking rates than any other single group in the community.[21,22] The picture is quite different for hospital nurses: not only are their smoking rates twice as high as those of their medical colleagues,[23,24] but they smoke as much if not more than professional women and than women in general.[25] This pattern is not peculiar to Britain, and research in both the US[26] and Australia[27] yields similar results.

Why are nurses more likely to smoke than doctors?

Although there are signs that smoking is now falling among nurses as well as doctors,[28,29] why has the decline been so much slower among nurses? Anti-smoking campaigners have been quick to suggest that nurses are either less aware of the health hazards of smoking or less likely to accept them. But all the evidence indicates that not only are more than nine out of ten doctors *and* nurses aware of the risks of smoking, but both see their role in advising patients to quit smoking as equally important.[30] And the differences cannot be explained in terms of age differences between doctors and nurses, because nurses have higher smoking rates in every age group than other health professionals.[31]

Class differences must contribute, because nurses are much more likely than doctors to come from working-class backgrounds – despite the fact that they are classified with other professionals in official statistics. A casual glance at those most likely to smoke among hospital nurses quickly reveals that the lower the status of your job, the higher your smoking rate. Although estimates vary, those at the bottom of the hierarchy – nursing auxiliaries and aides – have smoking rates well over 50 per cent compared with fully qualified nurses whose rates vary from 30 to 40 per cent.[32] It is easy to see how the stress of working in a hospital could also explain why many nurses seem reluctant to part with their cigarettes. Hospital work is emotionally and physically demanding and smoking does seem to be a barometer of high-stress specialities – with psychiatric nurses and, in some instances, cancer nurses having the highest smoking rates of all.[33] Certainly well over two-thirds of nurses see their work as stressful and often confirm that heavy workloads and night work drive them to cigarettes.[34] Small-scale research shows that nurses on high-stress wards are more likely to respond by increasing their smoking, whereas those on low-stress wards are more likely to cut down.[35]

But no one could rightly claim that a hospital doctor's work is stress-free by comparison. It is the *nature* of the stresses upon hospital nurses which are quite different. The nurse takes on the care of the sick and dying at a much earlier stage in her career than the doctor. And unlike the doctor, when she is on duty she is trapped on the ward with very little freedom or control over her own activities. Faced with a series of tasks dictated to her by the nursing hierarchy, from which she dare not deviate, her daily work is a series of crises punctuated by long periods of boredom – especially at night. When life is boring, the doctor can disappear for a game of squash. The nurse must stay put. Her 'cigarette break' represents one of the few ways open to her to relieve the frustrations of a long period of duty. It is no accident that community nurses, by contrast, have far lower smoking rates than those who work in hospital.[36] The community nurse has autonomy and responsibility, as well as the freedom to work with her clients as she sees fit. The hospital nurse works under the double medical *and* nursing hierarchy, and smoking is her way of dealing with the frustrations which they impose. But above all, nursing is *women's work* – the medical profession is still as quintessentially male as the nursing profession is female. And like women in other jobs, nurses are underpaid and undervalued. Smoking is a mark of their dissatisfaction with this state of affairs. Many qualified nurses with long years of experience are forced to continue living in shoddy hospital accommodation because they cannot afford to live elsewhere. Nursing, like motherhood, is regarded as menial work; it is about nurturing, caring and, above all, serving others. Although a nurse's work is as essential to the well-being of the patient as a doctor's, nurses are still regarded as doctor's handmaidens – especially within the hospital.

Beryl is a 25-year-old student nurse; she used to smoke 20 cigarettes a day when she was a nursing auxiliary. She is committed to becoming a nurse, but resents the power structure within the hospital and paints an uncompromising picture of life on the ward:

You are always the underdog, at the bottom of the pecking order. We have little control over our work. It is always determined by the nurse above us and the nurse above her. I resent being looked upon as a glorified waitress instead of the professional I'm training to become . . . you are conscious of being just a nurse – you simply don't exist. In nursing you quickly realise that medicine is a separate camp – and a more powerful camp than ours. We usually carry out what the doctor says we should do, which I accept as correct. But I also think that we do a hell of a lot that we don't get credit for. Patients are thankful, but professionals are not. It creates the impression that nurses are dispensable and doctors are not.

Doctors and health educators have accused nurses who smoke of letting the side down. Yet why should nurses' reasons for smoking be any less legitimate than those which keep other women smoking? Being a woman – nurse or otherwise – and working in an environment where all the key decisions are taken by men, can only exacerbate the frustrations and sense of dependence with which most women already grapple elsewhere. Smoking is merely a sign of anger at this subordination.

8: A society that keeps women smoking

Is it possible, from the pieces of evidence we have gathered so far, to offer a general explanation of why women smoke? According to the experts, smoking in women is an inevitable result of their growing emancipation. In their view, the cigarette is 'a symbol of emancipation' and 'a defiant gesture of independence'.[1,2] The American National Institute of Drug Abuse (NIDA) believes that, as we move towards equality in education and work, women's smoking patterns reflect that equality. 'Smoking,' says NIDA, 'may be perceived in some way as an indicator of increased power and independence.'[3] Some researchers go further and suggest that women smoke to 'increase their identification with the masculine mode of relating to the world'.[4] The assumption implicit in these conclusions is that the rise of smoking among women over the last 15 years is a consequence of the parallel rise of the feminist movement of the 1960s.

According to this view, women want to be like men, so they now smoke like men and are consequently dying like men. There is no substantive research to support these conclusions, which reflect the *intuitive* assumptions of a largely male establishment. This, according to Patti White, Deputy Director of ASH (UK), 'Betrays an astonishingly arrogant and common misconception among men, that women want to be like them. It represents a basic misunderstanding of the feminist principle.'[5] If women were really following in men's footsteps, they would be quitting smoking and *not* taking it up. Moreover, the research – most of which has been conducted by women – shows that emancipation has very little to do with the reasons for women smoking. First, the smoking epidemic among women gained momentum long before modern feminism began to have any impact, and it is beginning to decline in countries like Britain, the US and Scandinavia which have strong feminist traditions. Second, young

American non-smokers are just as likely as smokers to identify with the women's movement.[6] More importantly, research conducted among more than 1,200 women by sociologist and former Minister for Education, Ingrid Eide, shows that Norway's most emancipated women were the group most likely to have *quit* smoking, and they were no more likely to be smokers than women as a whole (see Table 8).[7]

Table 8:   Norway's Liberated Ex-Smokers

Emancipation Level	Smoking Status	
	Smokers %	Ex-Smokers %
Low	22	4
High	30	22
All Women	**35**	**4**

A similar picture emerged from Jane Ritchie's smaller-scale research among 250 women at the University of Waikato, New Zealand. She found that smoking rates among women students who identified themselves as feminist were below the national 30 per cent average for women,[8] and as few as 19 per cent of women from the overtly feminist New Zealand Women's Studies Group were smokers.[9] So the 'emancipated' woman smoker is more a fantasy foisted upon us by the tobacco companies and short-sighted researchers than a reality. In the long run, says Virginia Ernster, Associate Professor of Epidemiology at the University of San Francisco, 'Cigarette smoking represents not independence, but rather dependence . . . and is more an indication of manipulation rather than freedom.'[10]

However, it would be naive to assume that changing attitudes towards women and increased spending power have had no influence on their smoking. They have certainly contributed towards removing many of the remaining taboos against smoking in Western culture. But it would be unscientific – and incorrect – to blame the growth of the women's movement itself for a phenomenon which is much more complex. The influences which have led girls to catch up and even overtake boys in starting to smoke, owe much to the new climate of liberation, so effectively used by the tobacco industry. But there are other factors which explain why women continue to smoke and experience unique problems in quitting. The key to understanding this second part of the woman smoker's equation stems not so much from our new equalities, but from the continuing inequalities in our lives.

A glimmer of liberation

Smoking, to the teenager, becomes a symbol of liberation from childhood and parental controls – a symbol which is exploited to the hilt by the tobacco companies. The rugged 'he-man' and dynamic 'feminine' sex-symbols are deliberately calculated to entice the impressionable teenager to experiment with cigarettes. And sure enough, for boys, smoking represents entry into the tough male world which promises power and sexual adventure. Boys who smoke tend to be more rebellious, outgoing and anti-authority than their non-smoking classmates.[11] It is their attempt to buy an image which says: 'I'm cool and daring; I do what *real* men do.' But this does not fit the traditional female stereotype of girls who are supposed to be more demure, industrious, obedient and sexually inexperienced. Are smoking trends among girls running contrary to stereotype? Not until recently, for Scottish research shows that in the 1960s girls' smoking patterns and female stereotypes coexisted harmoniously. Fewer girls than boys smoked, and the girls took a highly moralistic attitude – strongly disapproving of other girls (but not other boys) smoking. A decade later this was no longer the case and the girls took a permissive view of their own as well as of boys' smoking.[12] This change of attitude among girls was borne out by American research in the late 1970s which concluded that girls – much more than boys – had adopted a set of 'new values' including greater sophistication, with more emphasis on sexual experience as well as the rebelliousness which had hitherto been a male preserve. 'It's not just in cigarette smoking that teenage girls are catching up with the boys,' it concluded.[13]

But the romantic era of 'new values', where many of today's single young women feel they can do and buy what they like – including cigarettes – is brief. For most women, the new hopes of equality continue to be disappointed. A decade and a half of change may have raised expectations for women who might previously have accepted their lot without question, but the inequalities persist. Although a majority of women in Britain and the US now have paid jobs, our work is still undervalued. We still earn far less than men in equivalent jobs, and society still concentrates us in a few low-paid and low status 'women's jobs'.[14] Women are still society's appointed guardians of men's, children's and elderly relatives' needs, and we are given little credit for the multiple juggling acts we perform every day – which goes a long way towards explaining why women are much more likely than men to report that 'pressures at home' stopped them from quitting smoking successfully.[15]

Smoking is one of the symbols of our lingering second-class citizenship. Whether we fulfil our boss's needs at work or our family's at home, there is little respite from our many duties – except momentarily in a cigarette. Because we have been taught to provide emotional support for those around us, we can't afford to get angry, irritated or even plain self-interested. So we smoke instead. It resolves nothing, but we go on doing it. Smoking is an outward sign of our constant battle to control our unvoiced frustrations; controlling these means we can be 'nice' to everybody all the time. To feel in control of our lives is just as important to men as it is to us, but the ways to exert this control open to us are more limited. We will tolerate unruly or drunken husbands or angry bosses who take it out on us, but who can we take it out on? Surely not our children. So we reach for the cigarettes instead.

Teaching women the myth of dependence

How does the carefree liberated teenage girl – who can take or leave cigarettes – become the woman who believes she is hooked on them? While lower-tar promotions aimed at women can delay a decision to quit, they cannot explain why women should feel *more dependent* on cigarettes than men. Nor can their dependence be explained by chemical addiction to nicotine. Rather, the strength of a woman's dependence on cigarettes is a reflection of the degree to which she *perceives* herself to be addicted. These perceptions are *learned*[16] in a society whose medical experts mistakenly view cigarette dependence as a 'sick-

ness' for which they must find a 'cure'. Thus many a well-
meaning doctor or health professional has inadvertently helped
to create the 'addiction' they are so anxious to cure. The more
convinced a person is of their 'addiction' to cigarettes, the less
likely they are to quit smoking.[17] The 'addict' thus uses addiction
as a justification, not for quitting, but for *continuing* to smoke.
Donald Cameron and Ian Jones, respectively Senior Lecturer at
Edinburgh University and Specialist in Community Medicine in
Fife, Scotland, see cigarette dependence not as a disease but as a
legitimate search for 'solace'; solace from the stresses of a society
which fosters vested interests in tobacco, and generates poverty,
unemployment and inequality of opportunity.[18] But what they
fail to explain is why women should depend on cigarettes for
consolation more than men. Think for a moment what 'addiction' itself really means. It is about feeling helpless, giving in to
forces you believe to be beyond your control; in the case of cigarettes, it is about letting cigarettes rule you. It is also about feeling
unable to cope with problems on your own, and needing help
from those 'who know better'. A woman's dependence on cigarettes is a metaphor for her sense of helplessness in a society
which grooms women to be 'dependent' and men to be 'independent'. The myth of the dependent woman is clearly exposed by
psychotherapists Susie Orbach and Luise Eichenbaum in their
book *What Women Want*, which is based on their experience as
therapists:

> The true picture of women and men's dependence *on each
> other* [my italics] is never acknowledged. . . In our culture
> both men and women come to feel ashamed of feeling depen-
> dent. It seems to signify weakness in both sexes, but in dif-
> ferent ways. Boys grow up on the other side of an unbalanced
> coin. Their dependency needs are hidden from view, but more
> successfully answered.[19]

Boys, they argue, go through life knowing that their emotional
support will come first from their mothers and later from the
women in their lives both at home and at work. Girls, on the
other hand, 'absorb early on that in the most profound sense
they must rely on themselves, there is no one to take care of them
emotionally. They cannot assume – as does the man – that there

will be someone for them to bring their emotional lives to.'[20] So men depend on women and women depend on cigarettes, and therein lies the crucial connection between a woman's emotional investment in cigarettes and her greater dependence on them. As women, we are trained to live up to the myth that not only do cigarettes satisfy key emotional needs, but also that we can *depend* on them to do so. We have learned to accept without question the idea that we are more emotionally needy than men. If we challenge this assumption, we are challenging the fabric of society, which functions more smoothly when we see ourselves as psychologically dependent on men. The irony is, as Susie Orbach and Luise Eichenbaum cogently argue, that while society forces women to be *economically* dependent on men it is they who are *emotionally* dependent on us.

Women and other drugs – a familiar story

Is there anything we can learn from women's dependence on other drugs which might point us towards a better understanding of why women cling to cigarettes? I put this question to 17 national and international authorities in the field. They represented 12 institutions including the renowned Addiction Research Unit and the Institute for the Study of Drug Dependence in the UK, the Addiction Research Foundation in Canada and America's National Institute of Drug Abuse. None could offer much help. Most had not looked for parallels between cigarettes and other drugs, preferring to stick to a single area of expertise such as smoking or alcohol. Despite this reluctance to take a broader view, many women's organisations are one step ahead of 'official' researchers. In the Women's Health Information Centre in London, the library classification for 'women and dependency' includes documents on cigarettes, alcohol, mood-altering drugs (tranquillisers and anti-depressants) and food. At first sight this seems a curiously disparate combination. Certainly cigarettes differ from alcohol in that they are always dangerous when used *as intended*, whereas occasional drinking can be harmless. Adequate food is of course essential, and tranquillisers prescribed for short-term use in a rare crisis can be helpful. But consider the parallels between cigarettes and other drugs:

Table 9: Women and Drugs – The Common Hidden Agenda

	The Drugs			
	Cigarettes	Alcohol	Tranquillisers	Food
Size Of The Problem	7¼ Million Women Smokers Slower Decline Among Women	30-40% of Alcoholics Are Women Faster Growth Among Women	14 Million Women Users	Most Women
Main Groups Affected	All Classes Of Women Girls	All Classes Of Women Young Women	Housewives With Children Older Women	Most Women
Special Health Implications	Special Risks In Young Women Lung Cancer Rising Faster In Women	Women More Susceptible To Damage	More Women At Risk	Equivalent Risk Of Heart Attack For Women And Men

Vested Commercial Interests	Tobacco Industry Government	Alcohol Industry Government	Drug Industry Government	Food Industry Government
Do Women Depend On It For Emotional Solace?	Yes	Yes	Yes	Yes
Official Recognition As A Problem For Women?	Slow	Not Recognised	Slow	Largely Unrecognised
Image Of Woman User	Sick	Bad	Sick	Silly
Those Most Likely To Ask For Help?	Women	Increasing Numbers Of Women	Women	Women

not only do they all pose substantial problems for women, but they are all (except tranquillisers) legal, widely available and tolerated – even encouraged – by governments which thrive on their misuse. And in each case the problem is exacerbated by industries which see women as a key means of boosting profits (see Table 9).

The similarities in the ways women depend on cigarettes and on other drugs do not stop here. Reading through the increasing number of helpful books written about women and drugs, one conclusion becomes glaringly obvious: *Women depend on cigarettes for the same reasons that they drink too much, take too many tranquillisers or over-eat*, and these reasons are social, political and economic as well as personal.

Brigid McConville, in her book *Women Under the Influence*, gives a detailed account of several women who are dependent on drink, as well as analysing the role played by government and the alcohol industry in promoting the growth of drinking among women. She concludes that, 'Women's drinking can only be understood in a wider social and political context.'[21] Women who depend on alcohol come from all walks of life and 'very different women drink (socially or otherwise) for the same reasons: oppression, inadequacy, anxiety, depression and lack of confidence.' For an increasing number of women, concludes Brigid McConville, drink offers a way of escape from boredom or frustration with home or work relationships. In her book *Women and Tranquillisers*, Celia Haddon offered similar reasons as to why twice as many women as men – especially married women with small children, and older women – take tranquillisers:

> Women's lives are more stressful than men's. Women do more work, make more adjustment and lose their financial independence [to men] . . . Popping a pill to deal with moments of stress is now considered to be quite respectable. What they do is take the sharp edge off life and blur out some of the reality.[22]

Womanly consolation – an enforced choice

Women are more likely to smoke heavily than to drink heavily, and men are more likely to do both.[23] Women in Europe,[24] in America[25] and in Australia[26] are all more heavily dependent on tranquillisers than men. Those who use tranquillisers are also more likely to smoke.[27] And food offers a particular kind of emotional support for women, but hardly ever for men. These differing patterns of drug use depend on a combination of social forces and commercial pressures which create the problems people havè, and also dictate which apparent solutions are available or acceptable. A unique piece of research commissioned by the German Health Education Bureau sheds new light on how women 'choose' differing drugs in order to cope with the stress in their lives. Its results in Figure 3 are striking: women with young children in paid work are far more likely to reach for cigarettes or alcohol in their most stressful moments than women at home, who are more likely to resort to food or pills (including tranquillisers).[28]

What do these different patterns of drug use mean? The taboos against women smoking and drinking in affluent cultures are now a thing of the past, and the image of the cigarette or the drink as an essential accoutrement of the successful, emancipated working woman are strongly promoted by the tobacco and alcohol industries. Alcohol is increasingly being seen as a normal part of the machinery of working relationships, and is both more available and more affordable to women working in (higher) paid jobs. At work, a woman's day is highly structured and going to the doctor for pills is not so easy to organise – especially if she has to rush home to look after her children after work.

On the other hand, the married woman at home is isolated from the newer and more permissive working environment. She has less money to spend on herself than her counterpart in paid work, and the idea that 'nice' mothers don't drink still lingers. Although her time is usually tied up with her children's needs, she has more control over how it is spent. The comfort of the refrigerator and larder are close at hand. Her doctor is nearby and he (it usually is 'he') *expects* her to have emotional troubles; he has been well-primed by the drug companies that she is an ideal candidate for tranquillisers.

But once a confirmed smoker, can a woman say 'no' to cigarettes without swapping one form of dependence for another? The evidence worldwide says 'yes'. When women quit smoking – and three-and-a-half million British women have already done

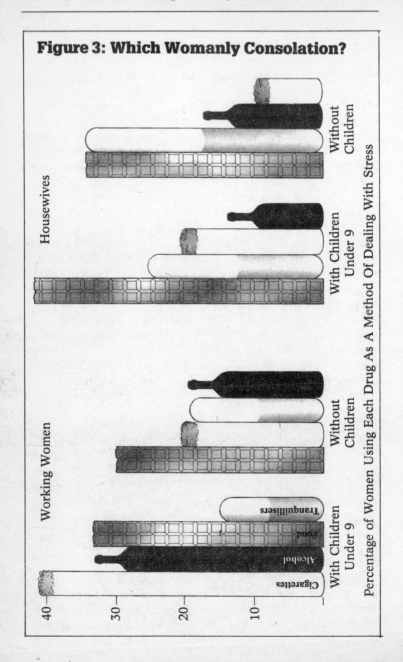

Figure 3: Which Womanly Consolation?

Housewives

Without Children

With Children Under 9

Working Women

Without Children

With Children Under 9

Cigarettes

Alcohol

Food

Tranquillisers

40

30

20

10

Percentage of Women Using Each Drug As A Method Of Dealing With Stress so – they resort neither to heavier tranquilliser *nor* alcohol use.[29,30,31] This is because chemical consolation is no longer necessary once a woman confronts the myth of her dependence.

Food for thought

Nearly all women – smokers and non-smokers alike – want to be thin. It is an international obsession among women in affluent cultures. Since cigarette advertising suggests that smoking is a passport to slimness, many young women are under the mistaken impression that smoking keeps them thin and that quitting results in inevitable weight gain. But why is weight an almost exclusively female preoccupation? Especially when men gain more weight than women when they quit smoking.[32] Food has a special meaning for women that it does not have for men. On the one hand, women are expected to feed and cook for other people, but no one is responsible for nurturing women. So they themselves reach out for food in an attempt to plug the emotional gaps in their lives. It is easier to quell that gnawing hunger with food than with love. At the same time, we live in a society which values women for what they look like – not for what they are or what they do. And current Western fashion dictates that to be beautiful you have to be thin. Being thin is one of the few sources of self-esteem society allows us. So powerful is this pressure that nine out of ten women who are normal weight see themselves as being too fat,[33] and nearly half of all American women are on a diet.[34]

So while women derive emotional consolation from food, society makes us feel guilty about eating. No wonder quitting smoking represents such a huge threat to a woman's equanimity! She sees her smoking as a means of maintaining her self-confidence in a world where she feels she has to be thin to be successful in her relationships with men. The thought of being fat, undesired and unsuccessful now seems far more difficult to face than the prospect of becoming ill from smoking at some undefined future date.

Undermining our confidence

If a woman is to quit smoking, it is obvious that she must believe she will be able to succeed. We have already seen how women are less confident than men of their ability to quit smoking, and feel more stressed and more dependent on cigarettes than men.[35] With the fear of weight gain, these act further to depress a woman's confidence in her ability to turn away from cigarettes. What women feel about quitting cigarettes represents a microcosm of what they feel about themselves in general. For research shows that most women not only hold a low opinion of themselves, but feel less competent than men under most circumstances.[36] By contrast, men commonly overestimate their ability to achieve *any* set task.[37] Women have little confidence in themselves or their ability to quit smoking because society has failed to encourage them to value themselves highly enough, and this is reinforced by guilt-inducing health education programmes (see Chapter 9).

PART II

Beating the Ladykillers:
Helping Yourself and Others

9: Beating the ladykillers –
a painful evolution

Smoking and health campaigners have begun to learn from their mistakes. Twenty years ago, when the seeds of the campaign were first sown in Britain and the US, women were conspicuously absent at all levels. Men dominated the research, the policy-making bodies and the health messages which ultimately emerged. This is changing, but its evolution has been painfully slow and has been brought about almost exclusively by women.

Before women existed

In 1962, London's Royal College of Physicians shattered the world with its first report on smoking and health.[1] Compiled by a committee of nine men, it summarised the damning evidence on the effects of smoking and made recommendations to government and other bodies for action. Its reference to women smokers was cursory and its emphasis, based on the research at the time, was on lung cancer among men. The US followed in 1964 with its first report masterminded by Luther Terry, the then Surgeon General, which reflected the same bias as the British report and dealt briefly with women in a short section entitled 'Other Conditions'.[2]

The early health education campaigns and TV documentaries mirrored what the experts had presented. Women did not figure in any of the early programmes as potential victims of the cigarette. Although health educators clearly intended their message to be heard by *all* smokers, the major impact was among men (see Chapter 1). And this continued to be the case for ten years in Britain.

The skin-deep sinner

In Britain one began to get occasional glimpses of women by the early 1970s. The Health Education Council gave birth to 'Fagash Lil', the woman smoker in the TV commercial whose attractions were judged by her male suitors to be 'just like kissing an old ashtray'. The British Medical Association's 'authoritative' Family Doctor booklet exhorted women to quit smoking in order to prevent premature wrinkles (even though there is no evidence to support such a theory).[3] The unavoidable message was: smoking put at risk men's lives, but only women's looks.

Receptacles for future generations

In 1973 women – or rather their unborn children – were put in the anti-smoking limelight. Evidence had gradually been accumulating that smoking during pregnancy could damage the unborn child, and had been highlighted in the follow-up reports from the American Surgeon General in 1973,[4] and the Royal College of Physicians in 1971.[5] Alastair Mackie, then newly appointed Director of the Health Education Council (HEC), dreamt up one of the most controversial anti-smoking campaigns in the Council's history.[6] The first poster series featured a nude pregnant woman, with pubic hair clearly visible, against the bold caption: 'Is it fair to force your baby to smoke cigarettes?' In the accompanying TV commercial showing a tiny underweight baby in an incubator, the medical voice of doom warned: 'You may deprive your baby of oxygen . . . you may poison its bloodstream with nicotine . . . it may even threaten his [*sic*] life.'

The acceptability of the campaign, let alone its likely impact, was not tested beforehand. It had no impact on pregnant women's smoking habits, let alone on women in general.[7] Looking back at those early days, the HEC certainly agrees now that this kind of emotional blackmail merely served to reinforce the guilt and anxiety women already feel, and could only undermine what little self-confidence they need to quit smoking. More recent HEC material avoids guilt-inducing messages, and for the first time the responsibility of the father as well as of the mother in producing a healthy baby is acknowledged.

The pregnancy campaign had far-reaching effects. It became synonymous with the *entire* anti-smoking campaign directed at women. In rich countries *most* women are *not* pregnant *most* of the time. Therefore a campaign directed solely at smoking in pregnancy *ignores most women most of the time*.

Other countries have followed suit. In January 1985 the American Cancer Society launched a 30-second anti-smoking commercial which featured a computer-simulated foetus smoking a cigarette. 'Would you give a cigarette to your unborn child?' asked a woman's voice as the foetus inhaled. 'You do every time you smoke when you're pregnant. Pregnant mother, please don't smoke.' The campaign was dreamt up by Irving Rimer, the Cancer Society's Vice-President for Public Affairs. It did not, he told me, form part of the Society's well-thought-out strategy on women and smoking, but was what is known in the trade as opportunistic advertising. Irving Rimer was approached by two computer animators who proposed simulating a foetus smoking; the Cancer Society did not like it, but he went ahead anyway. Two out of the three US TV networks refused to screen it, the anti-abortion lobby loved it because they saw it as furthering their cause, and the women's movement was outraged by it because they thought it was an anti-abortionist conspiracy. It is hard to see how such a deliberately emotion-ridden and uninformative manoeuvre could have achieved anything other than alienating the women it sought to influence.

It has at last become obvious that the way to deal with smoking in pregnancy is not in the media-man's isolated world of TV, but in the context of other relevant aspects of pregnancy and a woman's life as a whole. The most up-to-date research now shows that while all smoking is dangerous to all women, it is a major risk to the unborn baby's health *only* if its mother also suffers the other effects of poverty. It is the babies of black women, working-class women and undernourished women who are most at risk.[8,9,10] It can be no coincidence that one of the few major health education projects which took some of these factors into account was conducted by a group of women specialists, all of whom were feminists and had been pregnant themselves. Entitled the Pregnant Pause Campaign, this ambitious A$1m initiative was funded by the New South Wales Health Commission.[11] It set out to raise women's awareness of all drug use – including cigarettes – during pregnancy by using a positive approach which involved not only the women themselves, but the husbands/fathers and the wider community as well. And the results showed that this alternative to traditional, guilt-inducing health education did reduce smoking among pregnant women.[12]

Redressing the balance

While most rich countries continued in official oblivion of the growing smoking problem among women, Norway had already taken action. By 1973, the Norwegian Council on Smoking and Health had invited representatives of leading Norwegian women's organisations to collaborate on a strategy appropriate for women.

The US agencies concerned with smoking and health – especially the American Cancer Society (ACS) and the American Lung Association (ALA) – have had almost as long a tradition as Norway of appealing to women on their own terms. The ACS led the way in the mid-1970s, but was followed closely by the ALA. The ACS was also the first deliberately to highlight women as a special target for action in its five-year plan, 'Target Five', to reduce smoking.

By 1979, Joe Califano – the ill-fated Secretary of State for Health, Education and Welfare (HEW) – had come into office. He was a man who wanted to do something about smoking, and was the motive force behind the Surgeon General's 1980 report on smoking which was devoted entirely to women. Having helped get tobacco in general and women in particular onto the federal health agenda, the pro-tobacco lobby got him sacked.[13] Before Ronald Reagan took over the Presidency, the seeds of a new campaign on women had already been sown. There was to be an HEW-funded series of TV commercials featuring teenage heart-throb Brooke Shields. So powerful was her potential to reach American teenage girls that the White House pro-tobacco lobby managed to get the entire campaign shelved.[14] Fortunately it was handed over to the ALA, which used the material effectively.

By 1985, the prospect of lung cancer overtaking breast cancer as the No.1 cancer killer in women, spurred the Cancer Society into further action. At a press conference, the ACS President –

professor of surgery, Robert McKenna – announced a new drive by the Society to curb tobacco promotion, along with a new stress management programme which he said 'will be most beneficial to women'. An editorial in the ACS Journal *Ca*, put the ACS view in uncompromising terms: 'Lung cancer is a feminist issue . . . I urge women to refuse to be victims of manipulative advertising by the tobacco industry.'[15]

In central Europe, it has proved more of an uphill task to get women on to the smoking and health agenda. In 1979, the World Health Organisation made its first gesture towards women, and three were included in the membership of its second expert committee on smoking and health. But still women did not feature independently in their report.[16]

Following the publication of *The Ladykillers* in 1981, many women were galvanised into collective action. Under the energetic aegis of Eileen Crofton, Medical Director of ASH in Scotland, and her successor Alison Hillhouse, Scottish ASH were the first to produce 'woman-centred' materials. Nearly half of the numerous women's health events and conferences on smoking have also been in Scotland, which is also where the first move to put women on to the health policy map emanated.

Meanwhile, the much maligned media were quicker than the health policy-makers to spot a new way of telling an old story. Where the old headlines about women smokers used to read: 'Mum's Fags Linked to Teenage Flops', my press cuttings show that nine in every ten articles now deal with 'Why Women's Health is Going Up in Smoke'. The popular press has led the way, and the medical press is still trailing. The *Glasgow Herald* even launched its own women's campaign and organised a conference which set up self-help groups for women who wanted to quit smoking. In November 1983, Channel 4 television screened the first-ever British documentary featuring a woman dying of lung cancer. It took the health policy-makers another two years to follow suit, but nevertheless signs of change were afoot. Organised by Yvonne Bostock from SHEG and Ilona Kickbusch – Regional Director for Health Education at WHO's European office – the first ever international conference on women's health took place in Edinburgh. Amongst the many other issues raised, cigarettes were at last a matter of international concern.

By then the ultra-cautious English were ready to stir and with characteristic subtlety, the HEC upgraded its previously invisible women who now appeared alongside men in all their publications. Even their excellent booklet for general practitioners, *Give up Smoking*, was re-vamped to include a woman doctor. Deryk Lambert, the HEC's Medical Officer, made their concern for women explicit at a conference in 1984: 'It is of considerable importance to the health of this country that this aspect [women] – frequently neglected – is given some emphasis during our deliberations.'[17] And so it was. In an unprecedented visible effort to redress the balance of the sexes, both female and male pop stars and sports celebrities were selected to appear in the HEC's 'Pacesetters Don't Smoke' campaign aimed at teenagers. In 1985, and after more than two decades of health education on smoking, the HEC finally launched an initiative which concentrated directly on the impact of smoking on women's health (see Chapter 10). This was followed by a hard-hitting joint drive from the British Medical Association and the HEC to get cigarette advertising out of women's magazines.[18]

Women got another important break in 1983. We were to be made a topic of 'special concern' along with other underprivileged groups – children and people from poor countries – at the Fifth World Conference on Smoking and Health in Winnipeg. The international spotlight had finally hit women, and in all there were six other sessions devoted to them. To my surprise, I was invited to chair a session boldly entitled 'Smoking and Feminism'. Bob Wake, a professor of psychology and the conference programme chairman, warned me: 'You had better make it good. I've stuck my neck out on this one.' He had little cause to worry. The session was packed to capacity, delegates from more than 70 countries being eager to hear the long overdue contribution women had to make to the debate about smoking and health.

The Winnipeg discussions resounded widely, especially in Australia where the first big-budget anti-smoking initiatives were beginning to have an impact. Elaine Henry, then secretary of the New South Wales Cancer Council, felt that it was time the Council shifted its emphasis. She therefore organised a much-publicised lunch attended by well-known women who examined the impact of cigarettes on women's health. This was backed up by a media campaign whose uncompromising message was: 'Smoking discriminates against women.' Under Elaine

Henry's guidance, the Council was the first in the world to dir- ectly publicise the dual effects of smoking and the Pill: 'Smoking makes the Pill doubly dangerous' was its new message to young women. The Cancer Council initiatives formed a useful prelude to the New South Wales Health Commission's own smoking and health campaign: 'Quit for Life' (QFL). This A$1m extravaganza had also been launched in 1983 and was ambitiously aimed at all adults.

The QFL team at the Health Department were quick to high- light women in their follow-up in 1984. Their justification was simple: smoking was rising among young women and so was lung cancer. It was therefore time to concentrate on them before it was too late. With the benefit of hindsight and a generous budget of A$800,000,[19] they did not need to make the same mis- takes as their counterparts abroad. The most effective messages for women, concluded their research, were those which por- trayed women as 'winners'.[20] The resulting TV and radio com- mercials, which featured Lorrae Desmond, not only took women seriously but showed that they could quit as well as men.

But the Health Department also went for what their ad agency described as 'a strong emotional equation' based on 'horror and romance'.[21] In their view, young women were most likely to be impressed by such an approach. This led to a series of TV com- mercials portraying Mrs Holden, the homely grandmother who had genuinely had had a cancer of the larnyx removed which had left her with a permanent tracheostomy (a hole in her neck). The ads depicted her whispering in a staccato and hoarse fashion to her small granddaughter playing at her knee: 'I ended up with cancer of the throat . . . I breathe through a hole in my neck.' No one can deny that this was emotionally hard-hitting, but aside from the tears and horror it has little relevance to women smokers. For cancer of the larynx is a rare smoking-induced ill- ness in which nine out of every ten victims are *men*. Unlike lung cancer, which is soaring in women, cancer of the larynx is also a *curable* illness – which makes the ad's sensationalist approach even harder to justify. I asked several members of the QFL team whether the campaign had been effective, but none was prepa- red to show me their results.

Western Australia is well-endowed not only with a large smoking and health budget, but also with numerous women act-

ivists like Ruth Shean – director of the Australian Council on
Smoking and Health – and Debbie Fisher, then part of the
Health Department's Smoking Project Team. In 1984, WA launched its first statewide smoking and health campaign under the
banner: 'Quit. Take a fresh breath of life', aimed at adults.
Women were as visible a part of the campaign as men, and sure
enough women and men responded equally well to its message.[22]
A later ad depicted a young girl with a 'pretty face' transformed to
an unrecognisably gnarled old woman. 'What good's a pretty
face if you've got an ugly breath?' was the message. Although
clearly intended for girls, this ad had an equally powerful effect
on teenage boys. Whatever its effect, there is no evidence that
smoking turns 'pretty' young girls into wrinkled old hags. Moreover, the Women's National Commission found it offensive, so it
was hastily withdrawn.

The women's movement – a new voice

As far as the women's movement is concerned, smoking 'is
someone else's problem'. That was the unavoidable conclusion
of my research in 1979. Even *Our Bodies Ourselves*, the well-
known women's health bible, could 'not find sufficient room
for it' then. And most of the 50 women's organisations I wrote
to on both sides of the Atlantic – asking whether they saw
smoking as an issue for women – did not reply. The few who did
were largely hostile. Today the story is different – in Britain at
least. The new edition of *Our Bodies Ourselves* now contains a
whole chapter devoted to smoking and other drugs. This time I
surveyed over a hundred UK women's and general health organisations, and discovered that the most striking change of attitude was among the women's health organisations themselves.
Not only had they proliferated hugely in recent years but nearly
40 per cent responded this time and few were overtly hostile.
Most saw smoking as an important issue for women, and many
had already organised local or national events. While traditional
anti-smoking acitivities tend to focus on 'the smoker' rather than
wider issues, women's organisations have found a new political
home for smoking: within the context of women's health and
women's lives in general. The Scottish Women's Health Fair

dealt with smoking under the aegis of 'Head On', a group whose focus was mental health. Others focused on cigarettes together with other drugs, and the Northern Women's Health Conference covered smoking in a slot entitled: 'Women's Bodies – Women's Lives'. The Women's Therapy Centre in London offers quit smoking courses alongside others which help women to maximise their ability to beat smoking, such as dealing with stress, eating problems and feminist therapy. Remarkable among women's health groups was the lack of response from Well Women Centres and clinics. I wrote to 40 and only three replied, with two offering specific help for women smokers.

Whilst active on smoking in general, most of the medical and health organisations I contacted had not focused on women at all. Exceptions were the Spastics Society, Maternity Alliance and the Family Planning Association, who all emphasised the special risks smoking imposes on women. Among the responses in this group were those from the Coronary Prevention Group (CPG) and the Women's National Cancer Control Campaign (WNCCC). Both are run by women and both see women and smoking as a major issue. The CPG was preparing a booklet on women and heart disease and the WNCCC – under the aegis of its new director, Alice Burns – devoted its 21st Anniversary Conference exclusively to women and smoking. The WNCCC now plans a nationwide research project on smoking and cancer of the cervix, which is expected to reach 100,000 women through their cancer screening services.

Some women's organisations like DAWN (Drugs, Alcohol and Women Nationally) felt they should be concerned about cigarettes too, but did not feel they had the 'expertise' to do so. Others, like the GLC Women's Committee in London, did not want to 'spread themselves too thinly'. But even more important, many individual women wished to raise the issue within their own groups, but were frightened of infringing on the freedoms of other women in the group. Others – like the Medway Women's Health Group – felt that smoking could not be raised as an issue unless women themselves clamoured for it.

While new impetus has come from a wide range of women's organisations in the UK and Europe, the American women's movement remains largely silent; the National Women's Political Caucus – although committed to campaigning on women's health – still has no policy on cigarettes. Neither does the National Organisation of Women (NOW), the major feminist organisation in the US. Individual NOW members, like Iris Simon from NOW's Nassau branch, have publicly objected to Virginia Slims tennis sponsorship, which she sees as an attempt 'to sell us a hazardous substance through a perversion of feminist ideals'.[23] According to Marie Shear, a freelance journalist and member of NOW for 15 years, smoking has never been raised as a political issue except at the 1983 NOW Convention when she asked the President to ensure that a non-smoking rule was observed at the meeting. Both NOW and the Caucus accept cigarette advertising in their national convention brochures, and both have rejected written rebuttals of this by their members. The 1983 Caucus Convention booklet contained what Marie Shear described as 'the most repellent tobacco ad ever directed at girls and women'.[24] Using illustrations of well-known American feminists, the tobacco company – Brown and Williamson – exhorted readers to uphold personal freedoms against 'those who would chip away at them', for the betterment of mankind [*sic*]'. This, says Marie Shear, invokes the heroes of feminism and civil rights to sell addiction and death to the very people those heroes served.[25]

But money from tobacco advertising is not the only reason which causes American feminists to hesitate. In the face of repeated threats to women's reproductive rights from the 'moral majority', it is easy to understand why the American women's movement sees smoking as a peripheral issue. Yet it is dangerous to justify one priority by ignoring another. It is as urgent to deal with smoking as it is to fight for improved contraception and abortion facilities. If the European women's movement is able to begin tackling the smoking problem alongside other equally important women's health issues, surely there is room for the American women's movement to follow suit?

10: It takes all kinds

There are as many ways of beating cigarettes as there are ex-smokers. The elements of a worldwide action programme on smoking have been reiterated time and again: inform and educate; legislate to remove pro-smoking messages; increase cigarette tax; help quitters and promote an environment where non-smoking is the norm. But how can this be translated into action – and how do women fit into this process? One thing is certain: without individual action, there can be no change. Some do it privately within the confines of their personal lives, others at work or in public life. At the Fifth World Conference on Smoking and Health, women delegates from across the globe made a start by suggesting ways of 'Stopping the Female Smoking Epidemic' (see Appendix 1). Probably their most important recommendation was that any effort to reduce smoking among women should be a visible but integral part of any overall strategy, and that 'women should be involved at every level of such initiatives'. But telling us what to do at international conferences is one thing. How can women – smokers and non-smokers alike – turn the words into action?

Taking the law into your own hands

In 1979 a group of Australians decided that if the government was not going to stop the tobacco companies promoting death, then they would do it themselves. They formed an activist organisation called BUGA UP (Billboard Utilising Graffitists Against Unhealthy Promotions). Armed with no more than spray cans, BUGA UP activists deface (they call it 'reface') key cigarette billboards. 'Doing a billboard' is BUGA UP's way of exposing the tobacco industry's real intentions, and by operating in the industry's own arena it beats them at their own game.

BUGA UP's messages are uncompromising and funny: 'Tobacco is a pain in the arts' reads their sticker at tobacco-sponsored cultural events. 'What's this, a Van Cough?' is scrawled across Benson and Hedges' purportedly arty ads. One of BUGA UP's recent Winfield 'hits' when refaced read: 'Anyhow . . . Have a wank . . . It's healthier.' Although tobacco is probably BUGA UP's primary target, alcohol and sexist advertising also get their fair share of 'hits'. Many of their women activists 'specialise' jointly in sexism and tobacco – especially as the two often co-exist. An ad for 'Lace Perfects' women's underwear, described as 'the year's most offensive billboard', presented no challenge to BUGA UP who refaced the message smartly to read: 'The Pervert Billboard'.

BUGA UP is an organisation with a difference; it has few rules and no power structure. If you want to join, all you need to do is contact your local group (see Appendix 2) and bring a spray can. Some of its activities are more legal than others (all are justified), and many are linked to its other arm: MOP UP (Movement Opposed to the Promotion of Unhealthy Products). Several members have been charged, usually with 'malicious injury to billboard', and BUGA UP takes great delight in bringing bevies of expert witnesses and doctors to testify that the action was in the public interest. Judges tend to be uniformly sympathetic and either let off the 'defendant' altogether or impose a minimal fine. The tobacco industry dreads these show trials, because they know they cannot defend the indefensible. So successful has BUGA UP been in some areas that tobacco companies have been forced to re-do (and sometimes remove altogether) their billboards on a daily basis. The BUGA UP success has given birth to several sister organisations like AGHAST (Action Group to Halt Advertising and Sponsorship of Tobacco) – formed by Health Education Officer Cecilia Platts in Bristol and expanded internationally by the International Organisation of Consumer Unions – and COUGHIN (Campaign on the Utilisation of Graffiti for Health in the Neighbourhood), a group of health professionals in London. COUGHIN's other arm, TREES (Those who Resist an Early End from Smoking), made its debut at the Benson and Hedges Cup Final at Lords, sporting visors and T-shirts which read: 'Benson and Hedges stumps your growth.'

Melbourne BUGA UP has a long tradition of women activists known in the trade as 'BUGS', and the first person ever to appear in court on a charge of malicious injury to a billboard was a women radiologist, Josephine Kavanagh, from the Royal Melbourne Hospital. Other women health professionals have followed suit. In 1981 Marj White, a 55-year-old former teacher, appeared in court on a similar charge. She was not fined because the court could not decide who owned the paper on which the billboard was 'refaced'! 'I was taken with the idea of joining BUGA UP,' says Marj, 'because it offers a humorous way of telling people they are being conned.' Her two most recent coups were to hijack the Marlboro Open Tennis Tournament two seasons running. In 1983 – together with Peter Vogel, a leading Sydney BUG – she staged the 'Marblerow Cemetery' outside the tournament entrance. They erected a 'Marblerow' scoreboard, which showed the Australian death toll for cigarettes for that year, and a series of tombstones – one appropriately inscribed with a red chevron and 'Tomb of the Unknown Cowboy ... saddled with a dopey habit.' Another long, thin tombstone with an angel on top read: 'Alma (Al)pine ... who succumbed to a luxury length death.' The event got major coverage on every TV and radio station. The following year, the high point of the tournament was BUGA UP's huge hot-air balloon which hung over the courts. Its message was simple: 'Cancer Country.' Shortly after this fiasco, Marlboro pulled out of the tournament.

Sydney BUGA UP is also well-endowed with women graffitists. Wendy Varney is a 33 year-old journalist who has a predilection for Alpine ads because they are aimed at women. Her favourite 'hit' was an enormous Alpine billboard in the centre of Sydney which had a row of spotlights on it. The ad showed the usual snowy scene with the 'Alpine fresh' message. One night, with the help of a girl-friend – she re-faced the message to read: 'Fresh as a fart – fatal as an avalanche.' Wendy's reasons for becoming a BUG are both political and personal:

> I'm interested in the politics of health, or rather sickness. My interest goes beyond tobacco to the food we are cajoled to eat, and the hazards of the workplace. I am concerned that some people always get the raw end of the deal on health – especially women who are already discriminated against on so many

levels and are becoming the victims of tobacco. My actions
are spurred on by the daily hazard of breathing other people's
smoke . . . To go and reface a billboard for me is not only important because it demystifies the advertisers' message, but it
allows a voice to an otherwise silent and powerless public.

Martha Ansara is 42, has three children and describes herself as
a feminist film-maker. Her BUGA UP specialities are tobacco
and alcohol. Martha has become well-known in her neighbourhood for 'doing' billboards while pushing her third baby in her
stroller. 'I spray quite openly,' she said, 'and get a lot of satisfac-
tion from it . . . particularly when an old lady approached me and
said: "Good on you, love, my husband died coughing." ' Martha
was ultimately caught 'doing' a Benson and Hedges billboard
whose message read: 'Excellence in mild.' She had altered the
last word to 'mildew'. Martha pleaded not guilty to malicious
injury to a billboard, her barrister using in her defence the principle of 'lawful excuse'. She was fined A$80 and is currently
appealing against the decision.

Why does she do it? Partly because of the horror and misery
she has seen caused by tobacco and other drugs, and partly because she finds BUGA UP a liberating thing to do, but mainly to
protect children: 'I do this for my children and any other
children (and adults) – not because I am a "Mum", but because I
am a rational, thinking political person – as all women can be.'

One-woman power

Kathy Judge quit smoking four years ago and runs a group in
Nottingham to help local people do the same. It all started a year
ago, when she heard on the radio about the local self-help team
which was preparing to help anyone who wanted to start a self-
help group but was unsure how to go about it. 'I've always wanted to help people,' says Kathy, 'and having stopped smoking
myself I thought I might be able to help others. The team said
why not start your own group? So I did.' With a £20 starter from
the self-help team, Kathy set about her new task energetically,
advertising the group through the local paper and a radio phone-
in. She hired a room in town and 12 people came to the first
meeting – all housewives. The group met weekly for several

weeks, and for anyone who needed to talk between sessions Kathy operated her own 'Advisory Phone-in' from home every day between 2 and 4 p.m. She now runs an evening group for couples of the same age where both partners want to quit. On National Non-Smoking Day in March 1985, Kathy did her first-ever radio interview about the group. 'The phone hasn't stopped ringing since then,' she says. So successful has her venture been that the police were called to clear away potential customers from Kathy's meeting place, which was filled to capacity.

Sheila Ali-Oston has never smoked. As a journalist with strong views about the rights of the non-smoker, you would think she would be in a powerful position to defend her rights, yet she found herself in an impossible situation when she tried to arrange a smoke-free space for herself at work. At the time, she was working for IMS Publications as a medical editor. She worked in an office with four other people, one of whom – her senior editor – was a smoker. The office was small and smoky, so she asked her editor if she could be moved to the window. The answer was negative. From then on things became polarised between her smoking editor (also a woman) and herself: 'I know that the other non-smokers in the office felt the same as I did, but none was prepared to speak up. So I was seen as the trouble-maker.'

Early in 1984 Sheila developed a cough and had repeated chest infections which kept her off work, on her doctor's orders, for two months. Her doctor told her that her smokey working environment had almost certainly aggravated her illness. While she was at home, things got worse: 'I received a number of veiled threats from my editor, suggesting that my absence was making it difficult for them to produce copy on time, and that they would have to begin looking for a replacement for me.' By now, she was both upset and scared that she might lose her job, so she contacted ASH and her union – the National Union of Journalists (NUJ) – for help. The NUJ's advice was clear: 'Don't resign under any circumstances. Wait until they fire you and then act.'

Once back at work, the atmosphere in the office was intolerable: 'I was treated as persona non grata.' And still she was not allowed to shift her desk to the window. In her desperation to avoid both the acrimony and the smoke, Sheila resorted to heaving her typewriter into empty offices and corridors in order to do her work. Finally, there being no trade union structure at work, she had no alternative but to see her supervisor (also a smoker) and her managing director. Both told her nothing could be done and implied she was making a fuss about nothing. Things quickly came to a head and the management sent her home, giving her an ultimatum that if things could not be resolved she would have to resign. When she returned to work the next day, the managing director told her to resign or he would fire her. When she refused she was given a month's pay and an hour to get out of the office. The supposed grounds for dismissal were 'irretrievable break-down in relations'.

Together with the NUJ and with help from ASH, Sheila filed a claim for unfair dismissal. Several months of tense silence followed; then three days before the industrial tribunal, IMS conceded and settled out of court. They gave her £1,000 compensation as well as a good reference – which she no longer needed as she had already got another job. Despite all the unpleasantness and emotional hardship it caused, Sheila still felt it was worthwhile, not simply because she had won but because her claim had been vindicated. Her advice to anyone in a similar position: 'Be sure of your facts and your rights. Read ASH's book on smoking at work. If you're not a member of a trade union, join one, and take their advice.'

Brotherhood rules but sisterhood is powerful

In 1982 a unique event in the history of smoking and health occurred. Under the directorship of David Player, the Scottish Health Education Group (SHEG) set up what it called a 'consultative group' composed entirely of women to advise on how SHEG should run a proposed campaign devoted to women and smoking.

Our first task was to define the women the campaign should target, and the special problems it should address. Douglas Leathar and Gerard Hastings (from SHEG's Advertising Research Unit) were to conduct the research, using small discussion groups. We said we would prefer the research to be done by women, but in the event the two men did nearly all the interviewing themselves. Their report – based on 23 groups of women and only four groups of men – declared grandly that 'cigarettes for women (but not men) provide a very short-term relief from what are *invariably short-term problems*' [my italics], which they described as 'the trivial niggles that were so much characteristic of women's lives'. Examples of such 'trivia' were: 'daily domestic pressures of housework, getting the children off to school, cleaning the house and doing cooking'. Campaigns directed at women, they said, should emphasise the short-term and *not* the long-term benefits of not smoking – which is why campaigns on smoking in pregnancy were so appropriate, they argued. This, we considered, represented yet another classic misunderstanding of women as seen by men. If women did not spend so much of their lives being preoccupied with the long-term needs of others, they wouldn't need to cling so vigorously to their cigarettes in the first place. Despite our objections, these recommendations went to SHEG's smoking policy group in early 1983. They agreed that the women's campaign should be off the ground by May of that year, but it never took place. In the interim, David Player had left to become the new director of the HEC in London. When the new SHEG director, Stanley Mitchell, took over, women were once more shelved and although they were partially resurrected in a low-budget women's magazine campaign, the high profile initiative originally intended was ditched.

We were disappointed, but not beaten. Our next step was to go back to David Player in London and, together with ASH UK, organise a national conference to forge stronger connections with other women's organisations. We continued to meet as a group and devised a conference programme. The ASH Executive Committee tried to replace some of our women speakers with men whom they thought would do a 'better' job, but we stood our ground and insisted that this was a conference for women with women speakers. And at the end of 1983, 200 women representing a diverse range of organisations met to discuss the issues and consider what action to take.

Our experience so far had taught us a lesson: if we wanted to get women onto the agenda, we had to stop being a dismissable 'consultative' group. So we floated the idea of setting up a formal UK ASH Women's Committee and it was thus that the ASH Working Party on Women and Smoking was born. Our opening bid after the joint conference was to approach the HEC policymakers. We suggested that there was good reason to devote health education resources to women and that this might best be achieved by appointing a woman at the HEC whose job it would be to coordinate initiatives on women and smoking, and perhaps women's health in general. David Player was keen for this to happen: 'Women have always been as important as men,' he told me. 'Even more so, in the case of smoking.' This concern for women's health is evidenced in the grant given to the editorial collective producing a British version of *Our Bodies Ourselves*, as well as a large grant to the new Women's Studies Unit at Bradford University. However Donald Reid, director of the HEC's Smoking Programme, was not as enthusiastic. 'Why give preferential treatment to women when men who smoke still outnumber women?' he asked 'And if we are in a position where we have to choose, then it has to be men.'

Nevertheless, by summer 1984 the HEC had appointed a liaison officer to act as a coordinator on women and smoking. Women were the hot favourite for a campaign . . . should the money become available. And it did. In early 1985 a £½m windfall arrived from the Department of Health. There were only two strings attached. The money had to be spent before the end of the financial year (within the month) and it had to be a high-profile TV campaign. There was no time to argue or to do any research to see which approach might be the most effective. The result was an isolated 45-second TV commercial which was so inoffensive that most people did not even notice it. Following this, and the 'Pacesetters' campaign which deliberately used female as well as male celebrities, Donald Reid told a meeting at ASH that the HEC had been 'beaten about the ears' to focus more on women. This, he said, had had disastrous results, and was tantamount to 'throwing money down the drain'. Women still feature in the HEC's Smoking Programme objectives for 1985-6, but it remains to be seen whether any action will measure up to the words.

The right to choose

For Virginia Ernster, founder member of Women Against Smoking (WAS), and Rita Addison, former President of GASP (Group Against Smokers' Pollution), a woman's right to choose extends beyond the campaign for safe and legal abortion. It means the right not to be seduced into smoking by the tobacco companies, plus everybody's right to breathe smoke-free air.

Rita Addison is a single parent with a teenage son – a psychologist by training but an activist by inclination. She joined GASP in 1977, and became its first woman president. Lobbying, counselling, campaigning and publicising come easily to Rita, and in her characteristic style she signs her letters: 'Yours for Clean Indoor Air'. The results of her work at GASP are plain. Its membership increased more than five-fold, and non-smokers' rights are much more widely respected in the US than almost anywhere else. A majority of US states now have legislation which guarantees the provision of smoke-free areas in public places, and Rita has also founded a company – Clean Air Associates – which advises individuals and firms on how to implement smoking control policies at work. The paranoia generated about this issue within the ranks of the tobacco industry is a good gauge of the effectiveness of GASP and other non-smokers' rights groups.

One of Rita's other continuing campaigns has been to expose what she sees as the scandal of cigarette-sponsored women's tennis. She was spurred into action by DOC (Doctors Ought to Care), a doctors' pressure group which renamed the New Jersey Virginia Slims 'Emphysema Slims' in 1978. She and Massachusetts GASP have twice picketed the Virginia Slims tournament at Boston University. On the first occasion Rita, together with local nurses and women doctors, stole the show (and the press coverage) from Philip Morris by challenging Billie-Jean King for 'willingly promoting cigarettes'. Rita described the sponsorship as 'the ultimate insult to all athletes and all women'. When Virginia Slims returned to the campus the following year, so did GASP. 'Yes, Virginia, there *is* a Surgeon General,' read the placards. The embarrassment to both Philip Morris and the players was intense. Renée Richards, a doctor herself, dissociated herself from the tobacco circuit and Virginia Slims did not come back to Boston in 1985.

Virginia Ernster is an epidemiologist, mother of two and the motive force behind the group of women health workers who set up WAS. WAS also grew out of the non-smokers' movement, and has worked together with Californians for Non-Smokers' Rights – a citizens' action group. Central to the aims of WAS is to draw public attention to the growing smoking epidemic among women, and to campaign for a ban on all cigarette promotion. As a result of WAS's work, women began to feature more prominently in local as well as national newspaper coverage of cigarettes. In 1983, when lung cancer deaths overtook those from breast cancer among Californian women, WAS approached San Francisco's Mayor Diane Feinstein for help. Not only did WAS achieve tremendous publicity for women's health, but Mayor Feinstein sent every woman in the San Francisco electorate a leaflet on the effects of smoking on women's health. Unique among Virginia's many achievements is that she is the first woman to have got smoking onto the agenda at the Californian division of NOW, where she held a workshop and put up two resolutions for national action. She fought vigorously for the now famous 'Proposition P' which provides statutory smoke-free areas at work. This was contested – and lost – by a $6m tobacco-industry-funded counter-campaign. In 1984 WAS members took to the streets, or more strictly to the Virginia Slims tournament at the Oakland Coliseum. The aim, said Virginia, was to 'decry any promotions that attempt to associate liberation with a product whose users are really victims'. Their placards were tennis racquets converted into no-smoking female symbols, and their messages were: 'Cigarettes and tennis don't MATCH' . . . 'Virginia Slims is COURTing cancer'. As free cigarettes were being handed out at the door, the Coliseum management confiscated the WAS leaflets. As always, the media knew a good story when it saw one, and health won the day – in the press, at least.

Are you an activist?

There are millions of smoking and health activists around. Nine and a half million of them have already quit smoking in Britain alone, and millions more are teetering on the edge. What are you prepared to do about one of the biggest health tragedies of our time? The following quiz will help you to sort out your 'activist's potential'. Imagine yourself in each of the situations outlined and choose the answers you feel are most likely to represent how you might react. More than one answer for each question may be appropriate. Work out your score from the answers on pp. 145-7.

1. You smoke 20 cigarettes a day. Do you think:
   (a) It is hypocritical for a smoker to do anything about smoking?
   (b) Anti-smoking activists are a pain in the backside, and should leave smokers alone?
   (c) A smoker should stop smoking first and take action later?
   (d) Smokers have just as much right as anybody else to take a stance on smoking and health?
2. You are a non-smoker and you have worked in a small office with five other people for two months. Two of the people smoke – one heavily – and both are women. The ventilation in your office is poor and after a morning in there, your throat is sore and your eyes start prickling. Do you:
   (a) Feel that raising the issue of smoking amounts to victimisation of the women smokers?
   (b) Raise it with your non-smoking colleagues, but decide it's not worth losing a good working relationship?
   (c) Raise it at a union meeting to see if an amicable agreement can be reached?
   (d) Wish you had a union, but suffer in silence.
   (e) Deliver a tirade of abuse at the women smokers, pointing out how much they pollute your environment every time they exhale?
3. Both you and your husband smoke, but wish you did not. You walk into your 14-year-old daughter's room and discover her being offered a cigarette by one of her friends. Do you:
   (a) Immediately confiscate the cigarette pack from her, and forbid her to see that particular friend again?
   (b) Feel that it is not your role to interfere in your daughter's process of self-discovery?
   (c) Feel you should quit yourself before you have the right to say anything to your daughter?
   (d) Tell your daughter and her friend how much you disapprove of their smoking, and how you would never have started yourself if you had known then what you now know about its effects; also explain that you cannot prevent them from smoking, but that you will not allow it in your own house?

4. There is to be a general election in a few months. You read an article in the paper by the local parliamentary candidate whom you are thinking of voting for; it says that there is too much 'healthism' about, and that self-appointed doctors and pressure groups are trying to deprive us of cigarettes, alcohol, cream cakes, sex and the right to be idle. 'Preventing ill-health,' the article goes on, 'makes bad economic sense, because people will live longer and become a bigger burden on the state.' Do you:
   (a) Not take it seriously because one can't believe anything politicians say anyway?
   (b) Read it carefully and decide not to vote for her/him?
   (c) Write a letter to the editor of the paper, saying that anyone who subordinates people to economics is not fit to stand for election?
   (d) Write to the candidate explaining why you are going to vote for someone else, demand to know which of the anti-health industries paid him/her to make such statements and send a copy to the newspaper?

5. You belong to a women's group which is organising a local women's health fair. You suggest that smoking is a topic which should be covered, but you get a hostile reaction from the rest of the group. One of the women (who smokes) says that women should stick to women's issues, while another says that telling women what to do about smoking oppresses them. Do you:
   (a) Regret ever suggesting the idea?
   (b) Officially agree with the other women for the sake of peace, but secretly nurture your doubts?
   (c) Accuse the smoker of depriving women smokers of important information about their health?
   (d) Suggest that this is a subject which must be discussed irrespective of the divergent views on it?

6. You have just quit smoking. You receive in the post an un-solicited special offer from one of the cigarette companies which reads: 'Dear Smoker, With just 10 pack-tops of Killer Slims you can win a holiday for two in the Caribbean . . . Just fill in the form and state in not more than 25 words why Killer Slims are the best.' Do you:
   (a) Throw it in the bin, delighted that you are no longer in the grip of the cigarettes?

(b) Fill in the form and buy ten packs of cigarettes, vowing that you will never succumb to them? .

(c) Tear it up angrily and tell your children that this is how they try to keep you hooked?

(d) Send it to your local parliamentary representative, asking for immediate action to prevent future unsolicited marketing?

7. You plan to take a four-hour train journey and you have reserved a seat in a non-smoking compartment in advance. The train is full and you find the man opposite you lights up a cigarette. You remind him politely (and then less politely) that he is in a non-smoking compartment, but he carries on smoking and tells you to mind your own business. Do you:

(a) Match his abuse, but resign yourself to a smokey journey?

(b) Try to find another seat?

(c) Ask the guard to intervene?

(d) Complain in writing to the railway authority, and demand a refund for your ticket?

8. You know that your 16-year-old daughter has the occasional cigarette, but still regards herself as a non-smoker. You flip through one of her magazines and see not only 15 pages of cigarette ads, but one which takes the form of a cheap offer for a range of cosmetics with the same name as a cigarette brand. Do you:

(a) Forbid your daughter to buy the magazine any more?

(b) Discuss it with her to see if she is interested in the offer?

(c) Discuss it with her and write to the magazine's editor pointing out that this represents an inducement for young girls to smoke?

(d) Write to the national body which controls advertising (Advertising Standards Authority, or Advertising Standards Council in Australia, or the National Advertising Review Board in the US) demanding that they put a stop to cigarette advertising in teenage magazines in the interests of protecting young people, and send a copy to the magazine's editor?

How to score your activist's potential
Add up the points you have scored for each response as follows:
1.   (a) 1   (b) −5   (c) 2   (d) 7

Anyone has a right to take a stance on smoking and health, irrespective of whether they smoke or not. If you believe you are not allowed to show any concern until you have stopped smoking yourself, you are being unnecessarily defeatist. Getting involved may even help you to quit. When Simone Weil was Health Minister in France she was a heavy smoker, but this did not stop her from being the first to launch a series of hard-hitting anti-smoking initiatives during which she cut down on her own smoking. Lashing out at the 'self-appointed' guardians of our health is a telltale sign of your feelings of impotence. Their main interests are directed at reducing smoking, not people. Once you admit that there is a problem, you are half-way towards becoming an activist.

2.　　(a) 1　　(b) 2　　(c) 5　　(d) 2　　(e) −5

To get anything done, women have always had to stand up for their rights. No one else has ever done it for us. As a woman, you should be able to raise your concerns for the non-smoker without alienating the other women. It is distorted logic to suppress your own right to breathe smoke-free air in the interests of a minority – irrespective of their sex – who would probably welcome an incentive to reduce or quit smoking themselves. A good activist understands that smokers are not adversaries and that the way to proceed is by an amicable collective decision. Most smokers want to quit and most would also support more public control of smoking.

3.　　(a) −5　　(b) −3　　(c) 1　　(d) 9

Drawing the line between parental responsibility and permissiveness is hard. On the one hand you may want your daughter to discover things for herself, but on the other you don't want her to do something which may ultimately kill her. Being too dictatorial is no good, because it simply won't work; the activist always goes for what is feasible. Despite rebellion, children still look to their parents for an example to be set. Research shows that parental disapproval of the habit has an even more powerful impact on preventing children from smoking than a non-smoking parent. Why shouldn't you set the boundaries within your own home? Would you think twice about allowing heroin dealing or spitting at the dinner table?

4.　　(a) −5　　(b) 1　　(c) 3　　(d) 6

The woman who lets politicians get away with murder is accepting her powerlessness. Individuals, both women and men, can and must influence those they elect to act on their behalf. The activist not only acts for herself but for others too, which is why communicating a decision in a letter to the newspaper, and insisting that your parliamentary candidates make themselves publicly accountable, acts in the collective interest.

5.   (a) −3   (b) −5   (c) −10   (d) 10

If you are a woman who believes in a woman's right to be informed, as well as in the principle of being supportive to other women, then (d) can be the only response which scores you points. (a) is a cop-out and (b) is plain dishonest, and if you chose (c), then don't bother to join a women's group.

6.   (a) 1   (b) −5   (c) 3   (d) 6

If you chose (b), you are putty in the hands of the tobacco pushers. The difference between choosing (c) and (d) is again that of individual and collective effectiveness. The true activist knows that the more widely she directs her outrage, the more effective she is likely to be.

7.   (a) 1   (b) −5   (c) 3   (d) 6

In this situation you are not just voicing an opinion, you are in the right. Giving in to this man would be giving up your rights. The activist will ask those with authority to intervene, because it is their job to make sure that their own restrictions on smoking are observed. In the case of a defensive smoker, it is also the best way of ensuring a comfortable journey for you as well as others.

8.   (a) −3   (b) 2   (c) 3   (d) 5

Again, your ability to have any impact here is not by imposing prohibitions on one individual, but by directing action against the collective mechanism which *generates* inducements to smoke. In this way, the vital link between individual action and collective power is made.

How to assess your score

Over 50 points	· You are undeniably an activist.
30–50	You are well on the way to activism.
10–30	You are a potential activist, but there is a lot of room for encouragement.
Less than 10	You are oppressed, not so much by cigarettes as by a society which encourages you to keep quiet rather than defend your rights.

11: Thinking about quitting?

Telling people why they should quit smoking is the easiest thing in the world. You have heard anti-smoking campaigners doing it for two decades and you probably agree with what they say. Yet you still find you can't quit. Other people around you seem to have managed without much hardship. How did they do it? 'Sheer strength of character,' they say infuriatingly. Your doctor has probably told you it's all a question of willpower – 'as easy as throwing your last pack of cigarettes in the bin', Tanya's GP told her. But that didn't answer Tanya's question – she wanted to know how to cope with the craving. 'Run around the block when you get the urge to smoke,' he offered helpfully. 'I suppose he expected me to run round the bloody block 60 times a day,' said Tanya.

Nobody will tell you how to find that elusive willpower, or how to hang on to it – least of all the experts. It's all very well for anti-smoking enthusiasts to describe smoking as the 'largest avoidable hazard to health'; but to you it's just one of the many problems you have to cope with. You may not want to go to an early grave, but it seems pointless to lie awake at night agonising about it. The key to dealing with your smoking problem is to make it the number one priority in your life – for a short while, at least. The first step towards solving any problem is concentrating on it.

In this chapter I hope to help you focus your attention on smoking and the part it plays in your life. Then I'll give you a framework for quitting. There is no single miraculous cure for smoking; and despite what many people say, the key lies not so much in the method itself as in how you approach the problem.

The four key questions

If quitting smoking were simply a matter of acknowledging its dangers, you would probably have stopped a long time ago. Some smokers simply clicked their fingers and quit when they first heard about the risks. But you are still smoking today – despite knowing the dangers. So it is important that, before you throw away your last pack, you make sure you are quite clear about what is at stake. There are four key questions you must answer before you try to quit smoking and you will not be successful until you are clear about the answers.

1. Why should I stop? If you haven't got a good enough reason, you won't stop. Other people's reasons may not be yours.

2. Will I get more out of giving up than continuing to smoke? All the official publicity says how bad smoking is for you. But you know that you get something out of smoking. What is it? How important is it for you to smoke? What do you see as the benefits of quitting? The woman who has had a heart attack may feel she has more to gain than the woman who has not yet suffered any ill effects of smoking. Are you prepared to risk becoming ill?

3. Have I the confidence to stop? Quitting, as we have seen, is not just a matter of reason and motivation, but also depends on how much you believe in yourself.

4. How do I stop? Method itself won't see you through without effort on your part. You must choose the way that best suits your circumstances.

These four key questions are so crucial to your success that we need to look at each one in turn.

Why should I stop?

At first glance the answer seems obvious. 'Health,' say the experts. But before you accept this as your own reason, think about your attitude to your health. How much do you value it? Has smoking already affected it? How much discomfort are you prepared to tolerate? For example, do you consider your 'smoker's cough' to be a normal part of your daily life, or does that increasing tightness in your chest worry you a little? The importance you attach to the effects of smoking on health does not depend

on the lurid details I can give you about smoking, but on *the
extent to which you perceive yourself to be at risk.*

How can smoking affect me?

Try doing the following 'Smoker's Awareness Quiz'. It will help
you focus on what is at stake for you. Can you answer the following ten questions on smoking? Check your answers with those
on pages 151–5 (more than one answer may be correct in each
question).
1. Which of the following is responsible for the largest number
    of deaths per year?
    (a) Road accidents
    (b) Cigarette smoking
    (c) Suicides
2. Roughly what proportion of smokers are likely to die as a
    result of their habit?
    (a) 1 in 1,000
    (b) 1 in 300
    (c) 1 in 4
3. Which of the following statements are true?
    (a) It is safe to smoke ten cigarettes a day.
    (b) Those who smoke cigarettes with a low-tar yield have a
         reduced risk of developing lung cancer compared with
         high-tar smokers.
    (c) It is less harmful to smoke two packs of low-tar cigar-
         ettes a day than one pack of high-tar.
    (d) It is safe to smoke cigars.
4. What are the chances of a heavy cigarette smoker (25+
    cigarettes a day) developing lung cancer?
    (a) 1 in 5,000
    (b) 1 in 100
    (c) 1 in 5
5. Which of the following is currently the most important cause
    of chronic bronchitis (i.e. cigarette lung)?
    (a) Industrial air pollution, e.g. coal dust
    (b) Cigarette smoking
    (c) Car exhaust fumes
6. Which of the following are known causes of lung cancer?
    (a) Car exhaust fumes

(b) General air pollution

(c) Exposure to asbestos through work

(d) Cigarette smoking

(e) Inhaling other people's cigarette smoke

7. A person who has had a heart attack and quits smoking:

(a) Halves the risk of another attack

(b) Has the same risk of having another attack

(c) Reduces the risk of a further attack to that of a non-smoker

8. Cigarette smoking increases the risk of which of the following:

(a) Breast cancer

(b) An earlier menopause

(c) Influenza

(d) TB

(e) Duodenal ulcers

(f) Infertility

9. Women who both take the contraceptive Pill and smoke increase their risk of developing which of the following conditions:

(a) Cancer of the ovary

(b) Cancer of the cervix

(c) Heart attack

(d) Stroke

10. The following is a list of possible harmful effects that smoking in pregnancy can have on the baby. Which four has smoking been *proved* to increase?

(a) Having a premature baby

(b) Miscarriage

(c) Congenital abnormalities and deformities

(d) Permanent retarded intellectual function in the baby

(e) A reduced birthweight

(f) A reduction in the subsequent height of the child

Answers[1-6]

Add up your marks for correct answers as follows:

1. (a) −2   (b) +5   (c) −2

Smoking causes roughly *seven* times as many premature deaths as road accidents in the UK each year.

2. (a) −2   (b) −2   (c) +5

Overall, very few smokers get off scot-free. In a lifetime of smoking 20 cigarettes a day, you will inhale at least 100lb of tar.

  3.   (a) −2   (b) +5   (c) −2   (d) −2

(a)   The only safe cigarette is an unlit one! No matter how moderately you think you smoke, your risk of ill-health is always higher than a non-smoker's. Researchers have shown that smokers die on average 10–15 years before their time.

(b)   The more tar your cigarettes yield (see Tables in Appendix 3), the greater your risk of lung cancer.

(c)   Those who smoke low-tar cigarettes can reduce their risk of lung cancer by at least a quarter as compared with high-tar smokers. *This holds true if you do not inhale more, puff more often or increase the number of cigarettes you smoke.* That is why (c) is the wrong answer: your risk of ill-health is actually increased if you double the number of low-tar cigarettes you smoke. Low-tar cigarettes are no passport to protection from heart disease either (see p. 61).

(d)   Cigars carry the same (or even higher) risk of ill-health as cigarettes if you inhale the smoke. Cigars are less hazardous *only* if you do not inhale.

  4.   (a) −2   (b) −2   (c) +5

One in five people who smoke 25 or more cigarettes a day will develop lung cancer. Those smoking 15–25 a day have a risk of 1 in 8. So if you smoke 10–15 a day, you are *not* a moderate smoker!

  5.   (a) 0   (b) +5   (c) −2

There is no good evidence that car fumes have any measurable effect on the incidence of chronic bronchitis or emphysema (cigarette lung) (see p. 20). Although air that is heavily polluted by smoke from coal does contribute to lung diseases *other* than cigarette lung, (a) is incorrect because smoking is by far the most important cause of this disease. Even coal-miners with a huge exposure to coal dust owe their high rate of chronic bronchitis to cigarettes.

  6.   (a) −2   (b) −2   (c) +5   (e) +5

(a), (b) & (d)   Although city dwellers have higher rates of lung cancer than those living in the countryside, this is largely because they are more likely to smoke. Air pollution and car exhaust fumes contribute little to lung cancer compared with the enormous effect of cigarettes.

(c)   Those who work in the asbestos industry have a higher risk of developing lung cancer. If they smoke cigarettes as well, their risk of lung cancer can be 100 times as great as that of a non-exposed non-smoker.

(e)   Passive smoking, or inhaling other people's tobacco smoke, is not merely irritating – it can also damage your health. Certainly babies and young children suffer more chest problems, and colic, if either or both of their parents smoke. But more importantly, evidence is now accumulating that passive smoking can increase the risk of lung cancer in a non-smoker. The longer a person is exposed to it and the more heavily s/he is subjected to it, the greater the risk.

   7.   (a) +5   (b) −2   (c) −2

Smoking is undoubtedly a major cause of heart disease (see p. 17), although there are other causes (see Personal Risk Profile, pp. 155-7).

(c)   Is incorrect because a heart attack *always* causes some permanent scarring of the heart muscle. Cigarette smoking probably exerts its effects on the heart through carbon monoxide and/or nicotine by causing the walls of the coronary arteries – carrying the 'lifeblood' of the heart itself – to thicken to such an extent that blood can no longer pass through.

(a)   Is thus the only correct answer because smoking, while not fully reversing the damage already done, can halve the chances of a further attack.

   8.   (a) −2   (b) +5   (c) −2   (d) −2   (e) +5   (f) +5

Cigarette smoking is not in any way associated with breast cancer. (c) and (d) are incorrect because they are diseases caused by a virus and bacterium respectively.

(b)   Research has shown that the more you smoke, the earlier you are likely to have your menopause. This may be because some of the components of tobacco reduce levels of the female hormone oestrogen.

(e)   Eight or nine in every ten people with duodenal or stomach ulcers smoke cigarettes. Smokers are about twice as likely as non-smokers to develop ulcers, and smoking also delays the healing of such ulcers. Research shows that in non-smokers 70 per cent of ulcers healed within four weeks without extra treatment, as compared with only 30 per cent in smokers. This seems to be because ulcers thrive in an over-acid environment and smoking may prevent the secretion of adequate amounts of digestive juices – essential for neutralising the acid produced in the stomach – and thus encourage the development of an ulcer.

(f)   Yes, it now looks as if smoking can reduce a woman's fertility too. Research is beginning to show that women who smoke take much longer to become pregnant than non-smokers. Conception is delayed most in those who smoke heavily, and smoking seems to exert its effect independently of other factors related to their partners or to methods of contraception.

9.   (a) −2   (b) +5   (c) +5   (d) +5

(a)   Is incorrect because there is no evidence that either the Pill or smoking increases the risk of cancer of the ovary, which is actually lower among Pill-users than in non-users.

(b)   There is now evidence that smoking, independent of other risk factors, increases the risk of developing cancer of the cervix (neck of the womb) 2–3 times above that of non-smokers. The earlier a woman starts smoking and the more heavily she smokes, the greater the risk (see pp. 22-6). Together with the Pill, which is also associated with a higher risk of cervical cancer, smoking is likely to exacerbate that risk.

(c)   Both the Pill and cigarettes independently increase the risk of having a heart attack. *Either* taking the Pill *or* smoking increases this risk 3–4 times above that of a woman who does not smoke or use the Pill. But taking the Pill *as well as smoking* compounds the risk to ten times that of a non-smoking, non-Pill-user (see pp. 22-6).

(d)   Smoking and the Pill both increase the risk of subarachnoid haemorrhage – a stroke or haemorrhage between the linings of the brain. These can either be fatal or cause severe and lasting disability. The smoker who also takes the Pill multiplies her risk of developing such a haemorrhage by up to 22-fold, compared with a non-smoking, non-Pill-taking woman.

10.   (a) +5   (b) +5   (c) +5   (d) 0   (e) +5   (f) 0

With the exception of (d) and (f), pregnant women who smoke have a small but significantly increased risk of all the other complications listed. Some researchers have suggested that smoking in pregnancy may have long-term effects on the baby's subsequent intelligence and development, but the evidence is still tenuous. (The research suggesting that smoking affects a child's growth showed that children born to heavier smokers were, on average, 1cm shorter than those born to non-smokers; at age 16, this difference disappears altogether.)

How to assess your score
70–95 points: You have a high awareness rating, and fully recognise the dangers of the cigarette.
50–70 points: You have a fair awareness rating, but there is still room for improvement.
0–50 points: You have a poor smoker's awareness. Re-read the answers to the quiz and Chapter 2.
An overall minus score: You really have no appreciation of the effects of smoking. Re-read Chapter 2 and the answers to the quiz slowly and carefully!

Your personal risk profile

Now that you are fully aware of the risks that the smoker faces – and the woman smoker in particular – you can move on to assess your own personal risk. You may escape serious illness, but few smokers escape completely unaffected. Answer YES or NO to each of the following questions, and then score your Risk Profile at the end.

	Yes	No
1 Do you smoke cigarettes (as opposed to other forms of tobacco)?		
2 Did you start smoking at the age of 14 or earlier?		
3 Have you smoked for 20 years or more?		
4 Do you smoke 15 or more cigarettes a day?		
5 Do you inhale when you smoke?		
6 Do you smoke, or have you spent most of your 'smoking career' smoking cigarettes which yield 20mg or more tar per cigarette (check the tar yield of your brand with the tables in Appendix 3)?		
7 Are you 35 or over?		
8 Does your job involve regular contact with any of the following substances:		
(a) asbestos		
(b) lead		
(c) cadmium		
(d) copper		

	Yes	No
9 Do you live in an industrialised area where the air is polluted?		
10 Do you tend to wheeze? (Asthma sufferers discount this question.)		
11 Do you often feel a bit of phlegm (or infected mucus) sticks at the back of your nose/throat?		
12 Do you have a chronic cough which never completely goes away?		
13 Do you cough up phlegm – especially in the mornings, during winter?		
14 Do you find you get short of breath under any of the following circumstances? (Only part (c) applies if you are over 60):		
(a) When climbing two flights of stairs		
(b) When hurrying along the street		
(c) When getting dressed		
15 Do you eat a lot of saturated fat (e.g. butter, fatty red meat, milk, cheese) and fatty foods?		
16 Do you have high blood pressure?		
17 Are you taking the contraceptive Pill?		
18 Are you diabetic, or does diabetes run in your family?		
19 Have any of your parents, sisters or brothers had a heart attack?		
20 Would you describe yourself as aggressive, highly-strung and competitive?		
21 Have you had your menopause?		
22 Do you tend to take very little strenuous exercise?		
23 Are you 14lb or more overweight?		
24 Do any members of your family have duodenal ulcers?		
25 Do you have an 'acidic' stomach – i.e. do you tend to get stomach pains when you haven't eaten for a while, which are relieved by food or antacid tablets?		
26 Do you tend to get stomach pains when you feel anxious or upset?		

How to score your risk

Score as follows for all the questions to which you have answered YES. The higher your score the bigger the risk.

1–8: *5 points for each*   15: *5 points*
  9: *2 points*   16: *5 points*
 10: *1 point*   17 & 18: *5 points each*
 11: *1 point*   19 & 20: *2 points each*
 12: *3 points*   21: *5 points*
 13: *5 points*   22 & 23: *1 point each*
 14: *4 points for*   24 & 25: *2 points each*
     each part   26: *1 point*

Very high risk: 80–100
You could be in serious danger of developing any one of the smoking-induced diseases. Check below to see if you are especially at risk of developing a particular condition. If you are worried, consult your doctor.
High risk: 50–80
You are taking a big chance if you continue smoking.
Medium risk: 20–50
You are still taking a substantial risk.
Low risk: less than 20
Your risk of developing a smoking-induced illness is not high – yet. But it will increase as you continue smoking.

Specific rise profile

1. Your lung cancer risk:
Add up your scores for questions 1–8. Your total possible score is 40. You have a high risk of developing lung cancer if your score is 35 or more.
2. Your risk of chronic bronchitis:
Add up your scores for questions 1–14. Your total possible score is 64. If you scored 50 or more you have a high risk of developing chronic bronchitis.
3. Your risk of heart disease:
Add up your scores for questions 1–7 and questions 15–23. Your total possible score is 70. You are at high risk of heart disease if your score is 50 or more.

4. Your risk of duodenal ulcer:
Add up your scores for questions 1–7 and 24–26. Your total possible score is 40. If you scored more than 35, your risk of developing a duodenal ulcer is high.

The other reasons for quitting

Health is usually the 'official' reason for giving up smoking, but just as many people quit for financial reasons. You may have several kinds of reason for wanting to stop. In Claudia's case: 'Without a doubt, the most important reason for me was to have control over my body. It was very much a matter of pride to me that I should be able to control what I wanted to do. I found it humiliating and horrible to be dictated to by cigarettes.' Like Claudia, you must gather together as many reasons for quitting as possible. If you are not convinced by your own reasoning, you will undoubtedly fail.

Will I get more out of quitting than continuing?

Weighing up the forces

Anti-smoking leaflets and commercials will tell you about the undoubted value of quitting smoking, but will give you little insight into what *you* get out of cigarettes. Their job, after all, is to persuade you not to smoke. It is your responsibility alone to weigh up the benefits of quitting against those of continuing. What are the special pressures on you to smoke? Every woman will have her personal tug-of-war about it. It is not enough to consider the so-called 'rational' argument alone. Your success depends on the balance you strike between the rational and emotional factors in your life, which together keep you smoking and wanting to quit at the same time. When you have discovered that balance, you will be in a position to change it.

The benefits of quitting

Smoking – unlike any other serious health hazard – is a risk with a loophole. If you drive drunkenly into a head-on collision, you can guarantee yourself permanent damage, but even if you smoke for many years, you can actually *reverse* some of the cigarette damage by quitting. If you have smoked for ten years, and then quit, it will take roughly the same amount of time for your risk of lung cancer to return to that of a non-smoker. But you don't have to wait a decade for an improvement in your health; more than nine in every ten smokers with a chronic cough find it completely disappears or substantially improves in less than a month. And in as many as one-third, it vanishes within a fortnight.

Similarly, about three-quarters of smokers who are short of breath notice an improvement very soon after giving up. Thus while lung cancer and heart disease are the ultimate threats over smokers, people are often more acutely aware of the tell-tale early signs of ill-health, which disappear almost magically on quitting.

Although Tanya only managed to stay off cigarettes for two weeks, she immediately noticed a difference in her health:

> I felt miles better. I could breathe more easily within a couple of days. That's probably why I felt a lot more energetic. I felt, for the first time, that air was really getting down into my lungs when I breathed. Before I stopped, the air would go *down*, but none would go *in*. It was lovely to be able to lie back in bed and breathe properly – I could never breathe lying down before I stopped, I was too chesty.

Barbara, who quit six years ago, admits the main thing she noticed when she first stopped was:

> a marvellous sense of superiority over the poor sods who were still addicted . . . I don't know whether I was *actually* healthier, but I certainly felt great. I hadn't smoked long enough for cigarettes to visibly impair my health, but it felt so good to know that you could go anywhere at any time of day or night, without worrying where the nearest cigarette machine was. It felt like a release from a self-inflicted imprisonment.

What do you get out of smoking?

Having a good reason for quitting is not enough. You need to examine why you can't quit *in spite of* the many good reasons you may have for doing so. Is it something to do with the 'stress' in your life? Perhaps you smoke when you feel bored or insecure. But *why* is your life so stressful or boring? Why do you feel insecure and reach for your cigarettes when perhaps your husband, male friends or colleagues at work quit years ago?

Understanding your need to smoke

To understand this, you must take over where the research leaves off. There is a big difference between the way the researcher sees you as a *smoker*, and the way you see yourself as a person who happens to smoke. The researcher tries to understand your problem by isolating you and your smoking from your surroundings. Only you can place yourself back in the *real* world in order to see what kind of priority smoking has in your life. Because smoking is always a complex habit, I suggest that the best way to understand your own reasons for smoking is to look at the problem from three different perspectives:

1. Your smoking career
2. Your cues for smoking
3. Your feelings and your need for cigarettes

Your smoking career

Go back to the beginning. Try to remember your very first cigarette – who gave it to you and under what sort of circumstances. Most of all, try to think back to why you wanted that cigarette. Did you feel forced? What were you trying to prove? Or was it just curiosity?

Pursue your smoking career step by step and try to connect up important phases in your life with changes in your smoking. When did you become a regular smoker? When did cigarettes become an indispensable part of your life? Did leaving school, getting a new job or moving to a new place have any influence on your smoking? Were you ever aware of smoking a specific brand in order to create a particular impression? Who were you trying to impress? Think back, too, to the people who have been important in your life, starting with your parents. Can you single out any female or male friends who had any special influences on your smoking patterns? Try to match the amount you smoked with changing phases in your life, and you might surprise yourself with the picture you uncover. If there are any great fluctuations in the amount you smoke each day, what are the circumstances which lead you to smoke heavily? Do you smoke more just before a period, for example?

Tanya's smoking career began when she was 12 and she smoked to impress her stepsister. 'I smoked to prove to her that I could do it.' Having left school at 14, Tanya's first job was at a Hatton Garden jewellers. She began smoking regularly then – about ten a day. She didn't really enjoy smoking, but it was the first time she had had the money to buy them; it felt adult to smoke and she smoked the same brand as her stepmother. By the time she was 18 she was smoking 20 a day. Smoking was slowly becoming an indispensable part of her life and when her brother challenged her to quit she surprised herself by losing the bet. 'I never thought any more about it, and just carried on smoking,' says Tanya. She married at 23, and gradually built up the number she smoked to 40 a day. It was not until after the birth of her first child that she recognised her increasing dependence on cigarettes. She smoked 40 a day throughout her second pregnancy and developed a severe chest infection after the baby was born; she could neither breathe nor lie down, but still she continued to smoke. Her relationship with her husband had by this time become very strained. She suspected that he was seeing another woman, and he didn't want to take any responsibility for bringing up their children. By the time her youngest was two, Tanya could no longer escape the obvious connection between her shortness of breath and repeated chest infections and her cigarettes. She suddenly had a vision that she might die, as her own mother had, before her children reached their teens. This finally prompted her to get help in giving up at the local smokers' clinic. For the first time since she had started smoking, she managed to stay off cigarettes for two whole weeks, by which time the storm which had been brewing with her husband finally exploded. Discovering that he did indeed have a girlfriend, who was pregnant, she threw him out of the house. She immediately turned to her cigarettes again and is now smoking more than she ever did previously: 'I don't think I was ready to give up,' says Tanya. 'I couldn't have faced life at that time without cigarettes. I think I've bitten off more than I can chew. I don't feel I have the strength to look after two kids on my own any more.'

Claudia's smoking career began when she was 11. She remembers lying in bed feeling ill and bored: 'I saw one of my mother's cigarettes lying around, and I tried half.' She associated smoking with the important, serious things her mother did. After that, she only smoked the occasional cigarette when it was offered at the youth club or Guides. Her friends smoked; it was 'very much the thing to do then', says Claudia. She was smoking about 20 a week by the age of 17. When she became aware that her own untipped brand wasn't quite smart enough, she changed 'to a more sophisticated-looking American brand'. The decisive factor which changed her smoking pattern was leaving Yorkshire, where she grew up, to start a new job in London at the age of 19. Her consumption doubled; she felt nervous and insecure in the lonely adult world away from her family and 'cigarettes became a friend'. As time went on she increased from 20 to 30 a day and, by the time she was in her late 20s, began to view her smoking as a problem. At 28 she ended a very unhappy relationship with a man, after which her cigarette consumption soared to 60 a day. Cigarettes became her immediate response to every sign of distress and the amount she smoked fluctuated daily. She smoked heavily when she felt bad, but was able to cut down when she felt more confident. It was not until nearly ten years later that she felt sufficiently strong to stop. Her need to control her smoking had by then overwhelmed her need to continue smoking. She quit at the age of 37.

Cues for smoking

To describe smoking as 'just a habit' is a truism – and an unhelpful one at that. It is more important for you to distinguish between those parts of the 'habit' which relate to emotional aspects of your life, and those which do not. Your strategy for dealing with each will be different. The emotionally less important cigarettes are triggered by 'cigarette cues' – the many circumstances under which you find yourself automatically smoking. Don't underestimate the strength of these cues – they are an integral part of your habit. If you can change them, you can cut out the cigarettes which accompany them.

I suggest that the best way to rediscover your cigarette cues – which are often so well ingrained they are hard to recognise – is to try to stay off cigarettes for a whole day (or a morning if you can't manage a day). Then go slowly through the situations in which you almost always smoke. The following examples of cigarette cues should help you identify your own and you will probably be surprised at how much of your habit really *is* just habit.

The Early Morning Consciousness Cigarette: Is the first glimmer of life in your dream-world a cigarette cue? As you automatically reach out to stop the alarm clock, do you also reach out for a cigarette?

The Breakfast Cigarette: Is grasping that first cup of coffee or picking up the newspaper another cigarette signal?

The Commuter's Cigarette: Have you been sitting in the smoking compartment of the train or bus for years? If you travel everywhere by car, do you automatically reach for a cigarette the moment you get your car going?

The Telephone Cigarette: Do you have an automatic reflex in which you reach for the receiver with one hand and a cigarette with the other?

The 'Me Too' Cigarette: Do you always smoke when others offer or in situations when others are smoking? This response may be emotional in part, but it is also very much an automatic reflex.

The Mid-Morning Break Cigarette: Is your break somehow incomplete without a cigarette?

The 'Smoking Is Permitted' Cigarette: Do you always find yourself smoking in restaurants and cinemas where smoking is permitted just because it *is* permitted?

The Concentration Cigarette: Do you always smoke when you have to concentrate?

The 'What shall I do with my free hand' Cigarette: Do you find that under some circumstances, especially when you are sitting still in one place 'trapped' into inaction, you always smoke?

There are many other cigarette cues to which you are so accustomed that they have become subconscious – the TV cigarette, the after-dinner cigarette, and the ubiquitous drink cigarette, the after-sex cigarette and the night-cap cigarette.

Feelings and cigarette need

Your cigarette need forms the missing link between your smoking career and your cigarette cues. It is the emotional cement upon which your habit is founded and it is one of the outward signs of the stresses you experience as a woman. It may be a specific response – because you are angry with your boss, irritated by your children, humiliated by your lover. On the other hand, it may be part of a more general response to the long-term stresses in your life – the isolation of long periods at home with the children, for instance. Or you may feel you're too fat. Or you may be angry with your lot, but can't express it in any other way (see Chapter 7).

Or do you simply have an overwhelming feeling of being enslaved by cigarettes? In many cases, your cigarette need will be bound up with your cigarette cues, but you should be able to trace your smoking back to your feelings as well as to your cigarette cues.

Smoking for Mrs D. is a release from what she describes as the 'unendurable tensions' of being married to a schizophrenic. Her smoking patterns reflect both responses to immediate crises in her life, as well as the continuing stress of her marital responsibilities. On the one hand, says Mrs D.: 'My husband's aggro sends me rushing to buy cigarettes.' But she also recognises her underlying reasons for needing cigarettes too:

> I think that I smoke from boredom and despair, as there is no foreseeable end to my marriage predicament. I might as well go one way as the other. I know the risks, which in my case are aggravated by a tendency to bronchial troubles, but choose to ignore them.

Lorraine describes herself as a 'compulsive smoker, eater, sipper and nail-biter'. She was fat as a child and is constantly waging a battle against weight gain. She has always postponed any serious attempts to stop smoking because she feels she may gain even more weight: 'I've been told that I will put on even more weight if I stop. That, to me, is like saying that a ten-ton lorry-load will drop on your head tomorrow. I'm not prepared to run the risk of gaining even more weight.' Lorraine has high blood pressure and had to stop taking the Pill but, 'It is more disfiguring to gain weight,' she says, 'than to risk the consequences of continuing to smoke.'

Yet Mary Morley, writing to the *Daily Mail*, sees things differently: 'I was a smoker for at least 30 years, but four years ago I suffered a heart attack ... I never smoked again. Given a real choice, it was easy. I have put on weight, but I would rather be alive and overweight than a skeleton in a box six foot under.'

Have I the confidence to quit?

Ex-smokers – as we have already seen – are achievers. Have you reached the stage in your life when you feel sufficiently confident in yourself and your ability to succeed?

After numerous unsuccessful attempts to quit, Clara began to regard giving up as something that only others could achieve and each time she failed she felt less and less confident. Quitting became a crucial test of her self-esteem:

> I used to think that if I could stop smoking I could do anything. But smoking meant too much to me then. I didn't yet have the confidence or the emotional equipment to get through the panics without cigarettes.

When she finally did stop for good, she says her reasons for success were:

> not specifically connected with my smoking at all, but rather with the changing relationship I had with myself and the world. It was one which slowly enabled me to believe in myself a bit more. Giving up was part of starting afresh and leaving the old lack of confidence behind.

The big when?

Like Clara, you won't succeed until you're ready. And that readiness to quit, although it depends in part on your view of the health risks you are taking, also depends on your state of mind. If you are a feeling miserable and battered, it is hardly worth aggravating your mood with repeated unsuccessful attempts to quit. The courage in giving up lies not so much in the act itself but in how you perceive your personal power, and only you can decide when the time is right.

The confidence test[7]

How self-confident a person are you? Have you ever dared to sit down and assess yourself truthfully? This test should give you a rough guide to how you feel about yourself in general and about your ability to stop smoking in particular. Don't be dishonest – there is only one person you can cheat!

How to test your self-confidence rating

Tick the box which most closely resembles how you feel about each of the following statements. Try to avoid the '*uncertain*' box if you can:

	strongly agree	mildly agree	uncertain	mildly disagree	strongly disagree
1 I am satisfied with myself on the whole					
2 I feel that I have a number of good qualities					
3 I feel that I do not have much to be proud of					
4 I am able to do things as well as most people					
5 I wish I could have more respect for myself					
6 All in all, I am inclined to feel that I am a failure					
7 I believe that I shall be able to stop smoking for good					

8 Even if the circumstances were right, I would find it hard to stop smoking				
9 It would be relatively easy for me to cut down the number I smoke by half				
10 I know that I shall be successful in stopping smoking when the time is right				

How to score

Questions 1, 2, 4, 7, 9, 10:

Score 10 points if you **strongly agree** 5 points if you **mildly agree** 2 points if you are **uncertain** 1 point if you **mildly disagree** 0 points if you **strongly disagree**

Questions 3, 5, 6, 8:

Score 10 points if you **strongly disagree** 5 points if you **mildly disagree** 2 points if you are **uncertain** 1 point if you **mildly agree** 0 points if you **strongly agree**

Your general self-confidence rating

Add up your scores for *all* the questions. You could have scored a maximum of 100 points.

High self-confidence: 70+ points

Fair self-confidence: 40–70 points

Low self-confidence: Under 40

Your ability to stop smoking

Add up your scores for questions 7–10. You could have scored a maximum of 40 points.

If you scored 30+: you have a strong belief in your ability to quit smoking. It therefore follows that your chances of success are equally high.

If you scored 20–30: you are not quite as sure as you might be of your ability to quit smoking. But with a little encouragement you could acquire the confidence that will lead to success.

If you scored less than 20: you haven't got much confidence in your ability to stop smoking *at the moment*. You will need a great deal of encouragement and support if you are ever to quit for good.[7]

How do I quit?

The deciding factor

Assuming that you have found one or several good reasons to quit, and have convinced yourself that the benefits outweigh those of smoking – it is your Self-Confidence Rating that will decide how you go about quitting. A HIGH Self-Confidence Rating means you will probably be able to go it alone with a minimum of difficulty. But a FAIR or, especially, a LOW score on the Self-Confidence Test means that you need some help in your efforts to quit and that you will probably benefit from group support. Of course the kind of support you choose is entirely up to you. For some, a helping hand (or sympathetic ear) from a friend, lover or family may be enough; but others may want a different kind of back-up. If this is the case, the support offered by a self-help group may be just what you need.

The value of the self-help group

Although most women and men go it alone successfully, there is good reason to believe that the group approach has special value for women who feel they need extra help. Most women who have participated in women's self-help groups recognise that the support they derive from the group is *because it is all-female*. There is something uniquely powerful about being able to share experiences and confidences with other women. This has been borne out by research in Canada which shows that the success rates for quitting smoking can be as high among women as men – as long as the group is *all-female*. From her experience of setting up self-help groups as part of 'Operation Smokestop', Liz Batten sees the all-women group as having enormous potential. Women and men have different things to discuss and different reasons for smoking, so it makes sense (she says) to provide a supportive forum for a woman to explore her smoking so that she can ultimately leave it behind her. Many women have already done so, and the number of women's self-help groups is mushrooming (see Appendix 2).

Viv does not see herself as the kind of person who would go to a women's group, but she couldn't quit smoking and was not getting much help from her husband and family:

> I've tried various methods. I went to a hypnotist, had acu-
> puncture, but that didn't do it for me. I think the greatest help
> to me in giving up smoking has been going to a group in
> London. It was a women's group – something I've never been
> to before. I've often read about the strength of a group of
> women getting together and discussing and talking about
> things, but I didn't really believe it until I went to this group.
> And it was amazing. We were all heavy smokers. We'd all tried
> various ways at various times to give it up, and we spent a lot
> of time looking at what cigarettes meant to us. And then to
> take it from there in learning how to put them [cigarettes] out.
> I think that group gave me most strength towards stopping.

There is sense in smokers seeking out other smokers, rather than
'expert' non-smokers, to share their difficulties and progress.
Talking about quitting smoking is a bit like trying to describe a
very familiar pain that has finally resolved itself. When it is there
it is vivid and uppermost in your mind, but when it is gone, it
seems a vague indistinct memory. That is why ex-smokers will
frustrate you with their woolly nonchalance while non-smokers
may find it incomprehensible that you should allow yourself to
fall victim to such a 'disgusting' habit in the first place. Within a
group you will find that everyone has a vested interest in your
progress. No one will get bored and the support you derive from
it will help you prepare for quitting.

If you feel you would rather quit on your own or with a friend,
there is no reason why you shouldn't adapt my suggestions on
group work and methods. Remember that my outline is for you
to adopt, modify or reject.

How to find a group

If you already belong to a women's group or local women's
health organisation, then you have a ready-made group. Find out
from other group members if there are other women who would
seriously like to quit smoking. It's best to keep groups small, with
no more than six to eight people. If you are not a member of any
particular group, but would like to start one, you could try the

idea out with some friends, colleagues at work or neighbours. If you feel daunted by the idea of setting up a group on your own, then contact your nearest smoking-and-health agency (see Appendix 2) for advice. They will also be able to tell you about more formal groups for smokers, usually run by the local health authority. Check Appendix 2 for self-help groups which already exist in your area.

Meetings

It is important to meet regularly, and to keep in close touch with one another. Meet somewhere comfortable and private where you can talk freely. It is a good idea to stick to a non-smoking rule at meetings. The number of times you meet will vary according to the needs of individual members and you may well want to meet more than once a week initially. Once you agree to meet, stick to the arrangement. Group members can keep in close touch by phone or visits between meetings when support can be crucial. An emergency phone call at a moment of temptation may see you or someone else through.

Using the group

The great thing about using a self-help group is that there are no rights and wrongs. Whatever feels right *is* right. If you feel a bit unsure about how to get started, don't worry: you'll get better with practice.
1. Start by answering the four key questions (see p. 149). It is important to get these right. Take as much time as you need and make sure that *everyone* has enough time to discuss their answers as fully as possible. It may help to go away and think about it, or even write down what your cigarette cues and needs are and then bring your answers back to the group.
2. Inform yourself as fully as you can about the health and other issues raised by smoking. Make sure you are fully aware of how smoking affects your own personal health – the quizzes on pp. 150 and 155 should help. If you want any further information, the smoking-and-health organisations listed in Appendix 2 will be glad to assist.
3. How do you feel about cigarette advertising? Do you feel ex-

ploited by the tobacco companies? What are you going to do about it?

4. Agreeing on a date for quitting is essential. You must make sure all members are happy about the date and are prepared to stick to it. There is little point in collectively throwing your cigarettes away in a dramatic gesture at the very first meeting if you are not yet ready to see it through.

5. The method you use to quit is not of central importance. Anything goes, from carrot-chewing to using mechanical filters. You may want to try one method as a group, but quitting is a very personal matter and it may be easier for each of you to use whichever method suits you best – any of the six I suggest below, or one of your own making. Whichever you choose, it is important to discuss with the group how you plan to face up to quitting.

6. Don't forget that quitting smoking does not immediately make you into an ex-smoker. Don't assume you won't need any more support from the group the minute you quit. The period when you hover between being a smoker and an ex-smoker is dangerous; you may find you need more support at this stage than at any other time. And even if you find you can manage by yourself with the minimum of effort, you may find you can help others gain strength from your own success.

Six ideas

There is no reason why you should not use parts of each of these methods or combine several. The final decision on strategy rests with you. Use these suggestions as a guide only.

1. Quitting 'cold'
This means deciding when to quit, and then doing it. It sounds too easy, but is the commonest (and most successful) method used. Coming to your decision is, therefore, the most important part of this method. If you are a fastidious sort of person you can set yourself a date in advance, and do a countdown to 'D-Day'. Choose a special day, such as a pay rise or your birthday. Try to choose a time when you are likely to be under minimum stress. Alternatively, you could quit the moment you get a cold or cough – but don't use this as a method of evasion. Don't be deterred if you have tried this way before – and failed: it was probably be-

cause you were not really ready to face life without cigarettes.

2. Smoke yourself sick

Decide when you are going to quit and then smoke double the number of cigarettes you normally smoke two days beforehand. On the day beforehand, smoke three (or even four) times as many cigarettes as usual. The principle of this method, of course, is to disgust yourself and to smoke yourself to a point at which you find cigarettes revoltingly unpleasant. This should give you added will-power to stay off cigarettes when D-Day arrives. Smoke every last cigarette you can find! If you are used to smoking mild cigarettes, then smoke a different, strong-tasting brand in the two days before quitting. And don't forget that doubling the amount you smoke also means puffing twice as much as well. Chain-smoke on the last day and on the evening before D-Day, find yourself a couple of quiet hours – probably before you go to bed. All you need is your remaining cigarettes (keep five), a lighter and a watch. Light the first cigarette and, keeping an eye on the watch, take a puff and inhale deeply every six seconds. Carry on doing this until you feel sick, or can't take it any more. Give yourself no more than a few minutes' break, then start again. Continue the six-second puffing process until you have got through your five remaining cigarettes, or until you feel you really never want a cigarette again. Go to bed immediately; don't hang around contemplating your fate. Your ex-smoker's career awaits you.

CAUTION: DO NOT USE THIS METHOD if you already have chest or heart disease – it could be dangerous.

3. The miserly approach

This method is also based on simple but sound principles. Work out how much you spend on cigarettes each day. If you are attempting to quit as a group, set up a communal 'fund' into which you all place the amount you spend per day on cigarettes. If there are six of you in the group, all smoking two packs daily, then you will collectively accumulate more than £700 in only six weeks. If you really mean business, why not open an ex-smokers' bank account and make someone in the group responsible for paying your collective cigarette money into it? When money has accumulated over, say, an eight-week period, celebrate with some of the proceeds. There are, of course, many variations on this theme. You could get those who lapse back to the odd cigarette to pay a forfeit – say, 50 pence – into the fund, but do make sure that everyone fully agrees to being penalised, since it may serve to depress rather than encourage those who waver.

4. Temporary, permanent quitting

If the idea of giving up for ever still seems a daunting prospect to you, then set yourself a short-term target first. Your first task is to prove to yourself that you can stay off cigarettes for a specified time, *because you have decided to do so*. Try to think of it as a dress rehearsal for the real thing. The length of the 'test period' depends entirely on how difficult you perccive quitting smoking to be. For instance, if you have never been able to go without a cigarette for more than a day, then try for two days first. When you have reached the first milestone successfully, you should feel more confident about setting the next – lengthening the test period each time. This way may seem more painless than method No. 1, but in fact it is not very different, except that the decision you take seems less awesome than quitting cold.

Many smokers go through this process unconsciously – they attmept to quit, go back to cigarettes, and then regard themselves as failures. Don't be discouraged – nearly all ex-smokers have a series of 'false starts' before they stop successfully. The potential ex-smoker is only a failure until she is a success.

This method allows you to build up your confidence by planning your practice runs rather than feeling miserable each time you seem to 'relapse'. Each 'relapse' becomes a step towards your ultimate success.

5. Estranged smoking

This is a good method for very exacting people. It involves reversing the smoking cues and requires patient adherence. Set a date for quitting, perhaps one to four weeks ahead, and confound your habit little by little. Start by smoking a different brand of cigarettes, preferably one you don't like. Change the brand again as soon as you become accustomed to it. Smoke with the opposite hand. Hold the cigarette between your second and third fingers. Use matches if you normally use a lighter. Try to avoid the usual cigarette cues, and smoke at unusual times in-

stead. Why not ban smoking everywhere at home except in the
loo, or when sitting in a certain chair? If you find it hard to
handle all the cues at once, then concentrate on avoiding them
one by one.

This method can be fun and should give you an insight into
why you smoke. Discuss what you learn about your habit with
the rest of the group. This is an especially good method for dis-
tinguishing the 'habit' from the 'need' for cigarettes. Once you
have actually quit, you may need considerable support in the initial stages: although you will have learned in the early stages to
deal effectively with your cigarette cues, you will still have to face
your cigarette need (see pp. 164-5).

6. Gradual quitting

This method sounds the easiest, but is often the most taxing and
is much like running a guerilla offensive against yourself. Each
day you must cut down smoking a little, and each day will therefore confront you with many new decisions about smoking.
Nevertheless, if you stick to your regime the gradual approach
does have its merits. You can reduce your health risk whether
you stop completely or just end up smoking less.

This method should appeal to the planners and organisers. It
is important to devise a timetable for cutting down and this
should be reasonably strict, but flexible enough to alter if you
find it tough going. Try to think of it as a fitness programme that
operates in stages. Don't progress from one stage to the next until
you feel you are ready to handle it. If you feel yourself slipping
back, don't give up entirely; just go back a stage or so and build
up again. The time you spend on each stage is, again, entirely up
to you, but collective pressure from your group to reduce to nil by
a certain date – four to eight weeks, for example – may give you
the extra impetus you need to stick to your schedule. There are
two important points about this schedule. If your objective is to
quit, then you must plan not just cutting down but cutting down
to *nil*. Second, don't set yourself impossible tasks. The underlying principle of this method is gradual reduction – no more than
20 per cent each week. So if you smoke a pack a day, and decide
to stop over a five-week period, cut down to 16 a day for the first
week, and 12 for the second, and so forth. If you find it impossible to stick to the 12-a-day regime, you can always return tem-

porarily to 16 a day. It does not matter if your final nil-date is shifted back a little – what matters is that you reach it successfully.

There are, of course, other ways of gradually cutting down your smoking. For example, you could make it easier for yourself by alternating cutting down the number of cigarettes you smoke with a week of smoking the *same* number of cigarettes, but of a lower-tar brand. Or you could use one of the commercially available filters to further reduce your intake of toxic substance (see p. 178).

If you really can't quit

I believe there is a small group of smokers who will never be able to quit. It is very small and there are no easy ways of knowing whether you are likely to fall into this category. You are your own best judge of this. Learn to trust your own feelings about your need to smoke. You may know only too well that the time is not yet right for you. But remember not to judge how entrenched your smoking is by your previous attempts to quit. There are two questions you must answer before you can decide whether you really can't quit:

1. *Have I tried?* Don't settle for anything less than success until you have convinced yourself you really have tried. It is important to examine why you haven't been able to quit. Perhaps the group can help you adopt a more successful future strategy. It may seem obvious, but no one should accept that they can't stop *until they have tried* – at least once in earnest. There is little difference between the smoker who insists it's impossible to quit, and the non-smoker who insists that people smoke because they are stupid or ignorant.

2. *Have I tried hard enough?* You only have your own judgement to follow here. If you can convince everyone else in the group that you really can't quit, perhaps you are justified in rethinking your smoking problem. Don't fall into the trap of using previous half-baked attempts at quitting to justify never trying again. But whatever you decide, don't settle for failure. If you don't stop completely, there is other action that you can take. So far as your health is concerned, there is no alternative that is as good as giving up completely, but you can reduce the risk you

take even if you continue smoking. If you choose this option, try
to think of it as a step towards success in the future.

The strategy for reducing your risk
This depends on paying close attention to two things:
  What you smoke
  The way you smoke

What you smoke
Here are a few simple rules:
1. Make sure you always smoke a filter-tipped brand. You might
like to try switching to a brand that contains dark, air-cured
tobacco rather than the usual light Virginia tobacco (see
Appendix 3). (It is more difficult to inhale dark tobacco.)
2. The most important way of reducing your risk is to make sure
that you smoke a brand that produces as little tar and nicotine as
you can accept *without* increasing the number you smoke. Try to
opt for brands which produce less than 5mg tar per cigarette (see
Appendix 3). Watch out that you don't compensate for the lower
tar levels either by inhaling more deeply or puffing more frequently. Although it is important to reduce both the tar and nicotine intake, you only really need pay attention to the tar yields of
the brand you choose, because a low-tar cigarette is automatically low in nicotine too.
3. Researchers believe that the carbon monoxide you inhale in
cigarette smoke is implicated in heart disease. Minimising your
carbon monoxide intake is not such an easy matter because a
cigarette with a low-tar yield does not necessarily mean that the
carbon monoxide yield is also low. The guide to cigarettes low in
carbon monoxide (Appendix 3) should help.

The way you smoke
Again, there are a few simple rules to follow:
1. Try to inhale as little as possible, although this is easier said
than done.
2. Try to take fewer puffs of each cigarette, and make each one
short so that you have as little time as possible to inhale.
3. Never smoke the last third of the cigarette – it is the most dangerous part, where the tar and toxic materials in the smoke become concentrated. If you are likely to forget, then mark each

cigarette beforehand when you open a new pack.

4. Never re-light a half-smoked cigarette – however much it offends your sense of waste. When a cigarette goes out, some of the harmful tar condenses and concentrates at the burnt end and you inhale this when you re-light it.

5. Never leave a cigarette in your mouth between puffs. This will minimise the amount you inhale.

12: Coping

Are there any remedies which will help?

If you are looking for a magic pill to stop you smoking, forget it.
You can go out and buy all kinds of anti-smoking remedies, but
none is a substitute for determination. There are no short-cuts to
success – what you need is unadulterated effort and concentration. Having said that, there are a number of products on the
market which you may find helpful, provided you use them to
supplement and not to *replace* your will-power. As the pressure
on smokers to quit increases, anti-smoking remedies are becoming as potentially profitable as slimming devices. And like so-
called miracle slimming cures, they should be treated with a
healthy dose of scepticism. They can be divided into three main
groups: mechanical, astringent or 'aversion' therapy, and nicotine substitutes.

1. Mechanical aids

There are several kinds of cigarette holders which reduce the
amount of harmful substances such as tar, nicotine and carbon
monoxide you inhale. MD4 and its American equivalent Water
Pik are two examples. They comprise a set of re-usable filters
which extract progressively larger proportions of the harmful
substances out of the smoke you inhale. The theory behind the
filters is that the smoker gradually weans her/himself off cigarettes over several weeks and can then, according to the manufacturers, go on and quit. Whatever the theory, you still have to
quit smoking yourself whether you use a filter or not. But the
filters do reduce your exposure to some of the dangerous substances in cigarette smoke.

2. Aversion therapy

The active ingredient in aversion therapy is usually silver nitrate (or potassium permanganate), and the idea is that in combination with cigarette smoke, these chemicals generate such an awful taste in the mouth that it puts you off smoking. There are now a plethora of different tablets, mouthwashes and sprays available which contain the active ingredient. As long as you don't smoke they all taste vaguely minty, and their effect is supposed to last for several hours, but their efficacy has never been properly tested. You may find that one of these helps; on the other hand, you may find that you have to give up the remedy instead of the smoking! Your chemist or drugstore will have a selection of these products available – ask the pharmacist for advice.

3. Nicotine substitutes

Much has been claimed in the past about so-called nicotine substitutes containing a substance called lobeline, but the only serious development in this area is a chewing-gum which releases nicotine as it is chewed. This can be absorbed into the bloodstream through the lining of the mouth. This approach to quitting is of course based on the medical idea that the need for cigarettes stems from nicotine dependence alone, and that the gum can minimise the 'craving' for cigarettes and allow a person to quit. In practice, there is more to smoking than nicotine alone, and experience with the gum so far suggests that only a very small and specialised group of smokers are likely to benefit from it. If you want to try the gum as part of your quitting strategy, it is available in the UK and Australia on prescription only – and you have to pay for it!

Coping without cigarettes

To be able to cope effectively, you will of course want to know what to expect when you quit. How hard will it be? Is the so-called 'smoker's withdrawal syndrome' inevitable? What symptoms can you expect, if any, and how long will they last?

For Claudia, the first two days after quitting were the worst:

I became very physical. I hardly slept at all for the first few nights. I kept jumping up and down, and couldn't sit still. But it was all right because I knew I had made it. I did get some spooky feelings like – what if a cigarette finds its way into my hand? I was scared that I might find one there out of sheer habit. I even dreamt that I was smoking: there was a cigarette and an ashtray and I picked up the cigarette and smoked it. I was knocked out after the first day and night, but I began to realise that it wasn't so bad. It was quite a revelation to me that I managed to get through all that time without a cigarette – it was terrific. I wasn't going to give way that lightly: after the initial trial there was no longer any reason to give in.

Alison has tried to quit several times in the last two years, but she has not been able to make it:

After about 12 hours without a cigarette, I begin to feel faint. It's rather like the sensation one experiences when going without food for too long. I then experience a not-in-this-world sensation. People's voices seem to recede away from me.

Added to this, Alison says, her vision becomes blurred and she feels overwhelmed by a sudden weariness: 'By this stage I can't perform my job properly and I dare not drive my car.' And so Alison returns to her cigarettes after each attempt to quit. The alternatives, as Alison sees them, are, 'Crash my car or get fired from my job.'

Why was giving up for Claudia relatively painless, but insurmountable for Alison? Will your experience be like Claudia's or Alison's? As far as the research goes the majority of smokers, like Claudia, do find it easy to quit. Only a minority experience physical symptoms and substantial difficulty. There is, unfortunately, no way of knowing whether you will be in the majority, and you can't rely on past attempts to gauge how hard it will be. The difficulty you experience depends not only on the body's physical response to cutting off the supply of chemicals in tobacco, but also on your circumstances and frame of mind at the time. In other words, the more stressful your life is, the more aware you will be of being deprived of cigarettes. Alison sees her 'withdrawal symptoms' as entirely physical in origin, but there are other forces at work. For example, she has noticed that there *is* a time when she can go for longer periods without cigarettes: when she is gardening. Under normal circumstances she smokes a cigarette roughly every half an hour, yet when in the garden she can go without for several hours at a time: 'Gardening is good therapy. It makes me bodily tired, but mentally very much at peace and relaxed,' says Alison. Like most of us, Alison can't afford to spend the whole of her life gardening, and her difficulty in quitting is heightened by the daily stresses of normal working life. It is equally likely, therefore, that if she attempted to quit at a time when she was either away from work, or when pressures on her were minimal, that her 'withdrawal symptoms' could also be minimal.

Does there have to be a withdrawal syndrome?

The idea of a 'withdrawal syndrome', like the definition of the 'helpless addict', is firmly entrenched in our minds. Yet research shows that you may not experience a withdrawal syndrome at all. Although estimates vary, up to half of smokers who quit don't experience withdrawal symptoms.

I feel it is more useful to think of the period after quitting in a different way: I would divide the post-smoking phase into two stages of varying length: Stage I is that of the *Reluctant Ex-Smoker*. This is the period immediately after quitting during which you will, not unexpectedly, want or need cigarettes; and the strength of this need will vary from person to person. Stage II is that of the *Nostalgic Ex-Smoker* and follows immediately from Stage I.

Stage I: The reluctant ex-smoker – what to expect
Research shows that ex-smokers experience far fewer disabling symptoms than the spectre of a 'withdrawal syndrome' would suggest. Less than 20 per cent experience any restlessness, insomnia or loss of concentration. The most important 'symptom' which emerges from the research is that of *wanting a cigarette!*

When Liz quit smoking, she rediscovered the joys of feeling

well – through a fitness class: 'It wasn't nearly as bad as I thought it would be. All I had was a headache and difficulty sleeping for a couple of weeks. Every time I think of having one [a cigarette], I remind myself of how well I am instead.'

Although the 'withdrawal syndrome' is less than it's made out to be, you should not underestimate that need for a cigarette, which can vary from mildly missing cigarettes to a real and urgent craving. The best defence you have against such cravings is to *be prepared for them*. Cravings, as Clara found for example, come in waves: 'I simply learned to accept that they pass.'

Although it need not necessarily happen, you may experience a series of sensations ranging from the vague and niggling to clearcut physical responses. The commonest feeling, which just over half of ex-smokers experience, is the urge to 'have something in their mouth', especially when tense. Second commonest is what researchers describe as 'increased nervousness and irritability', which can mean anything from slight moodiness to frightening mood swings. Abrupt adjustment to life without cigarettes can also make you feel lethargic or shaky and even constipated in the early stages.

How long do the feelings last?
The immediate symptoms – if you experience any – usually appear within hours of your last cigarette. They will be most acute during the first 36 hours while your body is still expelling nicotine. Most ex-smokers find that they diminish within a week, though they may recur for a few weeks. If you do find that your mood changes, you will probably feel relatively all right in the mornings, but quite crotchety at night. You can help eliminate nicotine by taking extra vitamin C (perhaps in the form of orange juice) during this period.

While your body is cleansing itself of the chemicals in tobacco, it is at the same time beginning to recover from the damage that smoking may already have done. The repair process starts immediately, but don't expect miracles. If you have abused your lungs and arteries for 10 years or more, it is hardly fair to demand instant recovery. If you already have the early signs of chronic bronchitis – a persistent cough with which you produce a rather unappetising phlegm – don't be surprised if the immediate effect of giving up smoking seems to make you cough more profusely.

This is because the phlegm caused by your smoking inevitably gets 'stuck' in your lungs, so when you quit the first step in the recovery process is to cough up that trapped phlegm.

Stage II: The nostalgic ex-smoker
Once over the first few weeks you will reach a new danger period: you are no longer a smoker, but cannot yet regard yourself as safely on the ex-smoker's terrain. You have probably invested a lot of energy and effort into stopping and surviving Stage I and will – justifiably – feel thoroughly pleased with yourself. In Stage I the novelty and sheer sense of achievement will help cement your resolve to stay off cigarettes. Others will be impressed with your success and even non-smokers will take notice. But the accolade is short-lived.

As you progress into the world of the ex-smoker your audience – even you – will become less impressed by the impact of your new status. This is the danger period of Stage II, the time during which the rewards of quitting seem dim compared with those of smoking. You are still too close to your old cigarette-smoking status for comfort. And like the ex-problem drinker who gets the bottle of vodka for Christmas, one slip-up and all your effort will be wasted. It is a time when the group could prove important in helping to revive your flagging determination. Not only will it allow you to voice your doubts, but members will listen avidly to your stories of how you almost succumbed at a party last week, or how you valiantly fought the urge when you had a row with a colleague at work. The group will understand the importance of these continuing victories for you.

How long does it take to become an ex-smoker?
Quitting smoking, like any other complex human activity, is an enigmatic business. I can't give you a thermometer to gauge your ex-smoker status, but you will know when it has happened. You will stop thinking about cigarettes; you will no longer have to be vigilant over former cigarette cues and temptations; you will no longer even feel smug: just normal. You will become an ex-smoker when cigarettes cease to have any relevance in your life. Researchers themselves do not entirely agree over when to call someone who's quit an ex-smoker; they usually define successful ex-smokers as those who are still off cigarettes a year after they

quit. But this is a somewhat arbitrary threshold. The point at
which *you* know that you will never need another cigarette is
entirely individual, and varies enormously. I, for one, knew that
after I had weathered the first two months there was no question
of ever going back to cigarettes. In general, about half who quit
are likely to return to cigarettes within six months. By nine
months, most ex-smokers are 'safe' ex-smokers. But this is not a
hard and fast rule – I have known the odd smoker to still feel the
need for cigarettes for longer than a year.

Weight gain – is it inevitable?
Contrary to what most smokers think, *a gain in weight is not
inevitable* on quitting. Up to half of women do not gain any
weight at all. Some actually *lose* weight. Although most do gain a
few pounds, their weight usually returns to normal again within
a few months without any special effort being made. There are
several possible factors which could contribute to the weight
gain. First – and most obvious – food actually tastes better, the
ex-smoker's appreciation of food increases and she eats more.
Second, smoking hinders food absorption, and quitting improves it. There is also the possibility – as yet unproven – that
until the ex-smoker adjusts to her new status, she burns up food
less efficiently. And this could also contribute to a gain in weight.
But by far the most important factor for women is that quitting
smoking removes a vital means for both satisfying and controlling hunger (see pp. 99-101). Which means facing a doubly
powerful desire to eat. The woman in this position soon finds
herself caught in a vicious circle. Imagine: you quit smoking, and
without apparently over-eating you notice that you have gained
a few pounds. This depresses you, you feel out of control and you
eat to console yourself. You gain more weight and begin to feel
an increasingly urgent need for cigarettes – which is even more
depressing. You then begin to wonder if all the effort was worthwhile . . .

To many women there seem only two ways out of this
dilemma: to return to cigarettes – and thus the old (and ineffective) mechanism of weight control – or to make a supreme effort
to control both your smoking and your eating. Both solutions
perpetuate the vicious circle. In the first case, you will be back to
square one, only heavier. And in the second, not only will you be

diluting the all-important effort of will you need to keep off cigarettes, you will be in the impossible position of curbing two needs which are inextricably bound up with one another.

I could of course recommend low-calorie diets, or other ways of losing weight, *but I would only be helping to perpetuate the very pattern you are trying to break*. Instead of automatically struggling with your weight as if it were part of your job description, try instead to answer the following questions:

1. How will my life change if I gain a few pounds?
2. Why am I so preoccupied with being thin?
3. Who am I trying to please by striving to stay thin?
4. Is it more important to please others than to preserve my health?

I suggest that each member of the group talks about what the consequences of gaining weight will be for her. Will a few pounds *really* make you fat? Will you become a less worthy person? Do you value your body more than anything else about yourself? Do you feel that you have nothing else of value to offer? Your answer will, perhaps, help you to release yourself from a size-10 mental straitjacket.

When Barbara first quit smoking she couldn't and wouldn't come to terms with gaining weight. Instead, she guarded her despair like a guilty secret.

I gained half-a-stone in the first month, and another half-a-stone in the next two months. I felt gross and obscene. None of my clothes fitted me. Instead of being pleased with my success in stopping, I became more and more preoccupied with not being able to control my weight. I didn't dare talk to anyone about it – it seemed tantamount to admitting I was a failure. I kept postponing meetings connected with my job because I couldn't face people. I was relieved when my boyfriend and I made love in the dark so that he didn't have to see what I regarded as my mutilated body. I eventually became so depressed that my boyfriend finally forced me to talk about it. Although I don't think he could quite appreciate how I could be obsessed with something so seemingly trivial, he was amazed and hurt that I could think that his feelings for me were as superficial as the fluctuations of a set of bathroom scales. I began to feel increasingly ashamed and appalled that he should have more respect for me than I did for myself. As time went on, I began to feel more confident not only in my ability to stay off cigarettes – which I had by then long forgotten – but in *myself as a person*. I eventually stopped trying to starve myself and, after six months, not only was I still off cigarettes but I was back to my normal weight.

How they coped

Although every woman will ultimately find her own way of coping without cigarettes, comparing notes and sharing your experiences with other members of the group will probably help to spur you on, as well as giving you a wider range of ideas for how to deal with 'danger spots' if they arise.

Clara

Clara, without being fully aware of it, prepared herself for giving up for nearly a year. First, she switched to a low-tar cigarette then she cut down from 40 to 20 a day. After a while she was almost ready to go the whole way, but she still had to battle with the constant cigarette cues – especially from her heavy-smoking flatmates. She had her last cigarette before she escaped to the country to spend a weekend with some non-smoking relatives. She had almost, but not quite, assured herself that she could succeed. For Clara, the final support came from the local group she attended for two months:

When I arrived at the group meeting I was looking for excuses to start smoking again. But instead I found the confidence I'd needed for so long to actually see it through. I did several things that now seem silly in retrospect, but were desperately important to me then. I made a wall-chart, and I charted my progress on six large bits of paper. I covered the walls of my room. My success grew all around me and I used to number each day as I successfully got through it without a cigarette. I remember vividly that the 13th, 14th and 15th days were the hardest. You could tell from the incredibly ornate and tortuous numbering I chalked up on those days.

For Clara, Stage I of quitting lasted three weeks. During that time she learned to cope with the waves of cigarette panic that arose with gradually decreasing frequency:

> In those first few weeks I played all sorts of games with myself. I would recoil in mock horror whenever I saw an ashtray in my flat. I would fill it with water and throw it away because I couldn't trust myself yet. The only thing I couldn't stop doing was chewing Fox's Glacier Mints, eating Polos and chewing-gum all day. The only person who was really furious when I stopped smoking was my dentist. And I stayed just about as slim as I was before I stopped.

One of the most difficult things Clara had to face was experiencing the full blast of the volatile feelings she had been able to 'banish' previously with her cigarettes:

> I had to live my life from mood to mood, from moment to moment. Everything seemed to happen in a panic. Once I realised that I could actually work without smoking, I knew the panic was over. From then on it became surprisingly easy. It was much easier to *actually* stop than *trying* to stop for years.

Claudia

Claudia couldn't remember how many failed attempts she had made before she finally succeeded – there were so many. Her doctor's warning that she should quit brought her closer to the final decision, but it was two years before she was finally ready to succeed. Like Clara, Claudia sought the support and encouragement she felt she needed from a local group. After the first meeting she was resolute about quitting – or so she thought. It was in fact her last false start. A few hours later that evening she succumbed:

> I was watching this awful play about an alcoholic husband who was beating up his wife. I made myself watch it; I was so desperately trying to keep my mind off cigarettes. It was so horrific, I eventually couldn't bear to watch it without a cigarette. Once I started, I couldn't stop: I smoked a storm in bed –

which is not unusual for me anyway. I had all those familiar thoughts of being inadequate and useless. Just as I was wallowing in self-pity, I thought to myself: I really will try . . . tomorrow. I put the light out and had another cigarette half an hour later – in sympathy with the seriousness of the decision that faced me in the morning. I then had my very last cigarette and then concealed all the smoking utensils.

The next morning I just kept moving, not daring to stop. I had a few days off work. In the following nights I averaged about an hour's sleep a night. But I was on holiday and the sleep loss was trivial compared with the immensity of my achievement.

Claudia's way of dealing with her craving for a cigarette was to immediately fill her mind with something else. She was constantly trying to outwit herself, not letting up for one moment, not running out of alternatives. She developed a set of safe, almost mechanical responses. Take, for example, the day she stopped:

It was very hot, I was slowly going bananas. It was easy to recognise the signs. I was getting more and more fidgety. I grabbed hold of the carpet sweeper and knocked hell out of the carpet; it made a helluva noise and it took me hours. The sweat poured off me, but it was terrific. I felt so drained. By the time I'd finished I was too tired to even think about a cigarette.

Claudia rapidly became adept at devising a series of little rituals to foil herself and her cigarette panics:

Sometimes I'd mechanically go off and make a cup of coffee the moment a cigarette came into my head. I drank so much coffee in those first two weeks I thought I'd explode. It wasn't so much drinking it that was so helpful, but the whole preparation process was somehow reassuring: getting the milk from the fridge, filling the kettle, spooning out the coffee. Going through those familiar motions soothed me, kept me occupied.

No sooner out of a crisis, Claudia found herself in another later that day:

> I could feel the agitation welling up again. I had decided to go out that night, because I thought it would do me good, but I wondered how on earth I would deal with it without smoking. I remember getting ready, thinking: How am I going to get through the door, walk to the tube, find my way and cope with all those people? It was a social evening and I didn't have a cigarette I could hide behind . . . I decided not to say a word [about stopping] to anybody. I kept saying yes to more coffee, wondering how I didn't spill the cup each time because my hands were all over the place. But it worked: not only did I survive, nobody seemed to notice my difficulty.

After the first 36 hours, Claudia became good at dealing with her new status. She realised that it wasn't so bad after all. Having very rapidly overcome what she saw as the physical part of her smoking, she then had to come more slowly to terms with the emotional part:

> I know that I am a very needful person. The emotional need for cigarettes was far greater for me than any physical need. While I knew that cigarettes were always a response to intense feelings, I tried to keep everything at low key. I couldn't allow myself to get angry or upset because I knew I would immediately say: Sod it, I'm going to have a cigarette. So I tried to avoid conflict in the early days, keeping as placid and calm as possible.

As the weeks went by, and Claudia's confidence grew, she became less afraid to express herself more freely. She felt she had finally reached a point 'when it was no longer necessary to deal with my problems either by smoking or other chemical aids . . . I'm almost surprised now when people ask me how the smoking is going. I feel like saying: but I'm a non-smoker *now*.'

Like most other people, Madeleine needed a practice run before she could quit smoking for good. Her first attempt equipped her for ultimate success:

It's very odd when you start not to smoke. Because I remember I gave up smoking two years ago – seriously and for ever I thought – and I discovered a fund of energy and joy inside me that was wonderful. It made me feel that life was terrific, and that I was beginning to live for the first time at the age of 30. I noticed that I'd removed what used to be like a screen or a veil between me and the world. All my senses felt very alive. I had no idea that this was going to be the case – I thought nothing but pain would result from not smoking. I didn't believe anyone when they said, 'You'll feel better.' I thought, rubbish, no you don't.

Those months were full of good times for me. I felt happy and positive. Work was going well and my private life was going well. But then my dearly beloved grandmother died and I became completely distraught. I couldn't cope with being so churned-up and feeling like an abandoned two-year-old. I found I couldn't mourn for her in a decent, quiet way, so I went back on cigarettes.

Madeleine continued to smoke for a further two years, for fear that when she came up against another emotional crisis she wouldn't be able to deal with it without cigarettes. She has now quit, and learned to her surprise that cigarettes are neither emotionally essential nor helpful in her work as a writer. Quitting smoking has presented her with other possibilities:

> My not smoking has opened me up to how much my mouth wants to kiss other people. At the moment it's all right, because I've got someone I'm having a relationship with whom I can kiss 20 times a day. And he doesn't mind . . . So I recommend kissing as incredibly helpful for anyone who's trying to give up smoking!

Appendix 1

5th World Conference on Smoking and Health Winnipeg, Canada, 10–15 July 1983

Stopping the Female Smoking Epidemic

Rationale

The case for directing a campaign specifically aimed at women in both the industrialised and developing countries is justified on the following grounds:

(a) trends in smoking-induced disease: lung cancer rates in women are rising faster than those of men in many affluent countries, and signs of an epidemic in the Third World are evident; rates for many other cancers, heart disease and a variety of pregnancy-related conditions are much higher in women who smoke than non-smokers;

(b) striking differences in trends in smoking prevalence: women are quitting at lower rates than men and in many countries smoking rates among teenage girls are notably higher than those of boys; data on Third World countries is needed;

(c) women have become a key target of the tobacco industry in its contemporary advertising strategies;

(d) there has been a paucity of information about the specific health risks of smoking for women and of the magnitude of those risks;

(e) women tend to smoke for different reasons from men;

(f) health education efforts which emphasise women have so far been few and far between.

Recommendations for action

The overall objective is to contribute to the worldwide effort to control smoking. Women must be involved at all levels of this effort, including activities relating to education/information, legislation, and smoking cessation.

Political/organisational

(a) *International:* Organisations committed to smoking and health, such as the International Union Against Cancer, the World Health Organisation, International Union Against Tuberculosis and International Union for Health Education, should set up women's action committees to produce reports that describe the problem and recommend appropriate activities. The committees should, where possible, be largely female and drawn from representatives of developing and industrialised countries.

(b) *National:* All organisations concerned with smoking and health should designate an officer whose responsibility it would be to coordinate the women's programme, which should be complementary to other smoking and health initiatives, as well as women's health programmes.

(c) *Regional/local:* Health, educational and consumer organisations should be encouraged to launch their own community activities and, where possible, to coordinate such efforts. Women's organisations, both traditional and feminist, should be involved.

Education/information

The emphasis of mass media and other campaigns should be on the value of non-smoking to women themselves, in addition to the effects related to pregnancy and children.

(a) *Existing materials* on women and smoking already developed for public education purposes should be collected, and a clearing-house for such materials established;

(b) *Possible target groups:* For industrialised countries, no age or class groups should be ignored, but special attention should be paid to girls who have not yet begun smoking and to women who smoke and wish to quit;

(c) *Themes:* Increase women's awareness of the special risks of smoking for women, emphasise exploitation tactics of the tobacco industry, design programmes to boost women's self-confidence, including programmes that deal with stress and concerns about weight;

(d) *Training:* Training for health professionals and educators to ensure a positive approach towards smoking education directed at women is essential.

Research

(a) Why girls in many countries are now more likely to smoke than boys.

(b) Smoking and smoking-related disease patterns among women in Third World countries.

(c) Sex differences in motivation to smoke and in the process of quitting.

(d) Smoking trends in women by their own demographic characteristics, including occupation and family status.

(e) Which methods of health education are successful with women.

(f) How tobacco promotion directed at women recruits smokers and delays quitting.

Individual and community support

(a) *Smokers*
As a majority of women smokers wish to quit, more formal and informal support for women is needed, including materials and groups for women only at work and at home. Community education should encourage families and friends to provide support for the majority of individuals who quit on their own.

(b) *Non-Smokers*
Increased efforts should be made to enlist the support of the majority of women who do not smoke in an attempt to encourage the positive aspects of being a non-smoker.

Action Policy from Special Topic
Session: 'Smoking and Feminism',
Winnipeg, July 1983.

Appendix 2

Useful organisations in the UK

These organisations will back you up with information, advice and literature on smoking, health campaigns and facilities for quitting.

ASH National Office,
5–11 Mortimer Street,
London W1N 7RH.
Tel: 01-637 9843.

British Medical Association,
(Campaign Information only),
Tavistock House,
Tavistock Square,
London WC1H 9JR.
Tel: 01-387 4499

Health Education Council,
78 New Oxford Street,
London WC1A 1AH.
Tel: 01-637 1881

Scottish ASH
at Royal College of Physicians,
9 Queen Street,
Edinburgh EH12 1JQ.
Tel: 031-225 4725

Scottish Health Education
Group,
Health Education Centre,
Woodburn House,
Canaan Lane,
Edinburgh EH10 4SG.
Tel: 031-447 8044

Tenovus Cancer Information
Centre,
92 Cathedral Road,
Cardiff, Wales.
Tel: 0222 619846

Women's Health Information
Centre,
52 Featherstone Street,
London EC1.
Tel: 01-251 6580

Women's National Cancer
Control Campaign,
1 South Audley Street,
London W1.
Tel: 01-499 7832

Exeter Ash,
Royal Devon and
Exeter Hospital,
Barrach Road,
Exeter EX2 5DW.

Grampian ASH
c/o "Birchwood",
Bartle Moor,
Kincardine O'Neil,
AB3 5EE.
Tel: 033 984311

Norfolk ASH
Chest Clinic,
West Norwich Hospital,
Bowthorpe Road,
Norwich.
Tel: 0603 28377

Northern ASH
Brunton Park Health Centre,
Princes Road,
Gosforth,
Newcastle upon Tyne NE3 5NF.
Tel: 0632 362327

Northern Ireland ASH
c/o Ulster Cancer Foundation
40 Eglantine Avenue
Belfast BT9 6DX.
Tel: 0232 663281

Northwest ASH
The Uplands
Bury New Road,
Whitefield,
Manchester.
Tel: 061 796 0933

Project Smokefree,
North Western Regional
Health Authority,
Gateway House,
Piccadilly South,
Manchester M60 7ZP.
Tel: 061 236 9456

Solent ASH
c/o Community Health
Department,
Dunsbury Way,
Leigh Park,
Havant.
Tel: 0705 482154

South Western ASH,
The Health Education Service,
Central Health Clinic,
Tower Hill
Bristol BS2 0JD.
Tel: 0272 291010

Suffolk ASH
Health Education Centre,
46a St Matthews Street,
Ipswich.
Tel: 0473 216398

West Midlands ASH
Health Education Centre,
Brierley Lane,
Bilston WV14 8TU.
Tel: 0902 41834

Yorkshire ASH
Huddersfield Health
Authority,
Health Promotion Unit,
St Luke's House,
Blackfootmoor Road,
Huddersfield HD4 5RH.
Tel: 0484 654777

Associated organisations

COUGHIN (Campaign On
the Use of Graffiti
for Health in the
Neighbourhood),
P.O. Box 316,
London E2 9PP.

TREES (Those who Resist an
Early End from Smoking),
P.O. Box 316,
London E2 9PP.

AGHAST (Action Group to
Halt Advertising and
Sponsorship of Tobacco),
Central Health Clinic,
Tower Hill,
Bristol BS2 0JD.
Tel: 0272 291010

Self-help groups

It is in the nature of self-help groups that they come and go as
needs change. Check that each group is still running before re-
commending it or attending it.

*Organisations which can put you in touch with self-help
groups*

Community Health Initiatives
Resource Unit,
26 Bedford Square,
London WC1B 3HU.
Tel: 01-636 4066

Helpline,
College of Health,
18 Victoria Park Square,
London E2 9PF.
Tel: 01-980 6263

The Hull Stop Smoking
Project,
Institute for Health Studies,
University of Hull,
Hull, HU6 7RX.
Tel: 0482 497405/46311
ext 7405

Nottingham Self Help Project,
114 Mansfield Road,
Nottingham,
NG1 3HL.

'Operation Smokestop',
c/o District Health Education
Officer,
Oaklands House,
Winchester Road,
Southampton.
Tel: 0703 784278

Existing self-help groups

Ashington Women's Health
Advice Centre (women only),
6a Laburnum Terrace,
Ashington,
Northumberland.
Tel: 0670 853977

Bolton Well Woman Centre,
(women only),
3 Siemens Street,
Horwich,
Bolton BL6 5PR.
Tel: 0204 699673

Exeter Well Woman Centre,
(women only),
124 Topsham Road,
Exeter.
Tel: 0392 72870

Glasgow 2000/Glasgow
Herald,
20 Cochrane Street,
Glasgow G1 1HL.
Tel: 041 227 4438

Haringey Women's Health
Group,
Tottenham Town Hall,
Approach Road,
London N15.
Tel: 01-801 3152

Kathy's Stop Smoking Group,
3 St Helen's Road,
West Bridgford,
Nottingham.
Tel: 0602 231660

Self Stop Smoking Group,
9a Sandringham Road,
London E8.

'Stop', courses at:
St John & St Elizabeth,
Grove End Road,
London NW8.
Tel: 01-444 6876

Women's Therapy Centre,
(women only),
6 Manor Gardens,
London N7 6LA.
Tel: 01-263 6200

Useful UK films on women and smoking

All are available for sale or hire.

The 'Ladykillers', (37 mins video),
Concorde Films Council Ltd.,
201 Felixstowe Road,
Ipswich,
Suffolk IP3 9BJ.
Tel: 0473 715754

'The Ladykillers' (12 min video/
                      tape slide),
c/o ASH in Scotland,
(Address see p.194)

'The Feminine Mistake'
(approx. 30 minutes)
The Health Education
Council,
(Address see p.194)

Useful Organisations in Australia

New South Wales

Australian Cancer Society,
Rooms 311-12,
Third Floor,
Trust Building,
Corner King and Castlereagh
  Street,
Sydney, NSW 2000.
Tel: 02-231 2355

BUGA-UP,
P.O. Box 80,
Strawberry Hills,
NSW 2012.

Heart Foundation,
Ground Floor,
343–9 Riley Street,
Surry Hills,
NSW 2010.
Tel: 02-211 5188

New South Wales State
  Cancer Council,
Challis House,
10 Martin Place,
Sydney,
NSW 2000.
Tel: 02-233 2300

Non-smokers Movement of
  Australia,
399 Pitt Street,
Sydney,
NSW 2000.
Tel: 02-267 7722

Quit for Life,
Health and Media Education
  Centre,
P.O. Box 450,
Crows Nest,
NSW 2065.
Tel: 02-320 0643

Victoria

Action on Smoking and
  Health (Australia),
P.O. Box 179,
Carlton North,
Vic 3054.
Tel: 03-663 5533

Anti-cancer Council of
  Victoria,
1 Rathdowne Street,
Carlton,
Vic 3053.
Tel: 03-662 3300

BUGA-UP,
P.O. Box 285,
Fitzroy,
Vic 3056.

Health Promotion Unit,
Health Commission,
555 Collins Street,
Melbourne,
Vic 3000.
Tel: 03-616 7777

MOP-UP,
P.O. Box 47,
Clifton Hill,
Vic 3068.
Tel: 03-481 8625

National Heart Foundation,
464 William Street,
West Melbourne,
Vic 3003.
Tel: 03-329 8511

Western Australia

Australian Council on Smoking
and Health (WA) Inc.,
705 Murray Street,
West Perth,
WA 6005.
Tel: 09-321 2365
09-321 6224

BUGA-UP,
P.O. Box 598,
Subiaco,
WA 6008.

National Heart Foundation,
43 Stirling Highway,
Nedlands,
WA 6009.
Tel: 09-386 8926

Non-smokers Movement (WA)
705 Murray Street,
West Perth,
WA 6005.
Tel: 09-322 6474

Smoking and Health Project
Team,
Public Health Department,
3rd Floor,
533 Hay Street,
Perth,
WA 6000.
Tel: 09-425 9666

Queensland

Health Education Division,
Department of Health,
232 Adelaide Street,
Brisbane,
Qld 4000.
Tel: 07-225-0122

National Heart Foundation,
99-103 Mary Street,
Brisbane,
Qld 4001.
Tel: 07-221 2100

Non-smokers Movement
(Qld),
Department of Nursing
Studies,
Qld Institute of Technology,
G.P.O. Box 2434,
Brisbane,
Qld 4001.
Tel: 07-223 2761

Queensland Cancer Fund,
P.O. Box 201,
Spring Hill,
Qld 4000.
Tel: 07-839 7077

South Australia

Anti-cancer Foundation of the
Universities of South
Australia,
G.P.O. Box 498,
Adelaide,
SA 5001.
Tel: 08-228 5027

Australian Council on
  Smoking and Health,
Honorary Secretary,
RMB 725,
Blackwood,
SA 5157.

National Heart Foundation,
155–9 Hutt Street,
Adelaide,
SA 5000.
Tel: 08-223 3144

South Australian Health
  Promotion Services,
158 Rundle Mall,
Savings Bank Building,
Corner Pultney Street,
Adelaide,
SA 5000.
Tel: 08-218 5000

Northern Territory

Northern Territory Anti-
  cancer Foundation,
G.P.O. Box 718,
Darwin,
NT 5709.
Tel: 089-81 3556

Australian Capital Territory

ACT Cancer Society
Dr W. Birch,
Department of Nuclear
  Medicine,
Royal Canberra Hospital,
Acton,
ACT 2601.

Action on Smoking and
  Health (Canberra),
Trevor Francis,
P.O. Box 280,
Dickson,
ACT 2602.

National Heart Foundation,
51 Northbourne Avenue,
Canberra City,
ACT 2601.
Tel: 062-47 7100

Tasmania

ASH Tasmania,
Chairman,
Professor I.C. Lewis,
Department of Surgery,
University of Tasmania,
43 Collins Street,
Hobart,
TAS 7000.
Tel: 002-34 2866

Department of Health
  Services,
Public Buildings,
Davey Street,
Hobart,
TAS 7000.
Tel: 002-30 2259
    002-30 3173

Heart Foundation,
86 Hampden Road,
Battery Point,
Hobart,
TAS 7000.
Tel: 002-34 5330

Tasmania Cancer Committee,
c/o 34 Davey Street,
Hobart,
TAS 7000.
Tel: 002-30 3557

Appendix 3

Tar, Nicotine and Carbon Monoxide Yields of Cigarettes (UK) 1985

Tar Yield mg/cig	Brand	Carbon Monoxide Yield mg/cig	Nicotine Yield mg/cig
	LOW TAR		
Under 4	Embassy Ultra Mild King Size	Under 3	Under 0.3
	John Player King Size Ultra Mild	Under 3	Under 0.3
	Silk Cut Ultra Low King Size	Under 3	Under 0.3
4	Lambert and Butler Special Mild King Size	6	0.5
	Silk Cut Extra Mild King Size	5	0.5
7	Cartier International Luxury Mild	9	0.7
	Consulate Menthol	8	0.7
	Consulate No.2	7	0.6
	Du Maurier King Size	8	0.7
	Dunhill King Size Superior Mild	7	0.7
	Merit Extra Mild	9	0.5
	Peter Stuyvesant Extra Mild King Size	7	0.7
8	Belair Menthol Kings	14	0.6
	Berkeley Extra Mild King Size	9	0.8
	Craven 'A' King Size Special Mild	8	0.7
	Craven 'A' Luxury Length Special Mild	10	0.7
	Dunhill International Superior Mild	9	0.7
	Embassy Extra Mild	9	0.8
	Embassy Number 1 Extra Mild	9	0.9
	Embassy Number 5 Extra Mild	8	0.7

Tar Yield mg/cig	Brand	Carbon Monoxide Yield mg/cig	Nicotine Yield mg/cig
8	John Player Superkings (Low Tar)	8	0.9
	John Player King Size Extra Mild	9	0.8
	Peter Stuyvesant Luxury Length Extra Mild	9	0.7
	Player's No.10 Extra Mild	9	0.6
	Silk Cut	9	0.7
	Silk Cut Number 3	9	0.7
	Silk Cut Number 5	9	0.7
	Vanguard King Size	11	0.8
9	Gauloises Longues Caaporal Filter*	16	0.5
	Kent King Size	7	0.8
	Player's No. 6 Extra Mild	9	0.8
	Silk Cut King Size	10	0.9

LOW TO MIDDLE TAR

Tar Yield mg/cig	Brand	Carbon Monoxide Yield mg/cig	Nicotine Yield mg/cig
10	Gauloises Disque Bleu Caporal Filter*	17	0.6
	St. Moritz Luxury Length Menthol	13	0.9
11	Dunhill International Menthol	14	1.0
	Gauloises Caporal Filter*	18	0.6
	Peter Stuyvesant King Size	13	1.0
12	Acclaim King Size	15	1.0
	Benson and Hedges Sovereign Mild	9	1.0
	Carlton Long Size	11	1.1
	Carlton Premium	11	1.1
	Gitanes Caporal Filter*	16	0.7
	John Player King Size	13	1.2
	Kensitas Club Mild	11	1.1
13	Craven 'A' Luxury Length	14	1.2
	Crown Crest King Size	12	0.9
	Embassy No. 1 King Size	14	1.2
	Gitanes International*	17	1.1
	Guards	15	1.1
	Kensitas Club Mild King Size	13	1.2
	Kensitas Mild King Size	12	1.2

Tar Yield mg/cig	Brand	Carbon Monoxide Yield mg/cig	Nicotine Yield mg/cig
13	Kings Filter Virginia	13	0.9
	Lambert and Butler King Size	15	1.2
	Marlboro 100s	14	0.9
	Marlboro King Size	13	0.8
	More Filter 120s	16	1.2
	More Menthol Filter 120s	15	1.2
	Piccadilly Filter De Luxe	13	1.3
	Player's No. 6 King Size	14	1.3
	Regal King Size	15	1.2
	United Filter Virginia	13	1.0
	Victoria Wine King Size	12	0.9
	Winston King Size	15	1.2
14	Ardath King Size	15	1.2
	Benson and Hedges Longer Length	14	1.3
	Benson and Hedges Sovereign King Size	15	1.2
	Benson and Hedges Sterling King Size	15	1.2
	Berkeley Superkings	13	1.3
	Carrolls Number 1 Virginia	14	1.2
	Chesterfield King Size	14	1.2
	Dunhill Luxury Length	16	1.2
	Embassy Filter	13	1.3
	Embassy No. 3 Standard Size	13	1.3
	Embassy Regal	13	1.2
	Fribourg and Treyer Superkings	14	1.4
	Kim	11	1.1
	Lark Filter Tip	14	1.1
	London King Size	16	0.9
	Park Drive Tipped King Size	15	1.2
	Piccadilly King Size	15	1.1
	Raffles 100s	15	1.3
	Senior Service Cadets King Size	15	1.2
	Senior Service Superkings	13	1.4

MIDDLE TAR

15	Camel Filter Tip	14	1.2
	Dorchester Filter	17	1.0

Tar Yield mg/cig	Brand	Carbon Monoxide Yield mg/cig	Nicotine Yield mg/cig
	Dunhill King Size	14	1.3
	Embassy Gold	13	1.3
	Fine 120 Super Length	14	1.3
	Hyde Park King Size	17	1.1
	John Player Superkings	15	1.5
	John Player Special Filter	13	1.4
	Kensitas Club Filter Virginia	15	1.3
	Kent De Luxe Length	15	1.2
15	Land M Filter Box	14	1.3
	Pall Mall Filter Tipped	12	1.3
	Peter Stuyvesant Luxury Length	16	1.4
	Player's Medium Navy Cut Filter	15	1.3
	Player's No. 6 Filter	14	1.3
	Rothmans King Size	17	1.2
	Rothmans Royals 120s	15	1.5
	State Express 555 Filter Kings	15	1.3
	Woodbine Filter	13	1.3
	Benson and Hedges Gold Bond Filter	15	1.3
	Benson and Hedges Sovereign Filter	13	1.2
	Benson and Hedges Special Filter King Size	17	1.4
	Craven 'A' King Size	15	1.3
	Dunhill International	16	1.5
	Fribourg and Treyer No. 1 Filter De Luxe	18	1.4
	Gold Flake (P)	11	1.2
16	Gold Leaf Filter Virginia	15	1.3
	John Player Special King Size	15	1.4
	Kensitas Club King Size	17	1.4
	Kensitas Corsair Filter Virginia	14	1.2
	Kensitas Filter Virginia King Size	17	1.4
	Kingsmen Filter Virginia	16	1.2
	Lambert and Butler International Size	16	1.4
	Major Virginia Filter Extra Size	17	1.4
	Park Drive Special Virginia (P)	11	1.4
	Piccadilly Number One (P)	11	1.3
	Player's Medium Navy Cut (P)	11	1.3
	Player's No. 6 Plain (P)	10	1.3
	Player's No. 10 Filter	16	1.2

Tar Yield mg/cig	Brand	Carbon Monoxide Yield mg/cig	Nicotine Yield mg/cig
16	Rothmans International	16	1.5
	Rothmans King Size Filter	15	1.6
	Royal Standard King Size	17	1.1
	Spar King Size	17	1.2
	Weights Plain (P)	10	1.3
	Woodbine Plain (P)	10	1.3
17	Benson and Hedges Gold Bond King Size	17	1.5
	Benson and Hedges Supreme International	14	1.6
	Camel (P)	10	1.3
	Capstan Medium (P)	11	1.3
	Gallaher's De Luxe Green (P)	10	1.4
	Kensitas Fine Virginia (P)	11	1.4
	Senior Service Fine Virginia (P)	10	1.4

HIGH TAR

Tar Yield mg/cig	Brand	Carbon Monoxide Yield mg/cig	Nicotine Yield mg/cig
21	Gauloises Caporal (P)	18	1.2
22	Gitanes Caporal (P)	17	1.3
	'Sweet Afton' Virginia (P)	12	1.9
23	Gallaher's De Luxe Blue (P)	14	1.9
25	Capstan Full Strength (P)	14	2.6

New brands recently introduced but not yet analysed by the government chemist for a period of six months. Estimates by the manufacturers of the yields for these brands are as follows:

Tar Yield mg/cig	Brand	Carbon Monoxide Yield mg/cig	Nicotine Yield mg/cig
9	Silk Cut Extra	9	1.0
	Dorchester Extra Mild	10	1.0
14	Embassy President	14	1.4
	Regal 100s	14	1.4

(P) indicates plain cigarettes. All other brands have filters.

* These brands contain darn, air-cured tobacco.

Tar, Nicotine and Carbon Monoxide Yields of Cigarettes (Australia) 1984

Brand	Tar (mg/cig)	Nic. (mg/cig)	CO (mg/cig)
Local Brands			
Barclay	1	0.2	2
Now Filter	1	0.2	2
Now Menthol	1	0.2	2
Rothmans Ransom Mark III	1	0.1	2
Hallmark Ultra Mild	3	0.4	4
Peter Stuyvesant Ultra Mild	3	0.3	7
Rothmans Ransom Select	3	0.3	6
Hallmark Dual Filter Menthol	5	0.4	8
Ardath Extra Mild	5	0.4	8
Claridge Extra Mild	6	0.8	7
Courtleigh Satin Leaf Special Mild	6	0.8	7
Escort Extra Mild	6	0.8	7
Hallmark Dual Filter	6	0.4	11
Sterling Mild Menthol	6	0.7	7
Wills Super Mild	6	0.7	7
Courtleigh Satin Leaf Menthol Mild	7	0.7	8
Silk Cut	7	0.7	9
Sterling Special Mild	7	0.8	8
Summit Lights	7	0.8	10
Wills Super Mild Menthol	7	0.7	9
Benson and Hedges Extra Mild	8	0.8	9
John Player Special Mild	8	0.8	10
Albany Trim	9	0.8	9
Alpine Lights	9	0.9	10
Black and White Extra Mild	9	0.8	10
Cambridge Extra Mild	9	0.9	10
Country Life Extra Mild	9	0.9	10
Dunhill International Menthol Mild	9	1.0	11
Dunhill KS Superior Mild	9	1.1	10
Longbeach Extra Mild	9	0.9	10
Marlboro Golden Lights	9	0.9	9
Nelson KSF	9	0.9	10

Brand	Tar (mg/cig)	Nic. (mg/cig)	CO (mg/cig)
Park Drive Extra Mild	9	0.9	10
Peter Stuyvesant Extra Mild	9	1.1	10
Peter Stuyvesant Luxury Length EM 94mm	9	1.0	10
Peter Stuyvesant Luxury Length EM 100mm	9	0.9	10
Viscount Extra Mild	9	0.9	10
Albany Trim Menthol	10	0.7	10
Alpine Luxury Length	10	0.9	12
Ardath Menthol	10	0.9	11
Black and White Virginia	10	1.0	12
Cambridge Extra Mild	10	1.0	13
Cambridge Menthol Mild	10	0.8	10
Cartier Luxury Mild	10	1.0	13
Cartier Luxury Mild Menthol	10	1.0	13
Cartier Vendome	10	1.0	11
Chesterfield Extra Mild	10	0.8	11
Claridge Filter	10	1.0	10
Craven A Special Mild	10	1.2	12
Du Maurier Special Mild	10	0.9	11
Dunhill Deluxe Mild	10	1.2	12
Dunhill International Superior Mild	10	1.0	12
Escort Virginia	10	0.9	12
Kent KS	10	1.1	12
Kool	10	0.7	12
Marlboro Special Mild	10	1.0	11
Nelson Select	10	1.0	12
Rothmans Extra Mild	10	1.1	11
Salem Menthol Mild	10	0.8	10
Winfield Extra Mild	10	1.0	10
Winfield Menthol	10	1.0	10
Ardath Filter	11	1.1	12
Ascot	11	1.1	13
Black and White Menthol	11	1.0	11
Cambridge Extra Mild Menthol	11	1.0	13
Capstan Filter 20s	11	0.9	12
Cartier Vendome Menthol	11	1.0	11
Marlboro Lights	11	1.0	11
Park Drive	11	1.0	13
Peter Jackson Extra Mild	11	1.0	11
Rothmans International	11	1.1	13

Brand	Tar (mg/cig)	Nic. (mg/cig)	CO (mg/cig)
St Moritz Menthol	11	1.1	13
Turf Filter	11	1.1	13
Wills Virginia	11	1.1	12
Winfield Export	11	1.1	12
Albany King Size	12	1.0	12
Cambridge Virginia	12	1.1	14
Camel Filter 25s	12	1.1	13
Capstan KSF 25s	12	1.1	13
Consulate KS Menthol	12	1.0	14
Courtleigh Gold Band Filter	12	1.1	14
Du Maurier	12	1.1	13
Dunhill International	12	1.2	16
Escort Menthol	12	1.1	12
John Player Special International	12	1.2	17
John Player Special KSF	12	1.1	14
Park Drive Menthol	12	0.9	14
Park Drive Premium	12	1.1	14
Peter Jackson	12	1.0	14
Peter Jackson Menthol	12	1.0	12
Peter Stuyvesant Luxury Length 100mm	12	1.3	16
Rothmans International Special Filter	12	1.1	14
Rothmans International Special Mild	12	1.0	12
Salem Menthol	12	0.9	12
State Express 555	12	1.1	14
Sterling Virginia	12	1.1	14
Viscount Regular	12	1.1	14
Viscount Specials	12	1.1	14
Alpine	13	1.1	14
Ardath Cork Tipped	13	1.0	10
Benson and Hedges Special Filter	13	1.2	15
Capstan Special Mild Cork Tipped	13	1.0	10
Chesterfield Filter 20s	13	1.1	16
Chesterfield Filter 30s	13	1.1	14
Country Life Virginia	13	1.1	15
Craven A Corked Tipped	13	1.0	10
Kingford	13	1.1	13
Marlboro Menthol	13	1.1	12
Peter Stuyvesant KSF	13	1.2	14
Peter Stuyvesant Luxury Length 94mm	13	1.2	15

Brand	Tar (mg/cig)	Nic. (mg/cig)	CO (mg/cig)
Peter Stuyvesant Menthol	13	1.1	14
Players No. 6	13	1.2	14
Rothmans KSF	13	1.2	13
Rothmans KS Plain	13	1.3	10
Temple Bar	13	0.9	10
Turf Cork Tipped	13	1.0	11
Vogue	13	1.2	13
Winfield Virginia	13	1.2	14
Benson and Hedges Plain	14	1.6	10
Capstan Medium Cork Tipped	14	1.2	11
Capstan Medium Plain	4	1.2	10
Chesterfield King	14	1.2	10
Craven A Filter	14	1.3	15
Dunhill KSF	14	1.4	14
Longbeach Virginia	14	1.2	16
Marlboro 20s	14	1.2	14
Marlboro 25s	14	1.2	14
Marlboro Gold	14	1.3	14
Philip Morris Filter	14	1.2	15
Philip Morris Regular	14	1.2	8
Rothmans King Size Cork Tipped	14	1.4	10
Belvedere	15	1.2	16
Martins KSF	15	1.2	16
Philip Morris Executive	15	1.3	11
Imported Brands			
Carlton Filter	1	0.2	2
Gitanes Filter*	5	0.5	12
Gauloises Filter*	6	0.4	14
Kent Golden Lights	9	0.8	11
Madison St Filter	9	1.1	10
Astor Mild KSF	10	0.6	12
Camel Milds	10	0.9	10
Ms Blue	10	0.6	12
Senior Service Virginia	10	0.8	7
Camel Filter Soft Pack	12	1.1	15
Lucky Strike	12	0.9	10
Sobranie Jasmine Filter	12	1.1	15
Mahawat Filter	13	0.7	23
Mahawat Plain	13	0.8	18
Salem Box	13	1.1	15

Brand	Tar (mg/cig)	Nic. (mg/cig)	CO (mg/cig)
Sobranie Cocktail Filter	13	1.0	18
Camel Filter Box	14	1.2	15
Gitanes Plain	14	0.8	12
Salem Soft Pack	14	1.2	16
Viceroy Kings	14	1.0	16
Camel Regular	15	1.3	11
Gauloises Plain	15	0.7	13
L&M	15	0.9	15
Lark	15	0.9	14
Pall Mall	15	1.1	11
Winston Box	15	1.2	16
Bentoel Kretek Filter	16	1.4	7
Ms King Size Filter	16	1.0	16
Sobranie Black Russian Filter	16	1.0	21
Winston Soft Pack	16	1.2	16
Astor Gold Filter	17	1.2	18
More Filter	17	1.5	24
Ms International	17	1.2	17
Sherman's Havana Rounds	17	1.6	14
More Menthol	18	1.5	25

* These brands contain darn, air-cured tobacco.

References

(The place of publication is London unless otherwise stated.)

Chapter 1: Today's epidemic

1. Lord Kaberry of Adel, *Hansard*, vol.464, 22 May 1985, col.369.
2. *General Household Survey 1982*, Office of Population Censuses and Surveys, Social Survey Division, Series GHS no.12, HMSO 1983; and *OPCS Monitor*, Reference PP1 81/5, 14 July 1981.
3. *General Household Survey*, op. cit.
4. G.F. Todd, *Changes in Smoking Patterns in the UK*, Tobacco Research Council, 1975.
5. *ibid*.
6. ASH, personal communication.
7. *OPCS Monitor*, Reference GHS 85/2, 17 September 1985.
8. *ibid*.
9. *ibid*.
10. L.A. Loeb, V.L. Ernster, 'Smoking and lung cancer: an overview', *Cancer Research*, vol. 44, December 1984, pp.5940-58.
11. H. Cox, L. Marks, 'Sales trends and survey findings: a study of smoking in 15 OECD countries,' *Health Trends*, Department of Health and Social Security, vol.15, no.2, May 1983, pp.48–52.
12. D. Hill, N.J. Gray, 'Australian patterns of tobacco smoking and related health beliefs in 1983', *Community Health Studies*, vol.VIII, no.3, 1984, pp.307–16.
13. H. Cox, L. Marks, *op.cit*.
14. N.J. Gray, D.J. Hill, *op.cit*.
15. J. Van Reek, 'Rookgedrag in Nederland van 1958–1982', *Tabak, Alcohol, Drugs*, vol. 9, no.3, 1983, pp.99–103.
16. W.J. Millar, *Smoking Behaviour of Canadians* (1981), Health and Welfare, Canada, 1983.
17. H.I. Mørck and others, *Tobaksforbrug og Rygevaner i Norden*, Denmark 1981.
18. *OPCS Monitor*, *op.cit*.

19. *Tobacco Statistics Finland*, Central Statistical Office, Helsinki, 1985.

20. J.M. Cohen Solal, *La Situation du Tabagisme en France*, Summary of Symposium on Smoking and Health in Southern European Countries, Copenhagen, World Health Organisation, 1 May 1984.

21. U. Reuter, *Rauchen*, Effizienzkontrolle 1980 der Bundescentrale für Gesundheitliche Aufklärung, Köln, 1981.

22. B. Thassitis, 'Cigarette consumption increase continues in Greece', *Tabak Journal International*, vol.2, April 1984, pp.116–18.

23. A.G. Kafatos, *Smoking Behaviour and Health Knowledge of Greek Adolescents in Athens*, Symposium on Smoking and Health in Southern European Countries, *op.cit.*

24. C. La Vecchia, 'Patterns of cigarette smoking and trends in lung cancer mortality in Italy', *Journal of Epidemiology and Community Health*, vol.39, 1986, pp.157–64.

25. A. O'Connor, *Prevalence of Cigarette Smoking in the Irish Population* (16+ years), Dublin, Joint National Media Research Survey, 1984.

26. *Tobacco International*, 11 May 1984, p.22.

27. D.R. Hay, *Smoking and Health: New Zealand Statistics, 1984*, National Heart Foundation of New Zealand, Report no.40, February 1984.

28. P.M. Löchsen and others, *Trends in Tobacco Consumption and Smoking Habits in Norway*, A Report from the Norwegian Council on Smoking and Health, Oslo, 1984.

29. P. Oles, 'The extent of tobacco use in Poland', *World Smoking and Health*, Summer 1983, pp.38–43.

30. *Insight Sheet 2: Smoking Statistics: Stop-Press Update*, ASH Scotland, 1984.

31. T. Salvador i Llivina, *Smoking Prevention in Catalunya*, paper at Workshop on Smoking and Health, Suzdal (USSR), September 1983.

32. L.M. Ramström, *Smoking Control in Sweden*, Swedish National Smoking and Health Association, 1983.

33. R. Cooper, 'Smoking in the Soviet Union', *British Medical Journal*, vol.285, 21 August 1982, pp.549–51.

34. *General Household Survey and OPCS Monitor, op.cit.*

35. J. Dobbs, A. Marsh, *Smoking Among Secondary School Children in 1984*, Office of Population Censuses and Surveys, 1985.

36. A. Charlton, 'The Brigantia survey: a general review', *Public Education About Cancer; Recent Research and Current Programmes*, vol.77, 1984, pp.92–102.

37. P.A. Gillies, *Biosocial Aspects of Smoking in Children and Adolescents*, paper presented to Annual Meeting of British Association for the Advancement of Science, September 1984.

38.   F. Ledwith, *Smoking Prevalence Among Primary and Secondary School Children in Lothian*, Proceedings of Health Education and Youth Conference, Southampton, 1982.

39.   L.A. Loeb, V.L. Ernster, *op.cit.*

40.   P. Homel and others, *1983 Survey of Drug Use by School Students in New South Wales*, Sydney, New South Wales Drug and Alcohol Authority, April 1984.

41.   ibid.

42.   R. Masironi, L. Roy, 'Smoking and youth: a special report', *World Smoking and Health*, Spring 1983, pp.27–32.

43.   K.K. Ibsen, 'Smoking habits in 9000 Danish schoolchildren', *Acta Paediatrica Scandinavica*, vol.71, 1982, pp.131–4.

44.   J. Dobbs, A. Marsh, *op.cit.*

45.   A.G. Kafatos, *op.cit.*

46.   L.R. Ramstrom, personal communication, 1984.

47.   D.R. Hay *op.cit.*

48.   *The Health Consequences of Smoking for Women: A Report of the Surgeon General*, Washington D.C., US Department of Health and Human Services, 1980, p.275.

49.   W.J. Millar, 'Smoking Prevalence among Canadian Adolescents', *Canadian Journal of Public Health*, in press.

50.   *Young People and Smoking*, Fact Sheet, Health Education Bureau, Ireland.

51.   M. Rimpela, *Juvenile Health Habits*, University of Helsinki, Finland, in press.

52.   L.E. Aarø, 'Smoking among Norwegian school children 1975–80', *Scandinavian Journal of Psychology*, vol.24, 1983, pp.277–83.

53.   T. Salvador i Llivina, *op.cit.*

54.   *General Household Survey, op.cit.*

55.   *ibid.*

56.   *NOP Market Research*, unpublished results from questions commissioned by the Office of Population Censuses and Surveys, 1984.

57.   A. Marsh, J. Matheson, *Smoking Attitudes and Behaviour*, Office of Population Censuses and Surveys, Social Survey Division, HMSO, 1983.

58.   *ibid.*

59.   *The Health Consequences of Smoking for Women, op.cit.*

60.   B. Jacobson, *The Ladykillers – Why Smoking is a Feminist Issue*, Pluto Press, 1981, p.15.

61.   *ibid.*

62.   F. Ledwith, *BBC TV Series 'So You Want to Stop Smoking' Evaluation of Back-Up Support in Scotland*, unpublished, 1984.

63.   M. Raw, J. Heller, *Helping People to Stop Smoking*, Health Education Council, 1984.

64.   M. Jarvis, 'Gender and smoking: do women really find it hard to give up?', *British Journal of Addiction*, vol.79, 1984, pp.383–7.

65.   *General Household Survey, op.cit.*

66.   *The Health Consequences of Smoking: Cardiovascular Disease, A Report of the Surgeon General*, US Department of Health and Human Services, Rockville, 1984, p.365.

67.   M.H. Mushinski, S.D. Stellman, 'Impact of new smoking trends on women's occupational health', *Preventive Medicine*, vol.7, 1978, pp.349–65.

68.   *ASH Bulletin*, no.11, 13 September 1978, p.5.

69.   J. Gaiser, 'Smoking among Maoris and other minorities in New Zealand', *World Smoking and Health*, Summer 1984, pp.7–9.

70.   *ibid.*

71.   L.D. Cardozo and others, 'Social and obstetric features associated with smoking in pregnancy', *British Journal of Obstetrics and Gynaecology*, vol.89, August 1982, pp.622–7.

72.   *Symposium on Smoking and Health in Southern European Countries, op.cit.*

73.   B. Thassitis, *op.cit.*

74.   T. Salvador i Llivina, *op.cit.*

75.   *The Health Consequences of Smoking for Women, op.cit.* pp.172–3.

76.   E. Goddard, unpublished General Household Survey data presented in a paper at ASH Seminar: 'Women and Smoking', November 1983.

77.   D. Borgers, R. Menzel, 'Wer raucht am meisten?' *Münchner Medizinischer Wochenschrift*, vol.126, no.38, 1984, pp.1092–6.

78.   H. Rohrmoser, *Frauen und Rauchen*, Bundescentrale für Gesundheitliche Aufklärung, Köln, June 1984.

79.   D. Ram-Prakash (ed), *Social Trends 13*, HMSO, 1983, p.51.

80.   E. Goddard, personal communication.

81.   *Women in the Labour Market – A TUC Report*, March 1983.

82.   U. Reuter, *op.cit.*

83.   A. Marsh, J. Matheson, *op.cit.*

84.   U. Reuter, *op.cit.*

85.   A. Marsh, J. Matheson, *op.cit.*

Chapter 2: The price women are paying

1.   'Deaths by Cause', *OPCS Monitor*, Reference DH2 84/2, 19 June 1984.

2.   *Mortality Statistics*, extracted from Registrar General for Scotland, preliminary return for 1983.

3.   *Provisional Mortality Statistics*, General Register Officer,

Department of Health and Social Services, Belfast 1984.

4. *Smoking or Health: A Report of the Royal College of Physicians*, Pitman Medical 1977.

5. *OPCS Monitor, op.cit.*

6. *Mortality Statistics for Scotland, op.cit.*

7. *Provisional Mortality Statistics, Belfast, op.cit.*

8. *OPCS Monitor, op.cit.*

9. *Mortality Statistics for Scotland, op.cit.*

10. *Provisional Mortality Statistics, op.cit.*

11. *Mortality Statistics for Scotland*, extracted from Registrar General for 1984.

12. *OPCS Monitor*, Reference DH2 8513, 23 July 1985.

13. *Health or Smoking? A follow-up Report of the Royal College of Physicians*, Pitman Medical, 1983.

14. *ibid.*

15. Derived from the *Registrar General's Statistical Review 1963*, and *Mortality Statistics* (DH2) 1983, with permission of the controller of HMSO.

16. R. Doll, R. Peto, *Quantitative Estimates of Avoidable Risks of Cancer in America Today*, 1982.

17. J. E. Bishop, 'Lung Cancer Deaths Surpass Breast Among US Women', *Wall Street Journal*, 14 February 1985.

18. *ibid.*

19. 'Death and Drug Use in Australia 1969–1980', *Technical Information Bulletin*, No.69, October 1982.

20. *World Health Statistics Annual*, Geneva, 1981, 1982, 1983.

21. *World Health Statistics Annual*, Geneva, 1984.

22. R. Peto, personal communication.

23. *General Household Survey 1984*, Hong Kong.

24. R. Masironi, L. Roy, *op.cit.*

25. W.C. Chan and others, 'Bronchial carcinoma in Hong Kong 1976–77', *British Journal of Cancer*, vol.39, 1979, pp.182–92.

26. L.C. Koo and others, 'An analysis of some risk factors for lung cancer in Hong Kong', *International Journal of Cancer*, vol.35, 1985, pp.149–55.

27. W.C. Chan and others, *op.cit.*

28. L.C. Koo and others, 'Active and passive smoking among female lung cancer patients and controls in Hong Kong', *Journal of Experimental Clinical Cancer Research*, vol.4, October–December 1983, pp.367–75.

29. L.C. Koo, personal communication.

30. *Health or Smoking? op.cit.*

31. R. Peto and others, 'The relevance in adults of air-flow obstruction, but not of mucus hypersecretion, to mortality from chronic lung

disease', *American Review of Respiratory Disease*, vol.128, 1983, pp.491–500.

32.   J.L. Cronenwett and others,, 'Aortoiliac occlusive disease in women', *Surgery*, vol.88, no.6, December 1980, pp.775–84.

33.   *ibid*.

34.   *ibid*.

35.   K. Wellings, 'Contraceptive trends', *British Medical Journal*, vol.289, 13 October 1984, pp.939–40.

36.   P.M. Layde, V. Beral, 'Further analyses of mortality in oral contraceptive users', *The Lancet*, 7 March 1981, pp.541–6.

37.   *Health or Smoking, op.cit*.

38.   *ibid*.

39.   P. Layde and others, 'Incidence of arterial disease among oral contraceptive users', *Journal of Royal College of General Practitioners*, vol.33, 1983, pp.75–82.

40.   A. Singer and others, 'Genital wart virus infections: nuisance or potentially lethal?', *British Medical Journal*, vol. 288, no.6419, 1984, pp.735–7.

41.   *ibid*.

42.   *ibid*.

43.   R.W.C. Harris and others, 'Characteristics of women with dysplasia or carcinoma in situ of the cervix uteri', *British Journal of Cancer*, vol.42, 1980, pp.359–69.

44.   N.H. Wright and others, 'Neoplasia and dysplasia of the cervix uteri and contraception: a possible protective effect of the diaphragm', *British Journal of Cancer*, vol.38, no.2, August 1978, pp.237–79.

45.   D.B. Thomas, S. Holck, 'Invasive cervical cancer and combined oral contraceptives', *British Medical Journal*, vol.290, 30 March 1985, pp.961–5.

46.   I.M. Sasson and others, 'Cigarette smoking and neoplasia of the uterine cervix: smoke constituents in cervical mucus', *New England Journal of Medicine*, vol.312, no.5, 31 January 1985, pp.315–16.

47.   E. Trevathan and others, 'Cigarette smoking and dysplasia and carcinoma in situ of the uterine cervix', *Journal of the American Medical Association*, vol.250, no.4, 22/29 July 1983, pp.499–502.

48.   D. Hellberg and others, 'Smoking as a risk factor in cervical neoplasia', *The Lancet*, 24/31 December 1983, p.1497.

49.   E. Trevathan, *op.cit*.

50.   *ibid*.

51.   D.F. Austin, 'Smoking and cervical cancer', *Journal of the American Medical Association*, vol.250, no.4, 22/29 July 1983, pp.516–17.

52.   A. Singer, *op.cit*.

53.   *General Household Survey 1983*, Office of Population Censuses and Surveys, HMSO.

54. *General Household Survey 1982*, Office of Population Censuses and Surveys, Social Survey Division, Series GHS No.12, HMSO, 1983.
55. Derived from *Registrar General's Statistical Review 1963*, and *Mortality Statistics* (DH2) 1983, *op.cit.*
56. *Health or Smoking?*, *op.cit.*
57. P.M. Layde, V. Beral, *op.cit.*
58. T. Hirayama, 'Non-smoking wives of heavy smokers have a higher risk of lung cancer: a study from Japan', *British Medical Journal*, vol.282, 17 January 1981, pp.183–5.
59. D. Trichopoulos and others, 'Lung Cancer and passive smoking', *International Journal of Cancer*, vol.27, 1981, pp.1–4.
60. S.T. Weiss and others, 'The health effects of involuntary smoking', *American Review of Respiratory Disease*, vol.128, 1983, pp.933–42.
61. D. Rush, P. Cassano, 'Relationship of cigarette smoking and social class to birthweight and perinatal mortality', *Journal of Epidemiology and Community Health*, vol.37, 1983, pp.249–55.
62. *Health or Smoking, op.cit.*
63. J.C. Stevenson, M.I. Whitehead, 'Postmenopausal osteoporosis', *British Medical Journal*, vol.285, 28 August 1982, pp.585–7.
64. *ibid.*
65. *World Health Statistics Annual, 1983, op.cit.*
66. C. Holden, 'Can smoking explain ultimate gender gap?', *Science*, vol.221, 9 September 1983, p.1034.
67. L.A. Loeb, V.L. Ernster, *op.cit.*

Chapter 3: Third World women – a market waiting to be tapped

1. *Smoking Control Strategies in Developing Countries*, Geneva: WHO Technical Report, Series 695, 1983.
2. C.S. Muir, D.M. Parkin, 'The world cancer burden: prevent or perish', *British Medical Journal*, vol.290, 5 January 1985, pp.5–6.
3. B. Jacobson, 'Tobacco and the Third World: a growing epidemic', in *World View 1985 – An Economic and Political Yearbook*, Pluto Press 1985.
4. W.H. Chandler, *Banishing Tobacco*, Worldwatch Paper 68, Washington DC, January 1986.
5. 'Third World market for cigarettes expands', *Tobacco Reporter*, March 1978, pp.13–14.
6. *BAT Industries. 1983 Annual Report and Accounts.*
7. *Tobacco Reporter, op.cit.*
8. P. Taylor, *Smoke Ring – The Politics of Tobacco*, second edition, Bodley Head, 1985.
9. B. Wickstrom, *Cigarette Marketing in the Third World: A Study of Four Centres*, University of Gothenburg, 1979.

10.   'How the brands ranked. Maxwell International Estimates', *World Tobacco*, December 1983, p.53.

11.   B. Jacobson, *op.cit.*

12.   *ibid.*

13.   *Smoking Control Strategies in Developing Countries, op.cit.*

14.   D.M. Parkin and others, 'Estimates of worldwide frequencies of twelve major cancers', *Bulletin of the World Health Organisation*, vol.62, no.2, 1984, pp.163–82.

15.   *World Health Organisation Statistics Annual*, Geneva, 1983.

16.   K.P. Ball, personal communication.

17.   R. Masironi, L. Roy, *Smoking in Developing Countries*, Geneva, World Health Organisation, 1983.

18.   V. Kennedy, *Women's Research and Resources Centre Newsletter*, no.5, 1979.

19.   M. Aghi, *Tobacco and the Indian Woman*, Proceedings of the Fifth World Conference on Smoking and Health 1983, in press.

20.   *ibid.*

21.   P. Gupta and others, 'Mortality among reverse chutta smokers in South India', *British Medical Journal*, vol.289, 6 October 1984, pp.865–6.

22.   M. Aghi, *op.cit.*

23.   *Smoking Control Strategies in Developing Countries, op.cit.*

24.   P. Gupta and others, *op.cit.*

25.   P. Gupta and others, 'Mortality experience in relation to tobacco chewing and smoking habits from a 10-year follow-up study in Ernukalam district, Kerala, *International Journal of Epidemiology*, vol.13, no.2, 1984, pp.184–7.

26.   L.P. Shirname and others, 'Correlation of mutagenicity, tumorigenicity of betel quid and its ingredients', *Nutrition and Cancer*, vol.5, no.2, 1983, pp.87–91.

27.   N.A. Jafarey and others, 'Habits and dietary pattern of cases of carcinoma of the oral cavity and oropharynx', *Journal of the Pakistani Medical Association*, June 1977, pp.340–3.

28.   M. Aghi, *Intervention in the Tobacco Habits of Rural Indian Women*, Proceedings of the Fifth World Conference on Smoking and Health 1983, in press.

29.   M.R. Pandey and others, 'Prevalence of smoking in a rural community of Nepal', *World Smoking and Health*, Spring 1981, pp.15–18.

30.   *ibid.*

31.   N. Cohen and others, 'Smoking and respiratory disease symptoms in rural Bangladesh', *Public Health*, vol.97, 1983, pp.338–46.

32.   N. Khanum, *Tobacco in Bangladesh*, Proceedings of Commonwealth Institute Conference on Tobacco in Africa, 1982.

33. N. Cohen, *op.cit.*
34. *ibid.*
35. *ibid.*
36. *World Health Statistics Annual 1983, op.cit.*
37. N. Cohen, 'Smoking, health and survival: prospects in Bangladesh', *Lancet*, vol.1, 1981, pp.1090–92.
38. *ibid.*
39. R. Masironi, L. Roy, *op.cit.*
40. *ibid.*
41. D. Femi-Pearse and others, 'Respiratory symptoms and their relationship to cigarette smoking', *West African Medical Journal*, vol.22, 1973, p.57.
42. B.O. Onadeko, A.A. Awotedu, *Smoking Patterns of Students In Higher Institutions of Learning in Nigeria*, Proceedings of Fifth World Conference on Smoking and Health 1983, in press.
43. 'Third World market for cigarettes expands', *op.cit.*
44. *World Health Organisation Statistics Annual 1983, op.cit.*
45. 'Brazilian cigarettes are mainly for expanding domestic market', *Tobacco International*, 29 June 1979, p.28.
46. *World Health Organisation Statistics Annual 1983, op.cit.*
47. *ibid.*
48. P. Taylor, *op.cit.*
49. *ibid.*
50. A. Kalache, personal communication.
51. R. Masironi, L. Roy, *op.cit.*
52. F.L. Lokschin, F.C. Barros, 'Smoking or health: the Brazilian option', *World Smoking and Health*, vol.9, no.2, Summer 1984, pp.2, 26, 30, 31.
53. F. L. Lokschin, F.C. Barros, 'Smoking or health: the Brazilian option', *New York State Journal of Medicine*, December 1983, pp.1314–16.
54. *World Health Statistics Annual, op.cit.*
55. F. L. Lokschin, F.C. Barros, *op.cit.*
56. P. Taylor, *op.cit.*
57. *ibid.*
58. 'How the brands ranked. Maxwell International Estimates', *World Tobacco*, June 1983, p.57.
59. P. Taylor, personal communication.

Chapter 4: The ladykillers – a history

1. J.C. Robert, *The Story of Tobacco in America*, Chapel Hill, University of N. Carolina Press, 1967.
2. R. Sobel, *They Satisfy: The Cigarette In American Life*, Garden City, Anchor Press, 1978.

3.   B. Day, 'Admen open the closet door and give sex updated appeal', *Campaign*, 1 March 1985, p.33.

4.   H. Howe, 'A historical review of women, smoking and advertising', *Health Education*, May/June 1984, pp.3–9.

5.   G.F. Todd, *'Changes in Smoking Patterns in the UK*, Tobacco Research Council, 1975.

6.   R. Walker, *Under Fire: A History of Tobacco Smoking in Australia*, Melbourne, Melbourne University Press, 1984.

7.   *ibid.*

8.   G.F. Todd, *op.cit.*

9.   *The Health Consequences of Smoking for Women: A Report of the Surgeon General, Washington DC, US Department of Health, Education and Welfare*, 1980.

10.   G.F. Todd, *op.cit.*

11.   R. Walker, *op.cit.*

12.   G.F. Todd, *op.cit.*

13.   *The Health Consequences of Smoking for Women, op.cit.*, p.23.

14.   R. Walker, *op.cit.*

15.   *The Health Consequences of Smoking For Women, op.cit.*

16.   G.F. Todd, *op.cit.*

17.   P. Taylor, *Smoke Ring – The politics of Tobacco*, second edition, Bodley Head, 1985.

18.   B. Jacobson, *The Ladykillers – Why Smoking is a Feminist Issue*, Pluto Press, 1981.

19.   E.A. Weiss, 'Communicating with the smokers in Australia', *World Tobacco*, September 1984, pp.85–7.

20.   S. Woodward, personal communication.

21.   'Women and smoking reports conflict', *Tobacco Observer*, vol.5, no.1, February 1980, p.1.

22.   B. Jacobson, A. Amos, *When Smoke Gets in Your Eyes*, British Medical Association, Health Education Council, May 1985.

23.   'With women in mind', *Tobacco*, March 1984, p.13.

24.   J.J. O'Connor, 'Women top cig target', *Advertising Age*, vol.52, no.41, 28 September 1981, p.93.

25.   *ibid.*

26.   B. Kanner, 'Advice on targeting women', *Advertising Age*, 23 June 1980.

27.   D. Rogers, 'Targeting women' (editorial), *Tobacco Reporter*, February 1982, p.8.

28.   E. Reisman, 'Look to the Ladies', *Tobacco*, March 1983, pp. 17–19.

29.   *ibid.*

30.   *ibid.*

31.   E. Reisman, 'Female figures', *Tobacco*, March 1984, pp.11–12.

32.   J.J. O'Connor, *op.cit.*

33. R. Donovan, 'Boost from Bishops', *Tobacco*, February 1983, pp.18–19.

34. 'A new profile of the cigarette smoker', *Tobacco International*, 22 December 1978.

35. *ibid*.

36. R. Scott, *The Female Consumer*, Associated Business Programmes, 1976, p.155.

37. R. Donovan, *op.cit*.

38. B. Oliver, 'Spar outfit takes on tobacco giants with own label contender', *Campaign*, 29 June 1984.

39. R. Donovan, *op.cit*.

40. *Smoking and Health Now: A Report of the Royal College of Physicians*, Pitman Medical, 1971.

41. P. Wisson, 'Housewives: the end of a myth', *Campaign*, 10 October 1984, pp.71–3.

Chapter 5: The evolution of the female cigarette

1. 'How the brands ranked. Maxwell International Estimates', *World Tobacco*, September 1983.

2. P. Taylor, *op.cit*.

3. B. Armstrong, T.L. Butler, *Tobacco Smoking and Tobacco-Related Behaviour in Western Australia 1980-1983*, Public Health Department, Perth, 1984.

4. *ibid*.

5. P.P. Aitken and others, 'Monitoring Children's Perceptions of Advertisements', *Social Science and Medicine*, vol.21, no.7, 1985, pp.785–97.

6. S. Chapman, *Cigarette Advertising as Myth: A Revelation of the Relationship of Advertising to Smoking*, Ph.D Thesis, Department of Social and Preventive Medicine, University of Sydney, 1985.

7. S. Chapman, 'A David and Goliath story: tobacco advertising and self-regulation in Australia', *British Medical Journal*, vol.281, 1 November 1980, pp.1187–9.

8. S. Chapman, *Cigarette Advertising as Myth, op.cit*.

9. B. Armstrong, T.L. Butler, *op.cit*.

10. S. Chapman, *Cigarette Advertising as Myth, op.cit*.

11. *ibid*.

12. NOP Market Research Ltd, November 1984, unpublished results from questions commissioned by the Office on Population Censuses and Surveys.

13. 'Brand shares of the UK cigarette market 1983', *Tobacco*, September 1984, p.6.

14. 'How the brands ranked', *op.cit*.

15. B. Kanner, 'Advice on targetting women', *Advertising Age*, 23 June 1980.

16. *The 1980 Virginia Slims American Women's Opinion Poll: a study conducted by the Roper Organisation, 1980.*

17. 'How the brands ranked', *op.cit.*

18. J.J. O'Connor, *op.cit.*

19. 'How the brands ranked', *op.cit.*

20. 'Targeting the female smoker', *Tobacco Reporter*, April 1983, pp.44–5.

21. J.J. O'Connor, *op.cit.*

22. 'Targeting the female smoker', *op.cit.*

23. *ibid.*

24. *ibid.*

25. *ibid.*

26. *ibid.*

27. W.F. Gloede, 'RJR puts on the Ritz: PM goes to Rio', *Advertising Age*, 21 January 1985.

28. *American Cancer Society News Conference on Lung Cancer*, 7 February 1985.

29. G. Amber, 'Playing a king-size waiting game', *Campaign*, 19 November 1976, p.16.

30. M. Daube, letter to Advertising Standards Authority, October 1976.

31. P. Thomson, letter to M. Daube, October 1976.

32. 'Virginia Slims goes much too far – ASH', *Campaign*, 10 December 1976.

33. R. Moyle, parliamentary question, *Hansard*, 13 December 1976.

34. *The British Code of Advertising Practice, Appendix H: Advertising of Cigarettes, of the Components of Manufactured Cigarettes and of Handrolling tobacco*, Advertising Standards Authority, January 1983.

35. C. Barker, 'BAT aims at women with new cigarette', *Campaign*, 21 May 1982.

36. 'How the brands ranked. Maxwell International Estimates', *World Tobacco*, June 1984, p.51.

37. B. Armstrong, T.L. Butler, *op.cit.*

38. S. Chapman, P. Homel, *Cigarette Advertising, Brand Preference and Attitudinal Congruency in Adolescent Smokers*, NSW Drug and Alcohol Authority, 1985.

39. R.E. Shean, *Secondary School Smoking Survey Preliminary Analysis*, Australian Council on Smoking and Health, unpublished, 1985.

40. A. Marsh, J. Matheson, *Smoking Attitudes and Behaviour. An Enquiry carried out on Behalf of DHSS*, OPCS, HMSO, London 1983.

41.   *ibid.*
42.   S.D. Stellman, L Garfinkel, *A New Longitudinal Analysis of One Million Men and Women: Preliminary Findings on Distributions of Smoking Habits*, Proceedings of Fifth World Conference on Smoking and Health, 1983, in press.
43.   B. Armstrong, T.L. Butler, *op.cit.*
44.   'Low tar comes of age', *Tobacco Reporter*, December 1977, p.84.
45.   J.B. Richmond, statement accompanying *The Changing Cigarette*, a report from the Surgeon General, Washington DC, Department of Health and Human Services, 1981.
46.   R. Peto, *Control of Tobacco-Related Disease, CIBA Foundation*, in press.
47.   C. Lenfant, 'Are "low yield" cigarettes really safer?', *New England Journal of Medicine*, vol.309, no.3, 21 July 1983, pp.181–2.
48.   C. Borland and others, 'Carbon monoxide yield of cigarettes and its relation to cardiorespiratory disease', *British Medical Journal*, vol 287, 26 November 1983, pp.1583–5.
49.   R. Peto, personal communication.
50.   *The Changing Cigarette, op.cit.*
51.   S. Chapman, *Cigarette Advertising as Myth, op.cit.*
52.   Abbott, Mead and Vickers, SMS, personal communication.
53.   M. Jarvis, *Tar and Nicotine Yields of UK Cigarettes 1972–1983: Sales-weighted Estimates from Non-Industry Sources*, unpublished.
54.   'Low tar Values', *Tobacco*, December 1983, pp.2–3.
55.   'Low tar Brands', *Tobacco*, November 1984, pp.8–13.
56.   *The Health Consequences of Smoking: Cardiovascular Disease, A Report of the Surgeon General*, Washington DC, Department of Health and Human Services, 1983.
57.   F. Ledwith, M. Rimpela, 'Can we have safer cigarettes?', *British Medical Journal*, vol.290, 12 January 1985, pp.157–8.
58.   *ibid.*
59.   'Brand shares of the UK cigarette market', *op.cit.*
60.   M. Mulholland, personal communication.
61.   'With women in mind', *Tobacco*, March 1984, pp.13–14.
62.   *ibid.*
63.   J.J. O'Connor, *op.cit.*
64.   *TART Research*, Western Australia, 1984, unpublished.
65.   E.A. Weiss, *op.cit.*
66.   *TART Research, op.cit.*
67.   E. Reisman, 'Look to the ladies', *op.cit.*
68.   E. Reisman, 'Female figures', *op.cit.*
69.   'With women in mind', *op.cit.*
70.   *ibid.*
71.   'Targeting the female smoker', *op.cit.*

Chapter 6: Growing up in smoke

1.　*Health or Smoking: A Follow-up Report of the Royal College of Physicians*, Pitman Medical, 1983, pp.54–6.
2.　*ibid*.
3.　*ibid*.
4.　M.J. Waterson, *Advertising and Cigarette Consumption*, Advertising Association, 1984.
5.　'Institute reinforces stand against youth smoking', *Tobacco Reporter*, November 1984, p.8.
6.　G.F. Todd, *Changes in Smoking Patterns in the UK*, Tobacco Research Council, 1975.
7.　*Smoking or Health: A Report of the Royal College of Physicians*, Pitman Medical, 1977.
8.　B. Jacobson, A. Amos, *When Smoke Gets in Your Eyes*, BMA Professional Division, Health Education Council, May 1985.
9.　P. Taylor, *Smoke Ring – The Politics of Tobacco*, second edition, Bodley Head, 1985.
10.　*ibid*.
11.　P.P. Aitken and others, 'Children's perceptions of advertisements for cigarettes', *Social Science and Medicine*, vol.21, no.7, 1985, pp.785–97.
12.　*ibid*.
13.　A. Charlton, 'Children's opinions about smoking', *Journal of the Royal College of General Practitioners*, vol.34, 1984, pp.483–7.
14.　P.P. Aitken, *op.cit*.
15.　D. Fisher, P. Magnus, 'Out of the mouths of babes ... The opinions of 10- and 11-year-olds regarding the advertising of cigarettes', *Community Health Studies*, vol.5, no.1, 1981, pp.22-6.
16.　H.M. Alexander and others, 'Cigarette smoking and drug use in schoolchildren: 11 factors associated with smoking', *International Journal of Epidemiology*, vol.12, no.1, 1983, pp.59–66.
17.　*Cigarette Smoking Among Teenagers and Young Women*, Washington DC, US Department of Health, Education and Welfare, 1977.
18.　'How the brands ranked. Maxwell International Estimates', *World Tobacco*, June 1984.
19.　R.E. Shean, *Secondary School Smoking Survey. Preliminary Analysis*, Australian Council on Smoking and Health, in press.
20.　P. Homel and others, *1983 Survey of Drug Use by School Students in New South Wales*, New South Wales Drug and Alcohol Authority, Sydney, 1984.
21.　'Brand share of the UK cigarette market 1983', *Tobacco*, September 1984, p.6.

22. Media Expenditure Analysis Ltd, 1983.

23. F. Ledwith, 'Does tobacco sponsorship on television act as advertising to children?', *Health Education Journal*, vol.43, no.4, 1984, pp.85–8.

24. A.D. McNeill and others, 'Brand preferences among schoolchildren who smoke', The *Lancet*, August 3 1985, pp.271–2.

25. B. Jacobson, *Tar and Cigarette Advertising – A Teenage Perspective*, Report to Cancer Research Campaign, unpublished.

26. B.K. Armstrong, T.L. Butler, *Tobacco Smoking and Tobacco-related Behaviour in Western Australia 1980-1983*, Perth, Public Health Department, 1984.

27. S. Chapman, *Cigarette Advertising, Brand Preference and Attitudinal Congruency in Adolescent Smokers*, New South Wales Drug and Alcohol Authority, in press.

28. P.P. Aitken, *op.cit.*

29. *The Ladykillers*, post-production script from 'Picture of Health', Channel 4 Television, 25 November 1983.

30. *ibid.*

31. J. Patten, letter to Renee Short MP, 10 May 1984.

32. B. Jacobson, *Tar and Cigarette Advertising – A Teenage Perspective, op.cit.*

33. S. Chapman, *Cigarette Advertising as Myth*, A Re-evaluation of the Relationship of Advertising to Smoking, PhD Thesis, Department of Social and Preventive Medicine, University of Sydney, 1985.

34. *Smoking or Health, op.cit.*

35. A. Marsh, J. Matheson, *Smoking Attitudes and Behaviour*, Office of Population Censuses and Surveys, Social Survey Division, HMSO, 1983.

36. *ibid.*

37. B. Silverstein and others, 'The availability of low nicotine cigarettes as a cause of smoking among teenage females', *Journal of Health and Social Behaviour*, vol.21, December 1980, pp.383–8.

38. B. Jacobson, *op.cit.*

39. R.G. Rawbone, A. Guz, 'Cigarette smoking among secondary schoolchildren 1975–9', *Archives of Disease in Childhood*, vol.57, 1982, pp.352–8.

40. *ibid.*

41. A.H. Rimpela, M.K. Rimpela, 'The risk of respiratory symptoms is increased among young smokers of low-tar brands', *British Medical Journal*, vol.290, 1985, pp.1461–3.

42. B. Jacobson, A. Amos, *op.cit.*

43. *ibid.*

44. *ibid.*

45. *ibid.*

46. *The British Code of Advertising Practice, Appendix H: Advertising of Cigarettes, of the Components of Manufactured Cigarettes and of Handrolling Tobacco*, Advertising Standards Authority, 1983.

47. B. Jacobson, A. Amos, *op.cit.*

48. *ibid.*

49. E.A. Weiss, 'Communicating with the smokers in Australia', *World Tobacco*, September 1984, 85–7.

50. *TART Research*, Western Australia, 1984, unpublished.

51. S. Chapman, *Cigarette Advertising and Myth, op.cit.*

52. R. Shean, personal communication.

53. S. Chapman, *Cigarette Advertising and Myth, op.cit.*

54. *ibid.*

55. K.C. Dale, 'ACSH survey: which magazines report the hazards of smoking?', *ACSH News and Views*, vol.3, no.3, May/June 1982, pp.7–10.

56. J. Guyon, 'Health questions: do publications avoid anti-cigarette stories to protect ad dollars?', *Wall Street Journal*, 22 November 1982.

57. *ibid.*

58. E. Whelan and others, 'Analysis of coverage of tobacco hazards in women's magazines', *Journal of Public Health Policy*, vol.2, March 1981, pp.28–35.

59. J. Guyon, *op.cit.*

60. P. Magnus, 'Superman and the Marlboro woman: the lungs of Lois Lane', *New York State Journal of Medicine*, vol.85, no.7, July 1985, p.342.

61. J.F. Cullman, evidence to Senate Commerce Sub-Committee, July 1969.

62. 'IBA raises tobacco sponsors' TV hopes', *Campaign*, 16 November 1984.

63. S. Woodward, personal communication.

64. 'Sportscan', Sports Sponsorship Computer Analysis Ltd, 1984.

65. R. Richards, 'Cigarettes and sports stars', *New York State Journal of Medicine*, April 1984, p.162.

66. R. Addison, 'The rare courage of public role models', *New York State Journal of Medicine*, April 1984, p.162.

67. R. Richards, *op.cit.*

68. C.R. Davis, 'What's behind the end of the Slims era?', *Tennis World*, 1978.

69. *Tennis World*, June 1984.

70. *ibid.*

71. *Sponsorship of Sport by Tobacco Companies*, terms of a voluntary agreement between the Minister for Sport and the Tobacco Advisory Council, May 1982.

72. 'The twisted morality that the ad industry must avoid', *Campaign* (editorial), 16 July 1982.

73. M. Hood, 'Why the smoke stays under fire', *Marketing Week*, 8 July 1983.
74. B. Jacobson, *The Ladykillers – UK Style*, paper presented at ASH Seminar on women and smoking, November 1983.
75. C. Burkham, 'How to use rock to reach the UK's young spenders', *Campaign*, 24 August 1984, p.27.
76. *ibid*.
77. R. Addison, *op.cit*.
78. P.M. Lochsen and others, *Trends in Tobacco Consumption and Smoking Habits in Norway*, Oslo, Norwegian Council on Smoking and Health, 1984.
79. M. Rimpela, *Juvenile Health Habits*, University of Helsinki, in press.

Chapter 7: What really keeps women smoking?

1. F.F. Ikard and others, 'A scale to differentiate between types of smoking as related to the management of affect', *International Journal of the Addictions*, vol.4, no.4, December 1969, pp.649–59.
2. M.A.H. Russell, J. Peto, 'The Classification of smoking by factorial structure of motives', *The Journal of the Royal Statistical Society*, series A (general), vol.137, part 3, 1974, pp.313-46.
3. A. Marsh, J. Matheson, *Smoking Attitudes and Behaviour*, Office of Population Censuses and Surveys, Social Survey Division, HMSO, 1983.
4. J.S. Tamerin, 'The psychodynamics of quitting smoking in a group', *American Journal of Psychiatry*, vol.129, no.5, November 1972, pp.589–95.
5. Extract from 'The Ladykillers', Documentary, Channel 4, 25 November 1983.
6. *ibid*.
7. *ibid*.
8. *ibid*.
9. A. Marsh, J. Matheson, *Smoking Attitudes and Behaviour*, Office of Population Censuses and Surveys, Social Survey Division, HMSO, 1983.
10. *ibid*.
11. L. Batten, *Addiction and Perceived Dependence: An Empirical Analysis*, Report on Operation Smokestop to Cancer Research Campaign. Unpublished.
12. C. Bailey, 'Smoking', *Ms London*, 21 July 1975.
13. A. Charlton, 'Smoking and Weight Control in Teenagers', *Public Health*, 1984, vol.98, pp.277–81.
14. *Adult Use of Tobacco 1975*, US Department of Health, Education and Welfare, June 1976.

15. J. Gofin and others, 'Cigarette smoking and its relation to anthropometic characteristics and biochemical variables in Jerusalem 17-year-olds and adults', *Israel Journal of Medical Sciences*, vol.18, 1982, pp.1233–41.

16. J.A.H. Baeke and others, 'Obesity in young Dutch adults: I, sociodemiographic variables and body mass index', *International Journal of Obesity*, vol.7, 1983, pp.1–12.

17. B. Nemery and others, 'Smoking, lung function and body weight', *British Medical Journal*, vol. 286, 22 January 1983, p.249.

18. P.H. Blitzer and others, 'The effect of cessation of smoking on body weight in 57,032 women: cross-sectional and longitudinal analyses', *Journal of Chronic Diseases*, vol.30, 1977, pp.415–29.

19. J.A.H. Baeke and others, *op.cit.*

20. A. Marsh, J. Matheson, *op.cit.*

21. *Smoking and Professional People*, Department of Health and Social Security, 1977.

22. E.R. Seiler, 'Smoking habits of doctors and their spouses in South East Scotland', *Journal of Royal College of Physicians*, vol.33, no.254, September 1983, p.598.

23. J. Spencer, *The Postal Survey of Nurses' Smoking Behaviour*, Research Report no.1, Institute of Nursing Studies, University of Hull, 1982.

24. *Smoking and Professional People, op.cit.*

25. *General Household Survey 1982*, Office of Population Censuses and Surveys, Social Survey Division, HMSO, 1983.

26. J. Dalton, I. Swenson, 'Nurses. The professionals who can't quit', *American Journal of Nursing*, August 1983, pp.1149–51.

27. R.J. Kirkby and others, 'Smoking in nurses', *Medical Journal of Australia*, vol.2, 1976, pp.864–5.

28. D.R. Hay, 'Intercensal trends in cigarette smoking by New Zealand doctors and nurses', *New Zealand Medical Journal*, vol.77, no.754, 25 April 1984, pp.253–5.

29. J. Spencer, *op.cit.*

30. *Smoking and Professional People, op.cit.*

31. *ibid.*

32. A. Knopf Elkind, 'Nurses' smoking behaviour: review and implications', *International Journal of Nursing Studies*, vol.17, 1980, pp.261–9.

33. P.W. Wilkinson, L. Tylden-Patteson, *Smoking Habits of Nurses within the Leeds Area Health Authority (teaching)*, 1980.

34. L. Hawkins and others, 'Smoking, stress and nurses', *Nursing Mirror*, 13 October 1982, pp.18–22.

35. S. Hillier, 'Stresses, strains and smoking', *Nursing Mirror*, 12 February 1981, pp.26–30.

36. L. Hawkins and others, *op.cit.*

Chapter 8: A society that keeps women smoking

1. S.V. Zagona, L.A. Zurcher, 'An analysis of some psychosocial variables associated with cigarette smoking in a college sample', *Psychological Reports*, vol.17, 1965, pp.967–78.
2. L.P. Bozzetti, 'Group psychotherapy with addicted smokers', *Psychotherapy and Psychosomatics*, vol.20, 1972, pp.172–5.
3. L.G. Reeder, 'Sociocultural factors in the etiology of smoking behaviour: an assessment', National Institute of Drug Abuse Research Monograph Series No.17, Washington DC, US Department of Health, Education and Welfare, 1977, pp.186–200.
4. J.R. Fisher, 'Sex differences in smoking dynamics', *Journal of Health and Social Behaviour*, vol.17, June 1976, pp.155–62.
5. P. White, *A Woman's Need to Smoke – Does it Reflect Her Position in Society?*, Proceedings of Fifth World Conference on Smoking and Health, in press.
6. *Cigarette Smoking among Teenagers and Young Women*, Washington DC, US Department of Health, Education and Welfare, 1977.
7. I. Eide, *Smoking and Feminism – The Developed World*, Proceedings of Fifth World Conference on Smoking and Health, in press.
8. J. Ritchie, *Women, Smoking and Feminism: A Comparison between Women's Studies Association Conference Participants and Waikato University Students*, paper prepared for New Zealand ASH, unpublished.
9. *ibid.*
10. V. Ernster, *Selling Cigarettes – How Women are Used and Hooked*, Proceedings of Fifth World Conference on Smoking and Health, in press.
11. B.R. Bewley, J.M. Bland, 'Academic performance and social factors related to cigarette smoking by schoolchildren', *British Journal of Social and Preventive Medicine*, vol.31, 1977, pp.18–24.
12. P.P. Aitken, *Ten- to Fourteen-Year-Olds and Alcohol: A Developmental Study in the Central Region of Scotland*, Edinburgh, Scottish Home and Health Department Health Education Unit, HMSO, vol.III, 1978.
13. *Cigarette Smoking Among Teenagers and Young Women, op.cit.*
14. *Women in the Labour Market – A TUC Report*, March 1983.
15. British Thoracic Society, 'Smoking withdrawal in hospital patients: factors associated with outcome', *Thorax*, vol.39, 1984, pp.651–6.

16. A. Marsh, J. Matheson, *Smoking Attitudes and Behaviour*, Office of Population Censuses and Surveys, Social Survey Division, HMSO, 1983.

17. A. Furnham, V. Lowick, 'Attitudes to alcohol consumption: the attribution of addiction', *Social Science and Medicine*, vol.18, no.8, 1984, pp.673–81.

18. D. Cameron, I.G. Jones, 'An epidemiological and sociological analysis of the use of alcohol, tobacco and other drugs of solace', *Community Medicine*, vol.7, 1985, pp.18–29.

19. S. Orbach, L. Eichenbaum, *What Do Women Want?*, Fontana Paperbacks, 1984.

20. *ibid.*

21. B. McConville, *Women Under the Influence – Alcohol and its Impact*, Virago Press, 1983.

22. C. Haddon, *Women and Tranquillisers*, Sheldon Press, 1984.

23. *General Household Survey 1982*, Office of Population Censuses and Surveys, Social Survey Division, HMSO, 1984.

24. K. Biener, 'Alkohol – und tablettenkonsum berufstätiger Frauen – representativ studie in der Schweiz', in *Frau und Sucht*, Hamm, 1981, pp.621–70.

25. *Use Habits among Adults of Cigarettes, Coffee, Aspirin, and Sleeping Pills, United States, 1976*, Vital and Health Statistics data, Series 10, Number 131, US Department of Health, Education and Welfare, 1980.

26. *National Heart Foundation Risk Factor Prevalence Study*, Report No.1 (1980).

27. MIND, personal communication.

28. *Spezielle Problembelastungen und Problembewältigungen in der Gruppe der 20-60 Jährigen Frauen*, Kommentar zu ausgewählten Ergebnissen, IMW-Köln, November 1982.

29. K. Biener, 'Exraucherinnen', *Münchner Medizinische Wochenschrift*, vol.123, no.25, 1981, pp.1035–8.

30. *Use Habits among Adults of Cigarettes, Coffee Aspirin, and Sleeping Pills, op.cit.*

31. *General Household Survey 1982, op.cit.*

32. P.G. Lund-Larsen, S. Tretli, 'Changes in smoking and body weight', *Journal of Chronic Disease*, vol.35, 1982, pp.773–80.

33. K. Smith, 'World looks a weighty problem', *Derby Evening Telegraph*, 2 May 1985.

34. K. Madden, 'Women and food: the consuming passion', *Vogue*, May 1985, p.307.

35. A. Marsh, J. Matheson, *op.cit.*

36. E. Lenney, 'Women's self-confidence in achievement settings', *Psychological Bulletin*, vol.84, no.1, January 1977, pp.1–13.

37. *ibid.*

Chapter 9: Beating the ladykillers – a painful evolution

1. *Smoking and Health – A Report of the Royal College of Physicians*, Pitman Medical, 1962.
2. *Smoking and Health: Report of the Advisory Committee to the Surgeon General of the Public Health Service*, Washington DC, US Department of Health, Education and Welfare, 1964.
3. A. Yarrow, *So Now You Know About Smoking: a Family Doctor Booklet*, British Medical Association.
4. *The Health Consequences of Smoking*, Washington DC, US Department of Health, Education and Welfare, 1973, pp. 99–125.
5. *Smoking and Health Now – A Report of the Royal College of Physicians*, Pitman Medical, 1971.
6. B. Jacobson, *The Ladykillers – Why Smoking is a Feminist Issue*, Pluto Press, 1981, p.71.
7. *ibid.*
8. 'Tobacco – hazards to health and human reproduction', *Population Reports*, series L, no.1, March 1979.
9. *The Health Consequences of Smoking for Women: A Report of the Surgeon General*, Washington DC, US Department of Health, Education and Welfare, 1980.
10. D. Rush, P. Cassano, 'Relationship of cigarette smoking and social class to birth weight and perinatal mortality among all births in Britain, 5–11 April 1970', *Journal of Epidemiology and Community Health*, vol.37, 1983, pp.249–55.
11. A. Chapman and others, *The Pregnant Pause Campaign. An Intervention Programme to Reduce Drug Use in Pregnancy*, Division of Drug and Alcohol Services, Health Commission of NSW Department of Health, New South Wales, September 1982.
12. *ibid.*
13. P. Taylor, *Smoke Ring – The Politics of Tobacco*, 2nd Edition, paperback, Bodley Head, 1985.
14. *ibid.*
15. A. Holleb, editorial, *Ca – A Cancer Journal for Clinicians*, March/April 1985.
16. *Controlling the Smoking Epidemic. Report of the WHO Expert Committee on Smoking Control*, Geneva, WHO Technical Report Series no.636, 1979.
17. D. Lambert, *Looking Back with Foresight*, paper given at Operation Smokestop Conference, 5–7 November 1984.
18. B. Jacobson, A. Amos, *When Smoke Gets in Your Eyes*, British Medical Association, Professional Division, Health Education Council, May 1985.
19. A. Cripps, personal communication.

20.   D. Waddell, *Preliminary Research on the Creative Concepts Developed for the Women's Component of the Sydney Quit for Life Campaign*, February 1984.

21.   John Bevins Pty Ltd, presentation to Department of Health, NSW, February 1984.

22.   M. Daube, personal communication.

23.   I. Simon, 'Women and cigarettes: feminine Ms-stake', *New York State Journal of Medicine*, April 1984, p.164.

24.   M. Shear, 'The pro-death lobby', *The Women's Review of Books*, vol.11, no.16, March 1985, pp.6–8.

25.   *ibid*.

Chapter 11: Thinking about quitting

If you want to read more in depth about the health effects of smoking, references a–f give more comprehensive information about the risks discussed in this chapter.

a.   *Health or Smoking – A Follow-Up Report of the Royal College of Physicians*, Pitman Medical, 1983.

b.   *The Health Consequences of Smoking for Women: A Report of the Surgeon General*, Washington DC, US Department of Health, Education and Welfare, 1980.

c.   P.M. Layde, V. Beral, 'Further analyses of mortality in oral contraceptive Users', *The Lancet*, 7 March 1981, pp.541–6.

d.   'Tobacco – hazards to health and human reproduction', *Population Reports*, series L, no.1, March 1979.

e.   G. Howe and others, 'Effects of age, cigarette smoking, and other factors on fertility: findings in a large prospective study', *British Medical Journal*, vol.290, 8 June 1985, pp.1697–1700.

f.   M. Ounsted and others, 'Factors associated with the intellectual ability of children born to women with high risk pregnancies', *British Medical Journal*, vol.288, 7 April 1984, pp.1038–40.

g.   The basis for the self-confidence questionnaire on pp.166–7 was provided by the following two sources: the *Rosenberg Self-Esteem Scale*; and the *Smoker's Self-Testing Kit*, Scotland, Scottish Health Education Unit, 1976.

THE POLITICAL ECONOMY OF HEALTH
LESLEY DOYAL with IMOGEN PENNELL

The Political Economy of Health shows that ill-health is largely a product of the social and economic organization of society; that medical practice and research are strongly influenced by their roles in maintaining a healthy labour force, and in socializing and controlling people; and that the medical field provides a large and growing arena for the accumulation of capital.

'Readable and well researched... Altogether a stimulating book and a worthy contribution to current debates on the politics of health.' *Lancet*
'The best book on health and health care that I have read for a long time.' *Nursing Mirror*

360 pages
0 86104 074 0   £5.95 paperback

MAKING SPACE
Women and the Man-Made
Environment
MATRIX

Making Space challenges us to look at our environment in a new light. Seven women – architects, designers and builders, collectively known as MATRIX show how sexist assumptions about family life and the role of women have been built into our homes and cities, and still influence modern housing design.

This path-breaking book points to the possibilities of a feminist future where space is made by women for women.

'Well written, enjoyable and thought provoking.' *Housing and Planning Review*

160 pages. Illustrated throughout
0 86104 601 3   £5.95 paperback

SMOTHERED BY INVENTION
Technology in Women's Lives
Edited by Wendy Faulkner and Erik Arnold

Technology affects women's lives daily, yet women themselves are unable to affect the shape of that technology. *Smothered by Invention* explores why, looking at men's control of the institutions of technology and the effects of this on women in reproduction, housework and paid work.

Modern technology is a *masculine* technology, a powerful tool in men's oppression of women. This is a controversial position, but one that speaks directly not only to feminists and the Left, but also to students of technology, science and society, and above all to everyone interested in building a more just and humane technology for the future.

288 pages
0 86104 737 0   £7.95 paperback

GENDER AT WORK
ANN GAME and ROSEMARY PRINGLE
Introduction by Cynthia Cockburn

The number of trades and professions in which
women work is increasing. Newspapers dearly
love 'the first woman taxi-driver' stories. They
neglect areas, including housework, where
women's presence is a long-established reality.
The case studies in *Gender at Work* – on
manufacturing, banking, the retail trade,
computers, nursing and housework – reflect
established trends occurring in all advanced
capitalists countries, including the UK. Its
empirical richness makes the book essential
reading for everyone interested in
understanding the link between the oppression
of women through production in workplaces
and consumption at home.

'A welcome addition to the literature.'
Tribune
'One of the most interesting contributions to
women's studies to be published in a long
while.' Ursula Huws, *City Limits*

144 pages
0 86104 671 4   £3.95 paperback

GREENHAM WOMEN EVERYWHERE
ALICE COOK and GWYN KIRK

The women's peace camp at Greenham Common has been a focal point in the growth of opposition to the escalation of nuclear arms.

This book is the personal testimony of many of the Greenham women who have made the difficult transition from private anxiety to collective commitment.

'Perhaps it is the long unheard and ignored voices of women that may rescue the world in time from the nuclear madness which is absorbing all thought and action.' Dora Russell

'At once an inspiration and a shock... like the Greenham action itself, the book is moving.' *New Statesman*

'Valuable because it makes our feelings important... a nice blend of analysis and how-to-handle-it-advice.' *Peace News*

128 pages. Illustrated
0 86104 726 5   £3.50 paperback